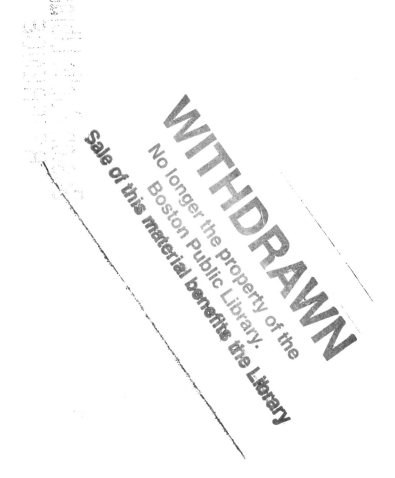

LESBIAN AND BISEXUAL
FICTION WRITERS

LESBIAN AND BISEXUAL FICTION WRITERS

Edited and with an Introduction by

Harold Bloom

CHELSEA HOUSE PUBLISHERS
Philadelphia

ON THE COVER: Romaine Brooks, *La Baronne Emile D'Erlanger*, ca. 1924. Courtesy of the National Museum of American Art, Smithsonian Institution; gift of the artist.

CHELSEA HOUSE PUBLISHERS

EDITORIAL DIRECTOR   Richard Rennert
PRODUCTION MANAGER   Pamela Loos
PICTURE EDITOR   Judy Hasday
ART DIRECTOR   Sara Davis
SENIOR PRODUCTION EDITOR   Lisa Chippendale

WOMEN WRITERS OF ENGLISH AND THEIR WORKS:
  Lesbian and Bisexual Fiction Writers

SERIES EDITOR   Jane Shumate
CONTRIBUTING EDITOR   Therese De Angelis
INTERIOR AND COVER DESIGNER   Alison Burnside
EDITORIAL ASSISTANT   Anne Merlino

Introduction © 1997 by Harold Bloom

First Printing
1 3 5 7 9 8 6 4 2

Library of Congress Cataloging-in-Publication Data

Lesbian & bisexual fiction writers / edited with an introduction by
   Harold Bloom.
      p.   cm. — (Women Writers of English and their works)
   Includes bibliographical references and index.
   ISBN 0-7910-4478-5 (hardcover). — ISBN 0-7910-4494-7 (pbk.)
      1. Lesbians' writings, American—Dictionaries. 2. Women authors, American—
20th century—Biography—Dictionaries. 3. Women authors, English—20th century—
Biography—Dictionaries. 4. Bisexual women—United States—Biography—Dictionaries.
5. Bisexual women—Great Britain—Biography—Dictionaries. 6. Lesbians—
Great Britain—Biography—Dictionaries. 7. Lesbians—United States—Biography—
Dictionaries. 8. American fiction—Women authors—Dictionaries. 9. English fiction—
Women authors—Dictionaries. 10. English fiction—20th century—Dictionaries.
11. Lesbians' writings, English—Dictionaries.   I. Bloom, Harold. II. Series.
PS153.L46L43 1997
813' .5099206643—dc21
[B]   97-4113
                                                                                   CIP

CONTENTS

THE ANALYSIS OF WOMEN WRITERS

HAROLD BLOOM

I APPROACH THIS SERIES with a certain wariness, since so much of classical feminist literary criticism has founded itself upon arguments with that phase of my own work that began with *The Anxiety of Influence* (first published in January 1973). Someone who has been raised to that bad eminence—*The Patriarchal Critic*—is well advised that he trespasses upon sacred ground when he ventures to inquire whether indeed there are indisputable differences, imaginative and cognitive, between the literary works of women and those of men. If these differences are so substantial as pragmatically to make an authentic difference, does that in turn make necessary different aesthetic standards for judging the achievements of men and of women writers? Is Emily Dickinson to be read as though she has more in common with Elizabeth Barrett Browning than with Ralph Waldo Emerson?

Is Elizabeth Bishop a great poet because she triumphantly meets the same aesthetic criteria satisfied by Wallace Stevens, or should we evaluate her by criteria she shares with Marianne Moore, but not with Stevens? Are there crucial gender-based differences in the representations of Esther Summerson by Charles Dickens in *Bleak House*, and of Dorothea Brooke by George Eliot in *Middlemarch*? Does Samuel Richardson's Clarissa Harlowe convince us that her author was a male when we contrast her with Jane Austen's Elizabeth Bennet? Do women poets have a less agonistic relationship to female precursors than male poets have to their forerunners? Two eminent pioneers of feminist criticism, Sandra Gilbert and Susan Gubar, have suggested that women writers suffer more from an anxiety of authorship than they do from influence anxieties, while another important feminist critic, Elaine Showalter, has suggested that women writers, early and late, work together in a kind of quiltmaking, each doing her share while avoiding any contamination of creative envy in regard to other writers, provided that they be women. Can it be true that, in the aesthetic sphere, women do not beware women and do not suffer from the competitiveness and jealousy that alas do exist in the professional and sexual domains? Is there something in the area of literature, when practiced by women, that changes and purifies mere human nature?

I cannot answer any of these questions, yet I do think it is vital and clarifying to raise them. There is a current fashion, in many of our institutions of higher education, to insist that English Romantic poetry cannot be studied in the old way, with an exclusive emphasis upon the works of William Blake, William Wordsworth, Samuel Taylor Coleridge, Lord Byron, Percy Bysshe Shelley, John Keats, and John Clare. Instead, the Romantic poets are taken to include Felicia Hemans, Laetitia Landon, Charlotte Smith, and Mary Tighe, among others. It would be heartening if we could believe that these are unjustly neglected poets, but their current revival will be brief. Similarly, anthologies of 17th-century English literature now tend to include the Duchess of Newcastle as well as Aphra Behn, Lady Mary Chudleigh, Anne Killigrew, Anne Finch, Countess of Winchilsea, and others. Some of these—Anne Finch in particular—wrote well, but a situation in which they are more read and studied than John Milton is not one that is likely to endure forever. The consequences of making gender a criterion for aesthetic choice must finally destroy all serious study of imaginative literature as such.

In their *Norton Anthology of Literature by Women*, Sandra Gilbert and Susan Gubar conclude their introduction to Elizabeth Barrett Browning by saying that "she constantly tested herself against the highest standards of male-defined poetic genres," a true if ambiguous observation. They then print her famous "The Cry of the Children," an admirably passionate ode that protests the cruel employment of little children in British Victorian mines and factories. Unfortunately, this well-meant prophetic affirmation ends with this, doubtless its finest stanza:

XIII
They look up with their pale and sunken faces,
    And their look is dread to see,
For they mind you of their angels in high places,
    With eyes turned on Deity.
"How long," they say, "how long, O cruel nation,
    Will you stand, to move the world, on a child's heart,—
Stifle down with a mailèd heel its palpitation,
    And tread onward to your throne amid the mart?
Our blood splashes upward, O goldheaper,
    And your purple shows your path!
But the child's sob in the silence curses deeper
    Than the strong man in his wrath."

If you read this aloud, then you may find yourself uncomfortable, on a strictly aesthetic basis, which would not vary if you were told that this had been composed by a male Victorian poet. In their selections from Elizabeth Bishop, Gilbert and Gubar courageously reprint Bishop's superb statement explaining her refusal to permit her poems to be included in anthologies of women's writing:

> Undoubtedly gender does play an important part in the making of any art, but art is art and to separate writings, paintings, musical compositions, etc., into sexes is to emphasize values in them that are *not* art.

That credo of Elizabeth Bishop's is to me the Alpha and Omega of critical wisdom in regard to all feminist literary criticism. Gender studies are precisely that: they study gender, and not aesthetic value. If your priorities are historical, social, political, and ideological, then gender studies clearly are more than justified. Perhaps they are a way to justice, or at least to more justice than women have received throughout thousands of years of male domination and aggression. Yet that is a very different matter from the now vexed issue of aesthetic value. Biographical criticism, like the different modes of historicist and psychological criticism, always has relied upon a kind of implicit gender studies and doubtless will benefit, as other modes will, by a making explicit of such considerations, particularly in regard to women writers.

Each volume in this series contains copious refutations of, and replies to, the traditionally aesthetic stance that I have advocated here. These introductory remarks aspire only to a questioning, and not a challenging, of feminist literary criticism. There are no longer any Patriarchal Critics; they are all dinosaurs, fabulous beasts fit for revival only in horror films. Sometimes I sadly think of myself as Bloom Brontosaurus, amiably left behind by the fire and the flood. But more often I go on reading the great women writers, searching for the aesthetic difference that yet may prove to be there, but which has not yet been found.

I N T R O D U C T I O N

BY ANY STANDARDS OF AESTHETIC JUDGMENT, Willa Cather must be considered the peer of the other major novelists of the United States in the 20th century: Dreiser, Faulkner, Fitzgerald, Hemingway. Though always lesbian, Cather declined to make her own sexual orientation an overt element in her fiction. I hesitate to name this evasiveness one of the strengths of her novels and stories, and yet great artists frequently have the resources to convert all manner of personal evasions into aesthetic values. In the best of Cather's works—*My Ántonia, A Lost Lady, The Professor's House*—we are given subtle intimations that certain male narrators and protagonists may well be female. Jim Burden, who tells the story of "his" Ántonia, is the archetype of these figures.

We come to understand that Jim is a kind of male lesbian, like some narrators in Henry James, Cather's master. Burden and Cather are never quite identified with one another, though they are difficult to distinguish. This seems to me one of the achievements, and not one of the failings, of *My Ántonia*. The beautiful ambiguity of deferred and finally lost sexual passion gives both to *My Ántonia* and to *A Lost Lady* a lyrical nostalgia unique in its overtones, yet also universal in its sense of loss. Lost love is, after all, the generic human nostalgia; virtually no one is immune from it. The dream of a more perfect love than any we have now is one of the starting points of imaginative literature. It has a deep relation to our desire to be different, to be elsewhere, a desire that vitalizes both reading and writing. Cather, an immensely subtle narrative artist, shares this dream or desire with her younger contemporaries Faulkner, Fitzgerald, and Hemingway. Doubtless, Cather's career would have been altered if she had not had her secret to "conceal," but I cannot see that it would have changed her for the better, in her aesthetic achievement.

Cather affords an interesting contrast to Virginia Woolf, her equal as a lyrical novelist. Woolf, molested in her youth by two older half-brothers, was more epicene than either bisexual or lesbian. Even her relationship with Vita Sackville-West could not be sustained, because of earlier traumas. Woolf's ambiguities of gender presentation are subtler even than Cather's. In her best works—*Mrs. Dalloway, To the Lighthouse, Between the Acts*—Woolf does not portray consciousness as being androgynous, as she does in the fantasy *Orlando*, but she finds ways of intimating an archaic mode of human consciousness that came before societies diminished men and women by estranging them from one another. If Cather's prime precursor was Henry James, Woolf's was Percy Bysshe Shelley, whose visionary poetry argues for a larger, more inclusive sense of the human than most of us are now able to recognize.

DOROTHY ALLISON

b. 1949

DOROTHY ALLISON was born on April 11, 1949, in Greenville, South Carolina, to Ruth Gibson Allison, a teenaged waitress and cook. She attended college at Florida Presbyterian (now Eckerd College) and received her M.A. from the New School for Social Research.

A self-labeled "lesbian-feminist" and incest survivor, Allison incorporates many events from her own life into her work, which she has described as "hard assed." She first attracted critical attention with her collection of poems, *The Women Who Hate Me*, in 1983. Her first book of short stories, *Trash* (1988), reflects the harshness and violence of her life in the South, the close ties she feels with female family members, and her lesbianism. The collection won two 1989 Lambda Literary Awards for Best Small Press Book and Best Lesbian Book.

Allison's first novel, the heavily autobiographical *Bastard Out of Carolina* (1992), was a National Book Award finalist and earned high critical praise for its stark portrayal of the brutal life of a young girl in a poor southern family and her determination to survive. Lillian Faderman attributes Allison's success to an attitude that "may be considered characteristic of post-lesbian feminism. She presents . . . an angry challenge to lesbian-feminist notions about appropriate sexual behavior (she is a defender of lesbian s/m), a fierce pride of (working) class, and an 'in your face' stance."

C R I T I C A L E X T R A C T S

MAB SEGREST

Dorothy Allison's writing shows the fierce refusal to deny any of her selves, a temptation at least as difficult within the feminist movement as beyond it. "A River of Names" sets out her dilemma. It is a story about stories, about storytelling—a narrative containing almost thirty separate tales. Its frame is a conversation between the narrator and Jesse, her middle-class lesbian lover, whose oblivion to class differences leads the narrator to lie in various ways about her own family, delivered by poverty into levels of violence and vulnerability unimaginable to the lover whose grandmother smelled like dill bread and vanilla. "Somehow it was always made to seem they killed themselves," the narrator writes of her cousins. "Somehow, car wrecks, shotguns, dusty ropes, screaming, falling out of windows, things inside them."

She mercilessly chronicles the fate of these cousins for the reader, while at times refusing to do so for the lover. Again, the theme is narration itself, and the ways it can be blocked or distorted because of the narrator's fears or the listener's insensitivity. Here the lover's bed, with all its cuddling and conventions of support, is not safe for the narrator. At times, she lies outright—inventing a grandmother who smelled like lavender instead of sour sweat and snuff, a character stolen from a novel. She also distorts through tone—drinking Bourbon to tell stories that "come out funny." There is distortion that acts out the listener's misinterpretations—Jesse's attributing her stories to a "fascination with violence" rather than to heartbreak and grief and a need to make peace with a violent past. Then there is silence, the absence of narration—"all the things I just could not tell her, the shame, the self-hatred, the fear."

"A River of Names" also shows the reasons for telling stories true, in spite of the obstacles. There is the need to establish a genuine relationship with the listener ("by not speaking I am condemning us"). There is an even greater need to be loyal to those she has survived, the need to address the self-hatred of the survivor, the "why me, and not her, not him?" by "saying something" about their lives. True narration carries a psychic risk for the woman who feels herself the "point of a pyramid, sliding back" under the weight of characters who are also kin; whose voice can mingle dangerously with the voices of "all those children screaming out their lives in my memory," making her "someone else, someone I have tried so hard not to be." ⟨. . .⟩

If "A River of Names" contains the impediments to narration, it also contains in its final sentence the moment when true narration starts—the moment of honesty in spite of risk, when Jesse says, again, "You tell the funniest stories," and the narrator replies, "but I lie." We can assume that it was such a moment that led to the narrator's ability to reveal to the reader the real stories, told without making the terrible funny, told for the narrator's own motives, with herself as her necessary first audience, that becomes the story "A River of Names."

—Mab Segrest, *My Mama's Dead Squirrel* (Ithaca: Firebrand Books, 1985), 129–31

DOROTHY ALLISON

Every evening I sat down with a yellow legal-size pad, writing out the story of my life. I wrote it all: everything I could remember, all the stories I had ever been told, the names, places, images—how the blood had arched up the wall one terrible night that recurred persistently in my dreams—the dreams themselves, the people in the dreams. My stepfather, my uncles and cousins, my desperate aunts and their more desperate daughters.

I wrote out my memories of the women. My terror and lust for my own kind; the shouts and arguments; the long, slow glances and slower approaches; the way my hands always shook when I would finally touch the flesh I could barely admit I wanted, the way I could never ask for what I wanted, never accept it if they offered. ⟨. . .⟩

The stuff on those yellow pads was bitter. I could not recognize myself in that bitchy whiny hateful voice telling over all those horrible violent memories. They were, oddly, the same stories I'd been telling for years, but somehow drastically different. Telling them out loud, I'd made them ironic and playful. The characters became eccentric, fascinating—not the cold-eyed, mean and nasty bastards they were on the yellow pages, the dangerous frightened women and the more dangerous and just as frightened men. I could not stand it, neither the words on the page nor what they told me about myself. My neck and teeth began to ache, and I was not at all sure I really wanted to live with that stuff inside me. But holding onto them, reading them, over again, became a part of the process of survival, of deciding once more to live—and clinging to that decision. For me those stories were not distraction or entertainment; they were the stuff of my life, and they were necessary in ways I could barely understand.

Still, I took those stories and wrote them again. I made some of them funny. I made some of them poems. I made the women beautiful, wounded but courageous, while the men disappeared into the background. I put hope in the children and passion in the landscape while my neck ached and tightened, and I found myself wanting nothing so much as a glass of whiskey or a woman's anger to distract me. None of it was worth the pain it caused me. None of it made me or my people real or understandable. None of it told the truth ⟨. . . .⟩

But a night finally came when I woke up sweaty and angry and afraid I'd never go back to sleep again. ⟨. . .⟩ But the desire to live was desperate in my belly, and the stories I had hidden all those years were the blood and bone of it. To get it down, to tell it again, to make sense of something—by god just once—to be real in the world, without lies or evasions or sweet-talking nonsense. I got up and wrote a story all the way through. It was one of those stories from the yellow pages, one of the ones I'd rewritten, but it was different again. ⟨. . .⟩

It was a rough beginning—my own shout of life against death, of shape and substance against silence and confusion. It was most of all my deep abiding desire to live fleshed and strengthened on the page, a way to tell the truth as a kind of magic not cheapened or distorted by a need to please any damn body at all. Without it, I cannot imagine my own life. Without it, I have no way to know who I am.

—Dorothy Allison, "Preface," *Trash* (Ithaca: Firebrand Books, 1988), 8–12

PUBLISHERS WEEKLY

In 14 gritty, intimate stories, Allison's fictional persona exposes with poetic frankness the complexities of being "a cross-eyed working-class lesbian, addicted to violence, language, and hope," rebelling against the Southern "poor white trash" roots that inevitably define her. Bridging the bedrooms, bars and kitchens of its narrator's adult world, and the dirt yards and diners of her '50s South Carolina childhood, this magnetic collection charts a fascinating woman's struggle for self-realization and acceptance through a sensual, often horrific tapestry of the lives of women to whom she is connected. In the mythically resonant early pieces, the conflicts of her foremothers, like Great-grandmother Shirley, "the meanest woman that ever left Tennessee," embody a grim legacy of drudgery that presages the seeds of her own rage and cavernous hunger, later finely played out through various love affairs. With a keen feel for the languid rhythms of Southern speech, Allison (*The Women Who Hate Me*) masterfully suspends the reader between voyeurism and empathy, breathing life into a vast body of symbolic feminine imagery.

—N.A., "*Trash*," *Publishers Weekly* (18 November 1988): 74

AMBER HOLLIBAUGH

Allison makes it clear that the treacheries that rip through her pages ⟨*Bastard Out of Carolina*⟩ began long before anybody in this book started drinking heavily, having kids or sleeping around. The novel works because she dares to take her readers home: she invites you into that hastily rented house with its broken-down yard, a place too many people have gawked at as they've driven past but never stopped to go inside. ⟨. . .⟩

⟨. . .⟩ For 309 pages she take you into that house so totally that you believe you'll never be able to leave it, never escape—and maybe, since she makes you fall in love with her people, never really want to. But at the same time she never lets you forget that inside that house, while you're sitting at that table listening to those stories, your life is perishing and so is everyone's you've come to love.

Allison drives the book ruthlessly to its final confrontation. "We do terrible things to the ones we love sometimes," says Aunt Raylene. "We can't explain it. We can't excuse it. It eats us up, but we do it just the same." All the strategies and silences that have been used to keep the family together begin to unravel relentlessly. It makes harsh, beautiful reading, the way an honest sentence is after too much hot air.

Allison doesn't let up, doesn't create heroines but gambles instead that her readers need truth more than pretty pictures and paper Goliaths. She goes back to the traditions forged in the earliest days of the women's movement and "speaks bitterness," letting the weight of what her readers already know come together with the power of her vision. She is right to say that her novel isn't easy to read, but neither are our lives. This is a book as consequential as our own stories: a novel that could save a life.

—Amber Hollibaugh, "In the house of childhood," *The Women's Review of Books* 9, nos. 10-11 (July 1992): 15

DOROTHY ALLISON

Throughout my work with the lesbian and gay, feminist, and small press movements, I went on reading the enemy—mainstream literature—with a sense of guilt and uncertainty that I might be in some way poisoning my mind, and wondering, worrying, trying to develop some sense of worth outside purely political judgments. I felt like an apostate who still mumbles prayers in moments of crisis. I wanted to hear again the equivalent of the still, small voice of God telling me: Yes, Dorothy, books are important. Fiction is a piece of truth that turns lies to meaning. Even outcasts can write great books. I wanted to be told that it is only the form that has failed, that the content was still there—like a Catholic who returns to God but never the church.

The result has been that after years of apostasy, I have come to make distinctions between what I call the academy and literature, the moral equivalents of the church and God. The academy may lie, but literature tries to tell the truth. The academy is the market—university courses in contemporary literature that never get past Faulkner, reviewers who pepper their opinions with the ideas of the great men, and editors who think something is good because it says the same thing everyone has always said. Literature is the lie that tells the truth, that shows us human beings in pain and makes us love them, and does so in a spirit of honest revelation. ⟨. . .⟩ It is the stance I assumed when I decided I could not live without writing fiction and trying to publish it for the widest possible audience. It is the stance I maintain as I try to make a living by writing, supplemented with teaching, and to publish with both a mainstream publishing house and a small lesbian press. What has been extraordinarily educational and difficult to accept these past few years of doing both has been the recognition that the distinction between the two processes is nowhere as simple or as easily categorized as I had once thought.

—Dorothy Allison, "Believing in Literature," *Skin* (Ithaca: Firebrand Books, 1994), 175–76

RACHEL PEPPER

⟨W⟩hile Allison's *Bastard* chronicles the fictionalized account of the abuse the author suffered as a child, in *Skin's* "Shotgun Strategies" she writes, "I have to be matter-of-fact about what happened to me for my own sanity, in order not to deny myself, nor ever to surrender to the constant pressure to do that. So I try to be straightforward about being a survivor of incest and violent contempt, but the things I still need to figure out, to talk about, are not the obvious issues . . ."

Allison's first book, a 1983 collection of poetry called *The Women Who Hate Me*, was well received, but she didn't reach her stride until five years later with *Trash*, a riveting volume of short fiction which won two Lambda Literary Awards in lesbian literature. I've always wondered what Allison was doing between books, and now I feel I know: she was writing articles for the *New York Native*! ⟨. . .⟩

Perhaps it is the perpetual curse of the politically aware writer always to balance the power of the pen with that of the sword. Allison ⟨. . .⟩ examines her own commitment to social change in *Skin's* "Sex Writing, the Importance and the Difficulty":

> I thought of myself as a dedicated politico with an accompanying belief in the importance of feminist political theory over the self-indulgent and trivial pleasures of writing fiction . . . Flirting and sex had nothing to do with writing, however, nothing to do with remaking the world . . . But everything is connected, Bertha Harris announced to us at the opening of one of her classes, and "Literature is not made by good girls." ⟨. . .⟩

The passion of Dorothy Allison ⟨. . .⟩ comes bursting forth unhindered from the pages of *Skin*. Most noticeably, the book presents a passion of survival, of learning to accept oneself, and of acting on that acceptance. In choosing to write out some of the most compelling personal and often troubling moments of her life, Allison succeeds in stirring both her readers' emotions and their consciences. This applies equally whether she's writing about strap-on dildos, butch-femme identity, or her extended working class Southern family.

—Rachel Pepper, "The Novelist as Activist," *The Harvard Gay & Lesbian Review* 1, no. 4 (Fall 1994): 24–25

MARTHA STONE

The title ⟨*Two or Three Things I Know for Sure*⟩ derives from ⟨Allison's⟩ Aunt Dot's saying that there were two or three things she knew for sure, but they were never the same things and she was never totally sure of them. Allison takes this refrain and with her sharp perceptiveness, applies it, mantra-like, to love and hate, evil and its perpetuation, to the importance of telling stories. One doesn't have to share Allison's need for connectedness to her family and roots to appreciate the power behind her words.

The art of story-telling, Allison remarks, had been used in her family both for survival and to keep some family members stuck in sad cycles of frequent pregnancies, cycles of abuse, abandonment and flight. Her Granny's stories, says Bone Boatwright, the narrator of *Bastard*, "made no distinction between what [Granny] knew to be true and what she had only heard told." ⟨. . .⟩

Allison's two or three things—which, unlike her Aunt Dot, she is always sure of—are sprinkled among these stories of short, unhappy lives, like that of her mother, who spent forty years as a waitress: an actress in the theatre of life, Allison observes. Some of *Two* is written about the feminist collective in Tallahassee, Florida, where Allison lived in the mid-70's. In this section, she discusses her feelings about sex and love. Love was a mystery, a calamity, a curse, an unexplored territory in her life, whereas sex was familiar, something she had been forced into as a young child, and which was central to the plot of *Bastard*. ⟨. . .⟩

In the 1994 introduction that Allison wrote for the Vintage edition of Blanche McCrary Boyd's *A Redneck Way of Knowledge*, she said that Boyd "tells us down home redneck truths about family and the wisdom to be found in grating your own nerves against the ones you both love and despise. I recognize it as a redneck variation on a Zen insight . . . it is the essential thing, the part of the redneck stance that must be felt from the inside—pain and great love, shame and enormous enjoyment." It may not be too much of a stretch to say that *Two or Three Things I Know for Sure* offers nuggets of wisdom, both mysterious and true, that have a lot in common with Zen koans.

—Martha Stone, "Not the Boatwrights," *The Harvard Gay & Lesbian Review* 2, no. 3 (Summer 1995): 45

DEB SCHWARTZ

The latest from the author of *Bastard Out of Carolina*, this short vivid narrative ⟨*Two or Three Things I Know for Sure*⟩ was written for performance and rings with the power of the spoken word. Allison brings together themes familiar to *Bastard* readers: the horrid tangle of love and hate, violence and tenderness that binds one family. She tracks her evolution as a writer from the girl who wove fictions to escape hideous realities, to the woman who refuses to whittle away at what's ugly or politically unsavory about her family and her desires— to read the cards she was dealt in the way she was taught she should. *Two or*

Three Things is unabashedly lyrical and forthright at once; Allison can break your heart recounting porchside conversation between sisters or standing eyes-open amid the wreckage of her life, defiantly full of hope.

—Deb Schwartz, "Dorothy Allison: *Two or Three Things I Know for Sure*," *Out* (September 1995): 54

JULIE ABRAHAM

In the quarter-century since Stonewall ⟨the landmark riot by gay patrons of New York City's Stonewall Inn when it was raided by police, launching the modern gay rights movement⟩, other literary forms besides the novel have flourished, and other forms of cultural production have proliferated: poetry, the essay, autobiography; video, performance arts, 'zines. But literature continues to be a significant source of representations of lesbianism, and anxieties about the parameters of "lesbian writing" have not been resolved, rendered academic, or ceased to undermine the possibility of our interpreting a range of writers and texts as lesbian. The novel continues to be the focus of these anxieties. When Dorothy Allison's *Bastard Out of Carolina*, nominated for a National Book Award in 1993, was not considered for the 1993 Lambda Literary Awards (for the best "lesbian and gay" books in a range of categories), the resulting debate was reported in the lesbian and gay community and mainstream media. Allison's novel was excluded from consideration because the judges decided to "focus on lesbian and gay content," which meant that "lesbian fictions" were "books whose main characters were lesbians consciously concerned with exploring their identity." Allison has a history of commitment to post-Stonewall lesbian and feminist politics and community ⟨. . . .⟩ But the story of Bone, the protagonist of *Bastard Out of Carolina*, ends as she reaches adolescence, before she is able to interpret her own story as lesbian or otherwise.

Allison's comments on the controversy illustrate the ongoing interpretive dilemma it reflects. In an interview in *The Nation* she recalls her own earlier battles with Bertha Harris, whose novels *Catching Saradove* (1969), *Confessions of Cherubino* (1972), and *Lover* (1976) were major contributions to the first wave of post-Stonewall lesbian writing. According to Allison, Harris "used to say there was no such thing as a lesbian novel because no little female books ever ran off with other little female books. I got into a furious argument with her in 1975 because I needed there to be a category called lesbian fiction. I realize now that what I really needed was to know that my life was a proper subject for fiction, that my life was as valid as heterosexuals' lives." The Lambda Awards decision suggests this desire for validation and the belief in fiction as a source of validation still flourish, as well as the assumption that stories of "female[s who] . . . run off with other . . . female[s]" are the only source of such validation. Even while Allison says, "I don't think I'm capable of writing a non-lesbian novel," she still talks about a given text as more or less lesbian, declaring that her "next book . . . is going to be much more lesbian in content, in the traditional definition."

These assumptions about the subject of "lesbian" texts still limit our interpretations of what it might mean to consider any given writer as a lesbian writer, and consequently our identification of writers as lesbian writers. Allison acknowledges the distinction between lesbian writers and lesbian novels: "Awards for lesbian writers," she concludes, "would in many ways be more valuable" than awards for lesbian fiction.

—Julie Abraham, *Are Girls Necessary? Lesbian Writing and Modern Histories* (New York: Routledge, 1996), xxii–xxiii

B I B L I O G R A P H Y

The Women Who Hate Me. 1983.
Trash. 1988.
The Women Who Hate Me: Poetry, 1980-1990. 1991.
Bastard Out of Carolina. 1992.
Skin: Talking About Sex, Class & Literature. 1994.
Two or Three Things I Know for Sure. 1995.

DJUNA BARNES

1892–1982

DJUNA BARNES was born in New York on June 12, 1892, to an unsuccessful American painter and an English violinist. Her father, who changed his own name several times before becoming Wald Barnes, gave his five children unconventional names and kept them out of the school system, believing that home education would make them better people.

Barnes attended Pratt Institute and the Art Students League in New York City. She became a journalist in 1913 to support herself and her family (her parents had divorced), writing for the *Brooklyn Journal* as "Lydia Steptoe."

Barnes published her first book, *The Book of Repulsive Women: 8 Rhythms and 5 Drawings*, in 1915. She continued contributing feature articles, short stories, poems, and illustrations to prestigious New York newspapers and to literary periodicals such as *Vanity Fair, The New Republic,* and *The New Yorker.*

In the early 1920s, Barnes traveled to Paris and became acquainted with a circle of British expatriate American writers, including Gertrude Stein, Ezra Pound, T. S. Eliot, and James Joyce. Joyce in particular greatly influenced her work; she was fascinated with his experiments in language and structure and his ability to express the unconscious mind. He was among the very few writers whom Barnes considered geniuses.

Barnes published another collection of poems and drawings, *A Book* (1923), and several one-act plays before completing two major works, *Ladies Almanack* (1928), a shrewd parody of Paris lesbians written in Elizabethan language, and the novel *Ryder* (1928). In the 1930s, Eliot persuaded Barnes to publish another novel, *Nightwood,* which has subsequently been considered Barnes's finest achievement. In his introduction, Eliot himself compared it to an Elizabethan tragedy in its accumulation of events, and he praised its rich, layered prose.

Barnes published only sporadically after *Nightwood,* claiming that the novel had drained much of her creative energy. She had begun drinking heavily in the early 1920s and was hospitalized several times in New York, Paris, and London for what she called her "famous breakdowns." She returned to New York at the outbreak of World War II, where she lived in isolation until her death in 1982.

CRITICAL EXTRACTS

JOHN HAWKES

Recently *Time* magazine, pernicious as ever, dismissed the *Selected Writings* of Djuna Barnes by saying that the best of her work, *Nightwood*, offered little more than "the mysterioso effect that hides no mystery," and even Leslie Fiedler has described Djuna Barnes' vision of evil as effete. Yet all her myth and fear are mightily to be envied. Surely there is unpardonable distinction in this kind of writing, a certain incorrigible assumption of a prophetic role in reverse, when the most baffling of unsympathetic attitudes is turned upon the grudges, guilts, and renunciations harbored in the tangled seepage of our earliest recollections and originations. It is like quarreling at the moment of temptation. Or it is like working a few tangerines on a speedily driven lathe. Djuna Barnes is one of the "old poets," and there is no denying the certain balance of this "infected carrier" upon the high wire of the present. She has moved; she has gone out on a limb of light and indefinite sexuality and there remains unshakeable. She has free-wheeled the push bicycle into the cool air.

Djuna Barnes, Flannery O'Connor, Nathanael West—at least these three disparate American writers may be said to come together in that rare climate of pure and immoral creation—are very nearly alone in their uses of wit, their comic treatments of violence and their extreme detachment. If the true purpose of the novel is to assume a significant shape and to objectify the terrifying similarity between the unconscious desires of the solitary man and the disruptive needs of the visible world, then the satiric writer, running maliciously at the head of the mob and creating the shape of his meaningful psychic paradox as he goes, will serve best the novel's purpose. Love, for Djuna Barnes, is a heart twitching on a plate like the "lopped leg of a frog"; for Flannery O'Connor it is a thirty-year-old idiot girl riding in an old car and tearing the artificial cherries from her hat and throwing them out the window; for Nathanael West, love is a quail's feather dragged to earth by a heart-shaped drop of blood on its tip, or the sight of a young girl's buttocks looking like an inverted valentine. Each of these writers finds both wit and blackness in the pit, each claims a new and downward sweeping sight and pierces the pretension of that sweet spring of E. E. Cummings. Detachment, then, is at the center of the novelist's experiment, and detachment allows us our "answer to what our grandmothers were told love was, what it never came to be"; or detachment allows us, quoting again from *Nightwood*, to see that "When a long lie comes up, sometimes it is a beauty; when it drops into dissolution, into drugs and drink, into disease and death, it has a singular and terrible attraction." But mere malice is nothing in itself, of course, and the product of extreme fictive detachment is extreme fictive sympathy. The writer who maintains most successfully a consistent cold detachment toward physical violence . . . is likely to generate the deepest novelistic sympathy of all, a sympathy which is a humbling before the terrible and a quickening in the presence of degradation.

—John Hawkes, "Fiction Today," *Massachusetts Review* (Summer 1962), in *The Chelsea House Library of Literary Criticism: Twentieth-Century American Literature*, vol. 1, ed. Harold Bloom (New York: Chelsea House Publishers, 1985), 306–7

ALAN WILLIAMSON

The typical hero in Djuna Barnes work suffers from a radical split in his identity between what he aspires to be and what he psychologically or physically is. The extremes of this dissociation are found among the doomed figures of *Nightwood*, whose lives constitute a revolt against the very facts of their physical being: the Jew who has built his whole concept of the meaning of his life around his fraudulent pretenses to aristocracy, and the sexual inverts. ⟨. . .⟩

This perpetual protagonist represents, in its most extreme form, the tragic encounter between an aspiring hero and a limiting universe, in that the antagonist is the protagonist's own nature rather than some external force pitted against him. This intensification is, however, also an internalization of the tragic process, and therefore non-dramatic. Comparing Djuna Barnes with other tragic writers, one discovers in her a curious repression of violence; introspective monologue is substituted for dramatic confrontation, and quiet acceptance of incurable suffering replaced the bloody catastrophe as a resolution. ⟨. . .⟩

The one external involvement with which Djuna Barnes is passionately concerned is love; and her vision of love always contains an element of incest. The important love relationships in the later works are nearly always either familial or homosexual. Love, as the externalization of the disoriented hero's quest, arises from the fragmented individual's craving for Edenic completion; therefore the most perfect love is that in which the lovers are mirror-images, complementary to each other but sharing the same basis of identity in blood and/or sex. Thus Djuna Barnes writes in "Six Songs of Khalidine," an early poem in the form of an elegy for a dead Lesbian lover:

> It is not gentleness but mad despair
> That sets us kissing mouths, O Khalidine,
> Your mouth and mine, and one sweet mouth unseen
> We call our soul. . . .
>
> *(A Book)*

In similar terms, Nora Flood in *Nightwood* describes her own Lesbianism: "A man is another person—a woman is yourself, caught as you turn in panic; on her mouth you kiss your own." The Lesbian lover is "yourself," but "caught as you turn in panic," a turned, inverse image. This element of complementarity within an integral, shared identity is fundamental in the two most fully explored love-relationships in the work of Djuna Barnes: the Lesbian relationship between Nora and Robin in *Nightwood*, and the filial relationship between Miranda and her mother Augusta in *The Antiphon*. Both relationships clearly represent a union of separate and opposed halves of a single identity. All of Nora's spiritual faculties are directed outward, in an intense interaction with other individuals; she lacks understanding or even awareness of her own subconscious. Robin, on the other hand, is sealed in a kind of trance in which she has lost the ability to communicate with the outside world. Thus Robin looks to Nora for a love which can penetrate through her trance, make her capable of antiphonal love, and save her from insanity, while Nora, in loving Robin, is attempting to capture and understand her own subconscious. Similarly, for Miranda, to accept her mother despite her mother's guilt towards her is to accept her family background as a part of herself, and thus is the only way to attain self-knowledge and a complete identity. For Augusta, the only atonement which can restore the integrity she has lost by her marriage is to gain the acceptance and love of her daughter Miranda, her chief victim. It is Miranda who memorably celebrates the antiphonal love between two halves of the same identity as man's only possibility for salvation, for escape from the fragmentation and solitude which are the "universal malady":

> As the high plucked banks
> Of the viola rend out the unplucked strings below—
> There is the antiphon
> I've seen loves so eat each other's mouth
> Till that the common clamour, co-intwined
> Wrung out the hidden singing in the tongue
> Its chaste economy—there is the adoration.
> So the day, day fit for dying in,
> Is the plucked accord.
>
> *(The Antiphon)*

Djuna Barnes is, however, pessimistic about the possibility of such an escape; both the Nora-Robin and the Miranda-Augusta relationships end in mutual destruction.

—Alan Williamson, "The Divided Image: The Quest for Identity in the Works of Djuna Barnes," *Critique* (Spring 1964), in *The Chelsea House Library of Literary Criticism: Twentieth-Century American Literature*, vol. 1, ed. Harold Bloom (New York: Chelsea House Publishers, 1985), 309–10

JANE RULE

There is no mystery about why ⟨Nightwood⟩ should have found acceptance, for its decadent elegance removes it from ordinary experience. The main character, a transvestite doctor who collects the tragic tales and confessions of the people around him, is a marvelously overblown monologuist who is given to statements such as, "No man needs curing of his individual sickness; his universal malady is what he should look to." "No, I am not a neurasthenic; I haven't that much respect for people—the basis, by the way, of all neurasthenia." "Pray to the good God; she will keep you. Personally I call her 'she' because of the way she made me; it somehow balances the mistake." His ironic cynicism and self-pity set the tone of the book, heavy with religious symbols and melodrama. What saves him is both his wit and his silliness.

Unfortunately the women characters are not so redeemed. Nora is tragically in love with Robin, a vague sort who has wandered into marriage and motherhood, wandered out again, wandered into Nora's life and out again because Nora wants to hold her and she will not be held. Robin wants to drift through the night, picking up women and making love to them so that the whole world will be happy. When Nora objects, Robin rages, "You are the devil! You make me feel dirty and tired and old." She goes off with Jenny, who has no more luck at keeping her home than Nora did. Nora meanwhile tries to understand her love, first by talking about Robin, then by trying to lead the same life Robin did. Encountering a young whore sitting before a statue of the Virgin, "looking from her to the Madonna behind the candles, I knew that image to her was what I had been to Robin, not a saint at all, but a fixed dismay." Fixed dismay she remains for Robin, who finally returns to Nora's neighborhood and camps in a deserted chapel. There Nora's dog tracks Robin down, and they grovel, snarl, and bark at each other and finally lie down together as Nora stands stunned in the doorway. It is really too bad that a book, so often beautiful and insightful, finally becomes pretentious and embarrassing. But just that failure allows T. S. Eliot his admiring introduction, in which he can moralize, "all of us, in so far as we attach ourselves to created objects and surrender our wills to temporal ends, are eaten by the same worm." We can all be sinners together. The chapel is the doghouse for us all.

—Jane Rule, "Four Decades of Fiction," *Lesbian Images* (New York: Doubleday & Company, Inc., 1975), 186–87

DONALD J. GREINER

⟨T⟩he following is suggested as a working definition of black humor: it makes no attempt to minimize the terror of the post-World War I universe; it uses comedy to encourage sympathy as well as to expose evil; it suggests futurity;

it celebrates comic distortion as an indication that anything is possible; and it is related to the poetic use of language. Three primary characteristics remain especially significant: extreme detachment on the part of the author; the comic treatment of horror and violence; and disruption or parody of conventional notions of plot, character, theme, and setting. The result is highly conscious, unrealistic, militantly experimental comic fiction.

Nightwood is one of the first American novels to reflect the working definition, yet apparently only Sharon Spencer has mentioned its comic spirit. Briefly commenting on the chapter "Watchman, What of the Night?" she describes the dialogue between Dr. Matthew O'Connor and Nora Flood as "intense, extremely funny, and extremely ludicrous. . . . The setting is the doctor's rented room in a cheap Paris hotel, a room that is in itself so terrifying and ridiculous that it might inspire pages of analysis of its 'black comedy.' " The black humor of *Nightwood* is, indeed, particularly illustrated in the grotesque, violent characters, the detached attitude toward the descriptions of outrageous clothes and houses, and the parody of the novelist's role.

These comic elements are part of Barnes' larger thematic concern with modern man's separation from a more primitive animal nature—at first glance, hardly the theme for a humorous novel. Only Robin Vote is united with her bestial side, yet she wanders through Europe from city to city and from lover to lover in a futile effort to attain full humanity. In *Nightwood*, humanity, day, and present contrast with beast, night, and past. Thus Robin is introduced as an "infected carrier of the past" and as having "the eyes of wild beasts." Her various love affairs with Felix, Nora, and Jenny illustrate a search for someone to tell her that she is innocent, for, as Barnes suggests, awareness of innocence leads to consciousness or moral values and, in turn, to humanity. Robin's three principal lovers, however, are unable to help her achieve the human state. Caught up in their own senses of alienation, and goaded by selfish love of Robin, they become animal-like themselves in their desperation to appropriate the bestial woman.

The numerous love affairs are destructive, painfully pursued, and selfishly concluded, for each character searches for a lover who might alleviate his sense of incompleteness. The longed-for reunion between animal and human states never takes place, and the characters are left with an impossible choice: to be primarily human, which means the painful awareness of alienation; or to be primarily animal, which means the longing for moral consciousness. Barnes suggests that the scale has tipped too far on the side of humanity, and she would probably agree with Dr. O'Connor's advice to Nora: "Be humble like the dust, as God intended, and crawl."

The discussion of theme might suggest to the unprepared reader that *Nightwood* is anything but comic. Happily, however, Barnes has not written a novel of unrelenting gloom. Her sense of humor is evident from the beginning, and her use of funny elements with a depressing theme reflects the perplexing mixture so vital to black humor. . . . Recognition of the comedy, however, depends upon the individual reader, for Barnes maintains total authorial detachment. Hedvig and Guido are not singled out as comic dupes, as characters who deserve only our laughter. Seen in the context of the novel, they are no more grotesque and ridiculous than the major characters who are damned by alienation and cursed by thwarted love. . . .

None of these people can be called characters in the conventional sense. They do not "live," nor are they "round," and the reader is never encouraged to identify with them. Like the characters in many contemporary black humor fictions, Barnes' people are static and subordinated to theme. *Nightwood* provides insight into the disordered human condition by conveying generalizations about love, bestiality, and religion, and it avoids the reader's expectations of verisimilitude and character development. In most instances, Felix, Nora, Robin, and Jenny act as vehicles for the poetic prose, for the "saving beauties of language"; they are not essential to Barnes' ideas nor to her means of expressing them. Specific details and descriptions are purposely omitted so that upon finishing *Nightwood* one cannot define what the characters wear or how they look. Poetic generalizations about homosexual or heterosexual love in the midst of discussions about bestiality, the night, and religion do not need living characters or realistic events. O'Connor's reaction to Jenny perhaps best expresses the reader's complex feelings about the characters in experimental black humor fiction: "That poor shuddering creature had pelvic bones I could see flying through her dress. I want to lean forward and laugh with terror."

—Donald J. Greiner, "Djuna Barnes' *Nightwood* and the American Origins of Black Humor," *Critique* (August 1975), in *The Chelsea House Library of Literary Criticism: Twentieth-Century American Literature*, vol. 1, ed. Harold Bloom (New York: Chelsea House Publishers, 1985), 308

CAROLYN ALLEN

In *Nightwood*, what readers hail as stylistic innovation begins not so much with Barnes's desire to experiment as with her recognition that current modes of discourse were inappropriate for her subject. In *Nightwood*, she eschews the language of rationality, often nominal in emphasis, dichotomous in argument, and factual in description, because it cannot adequately portray her subjects, the power of the night, of irrationality and the unconscious; and the nature of love, particularly love between women. To evoke them, Barnes uses instead an indirect, associative style that depends on reader intuition rather than on logic. The style of *Nightwood* tries to avoid naming directly, and so concentrates on not-naming, on using syntactic and semantic structures that signal indirection. Direct description would, for example, place in too distinct a relief a woman like Robin Vote, the novel's central force, who is best conceived as a presence rather than as a character. In passages describing her there is a syntactic preference for the passive voice suitable to her title, "la sonambule," and frequently for negation in keeping with her "presence-in-absence." In addition, love between women, in which self-knowledge comes from loving one who is different from yet resembles the self, requires a language tending toward synonymy rather than antonymy. Appropriately then, the principal mark of Barnes's style is the analogy, the terms of which are basically alike though superficially different. ⟨. . .⟩

Enclosure as a condition of emotional pressure exemplifies the metaphoric method by which Barnes writes indirectly rather than directly about her subjects. Both narrative presentation of characters and ideas of the characters themselves testify to Matthew's (and Barnes's) belief that it is not possible to "dress the unknowable in the garments of the known." That is, abstractions like love, memory, irrational passion, and emotional pressure are discussable only in terms of something concrete, like cluttered rooms. The psyche remains in part mysterious and the reader, like the characters, can only intuit what might be occurring in the unconscious.

At the same time, her presentation of the unconscious is always self-conscious on the part of the characters, and one of the most singular features of *Nightwood* is the way Barnes makes interior feeling a topic of exterior conversation. ⟨. . .⟩ Furthermore, the style of *Nightwood* as a whole is so idiosyncratic that it often seems as if Barnes were writing an essay instead of a novel. All the characters talk in the indirect style used in the narrative descriptions. Though in one sense Barnes keeps her reader at an impersonal distance by her indirection, in another she creates a personal voice which the characters all share. ⟨. . .⟩ As a result, the largely undifferentiated and highly self-conscious language may be thought of as Barnes's own "interior monologue" though formally there is nothing interior about it. Like Joyce and Faulkner, she is interested in what goes on in the mind, but instead of mimetic "streams" of consciousness or unconsciousness she relies on indirection in narrative observation, characterization, and figurative language.

In her slow coming to speech, Nora articulates for the first time the source of her passion for Robin and the reason for Matthew's failed efforts to dissuade her. In loving a woman she comes to know and love herself as well: "A man is another person—a woman is yourself, caught as you turn in panic; on her mouth you kiss your own. If she is taken you cry you have been robbed of yourself." To express the "outsideness" of love between women, Barnes reorders the patterns of ordinary discourse, eschews its propensity for naming directly, and creates a sense of doubleness in which states of mind are understood only in terms of metaphors that gather force from a context of related associations. In so doing she forges a style apart from the standard "great tradition," one perfectly suited to the novel's exploration of sexual possession, threat, pain, and love outside and beyond the conventional.

—Carolyn Allen, "'Dressing the Unknowable in the Garments of the Known': The Style of Djuna Barnes' *Nightwood*," *Women's Language and Style* (Studies in Contemporary Language 1). © 1978 by E. L. Epstein (L & S Books, 1978), in *American Fiction 1914 to 1945*, ed. Harold Bloom (New York: Chelsea House Publishers, 1987), 149–50, 152, 161–62

ANDREW FIELD

It is a lusty little book, but it is quite possible not to see this aspect of *Ladies Almanack* too clearly because of its convoluted language. Both *Ladies Almanack* and her novel of the same period, *Ryder*, are full of Joycean wordplay. The influence is clear. Barnes herself had written in one of her 1922 articles on Joyce how he had impressed upon her that all great talkers spoke in the language of Sterne, Swift, and the Restoration. Her own description of *Ulysses* as a—great Rabelaisian flower also suits *Ladies Almanack*. The language is a tossed salad of uncertain ingredients. It has largely the vocabulary and diction of the seventeenth and eighteenth centuries, but there are neologisms and usages to make any linguist frown, and there are strangenesses in the punctuation as well ⟨. . . .⟩ ⟨The⟩ opening note of arch sexuality which likens the woman's sex to the intricate patterns of a Persian carpet design (and concludes with—the consolation every Woman has at her Finger Tips . . .) is sustained as a leitmotif throughout the short work. A woman's genitals are compared to various flowers and then to a garden of Venus. They are also described as whorls and crevices, an escutcheon, a nook, a path, a hollow tree, a furrow and numerous other things. Many of the descriptions are decidedly bawdy: a toll-gate, an empty hack, a cow's trough, her Jollies, a Sword with no Rust, and her Nothing. Women in their periods sit—on a stack of Blotters. But many of these descriptions nestle in long and intricate sentences, which are as firmly neutral and flat as the drawings which illustrate the book.

The work, in fact, presents itself as a protest against the indelicacy of sexual manners of the time. Dame Musset is presented as a pioneer woman, and she laments the way in which shyness and privacy have given way to vulgar brazenness. The narrator may from time to time be heard sadly to disapprove, and her companion, Patience Scalpel, more firmly disapproves and fails to understand. Mina Loy was accepted as the token heterosexual among the Barney women.

There are whimsical passages in *Ladies Almanack* which are strangely and sadly moving, such as the conclusion to the month of April where the major

Freudian premise about women becomes a wry poetic silhouette of the unawakened Everywoman for whom death is but the second castration ⟨. . . .⟩ The finest portions of *Ladies Almanack* are about melancholy, and the words anatomy and melancholy occur frequently enough to force us to think of Burton's *Anatomy of Melancholy*, a title which is literally personified in some of the drawings where parts of the female body are presented to us as floating truncated sections of a corpse. *Anatomy of Melancholy* was one of her favourite books.

> —Andrew Field, *Djuna: The Life and Times of Djuna Barnes* (New York: G. P. Putnam's Sons, 1983), 125–27

ANDREW FIELD

Djuna Barnes has consistently inclined towards the framed scene rather than the flowing story in her writing. There is also her own word, from a letter to Charles Henri Ford (April 10, 1934), that she always found it extremely difficult to think up plots. There is both as much and as little plot in *Nightwood* as in any other Barnes work from as far back as her 1919 *Passion Play*. The notions of the "spatial narrative" and the "archictectonic novel" (a phrase used by another Barnes critic) have a certain use but should not be carried too far.

The most important and key sentence in ⟨Joseph Frank's discussion in his *The Widening Gyre*⟩ presents us with an image rather than a theoretical proposition, and the image speaks very well indeed to the formal reality of *Nightwood*.

> —The eight chapters of *Nightwood* are like searchlights, probing the darkness each from a different direction, yet ultimately focusing on and illuminating the same entanglement of the human spirit.

That sentence is true beyond question, for, as Frank and others have indicated, the initial chapters introduce us one after another to the major characters: Felix Volkbein, the foolish Jew who extinguishes himself by bowing before all signs of purported nobility; Robin Vote, the animal-beauty who is outside language and is attended by every other character in the novel; Nora Flood, who is the heroine and the victim of the tale; Jenny Petherbridge, a spiritual capitalist who collects people and plaster madonnas; and Dr. O'Connor, who talks a lot. By the midway point of the novel Dr. O'Connor and Nora virtually take over the narrative, and her plaints and his long responses simply curl back over and over upon the one time that is the story. The plot does not move forward, it merely is, like the portraits of the individual characters, or a scene set in a paperweight.

It is, however, a fundamental error to claim as Joseph Frank does that *Nightwood* lacks a narrative structure in the ordinary sense and cannot be reduced to any sequence of action for purposes of explanation. Whatever "in the ordinary sense" may mean, there is a simple and main story in *Nightwood*, and it is, moreover, a story which repeats rather closely a series of events which really did occur. That story is the profound and impossible love of a woman who contemplates and understands for a woman who rages and destroys. This plot may, granted, be slightly difficult to specify at the very first encounter, primarily because of the narrative lines that are tossed out and then not followed through. There is, too, the very great problem of perspective because Dr. O'Connor is both of and not of the main story. Dr. O'Connor is an entire Greek chorus put into a single character, and that character, moreover, stands very near to the reader so that his apparent dimensions are much enlarged. Once that is seen, once the painterly trick of perspective is grasped, whereby the main story is moved upstage where it must appear somewhat reduced, then *Nightwood* has a plot. The heat may be less, but the light which is shed on a whole range of matters beyond the particular lesbian love affair is considerably greater.

   —Andrew Field, *Djuna: The Life and Times of Djuna Barnes* (New York: G. P. Putnam's Sons, 1983), 146–47

SANDRA M. GILBERT AND SUSAN GUBAR

⟨In *Ladies Almanack*,⟩ Barnes used the formation of the female coterie around Saint Musset to explore the differences among lesbians, just as she adopted Renaissance diction and orthography, as well as the chapbook-calendar framework, to present the lesbian "Crusade" as a genuine Renaissance for women. Loving without the "trifle" that men possess, the followers of Dame Musset engage in "Slips of the Tongue" and "bringing up by Hand" while they "ride," "Tamper," "come down," or "thaw" together, as Barnes documents what is "nowhere" described, namely "how a Maid goes at a Maid." Although, with its rhythmic archaisms, its encyclopedic catalogues, its astrological, alchemical charts, and its riddling, punning prognostications, Barnes's English sounds and looks like a foreign language, it is Renaissance English—not ancient Greek—that she exploits to express the expatriation of lesbian culture from contemporary literary history as well as the lure of lesbian lore. Threatening to begin a whole new literary history for a coming age that liberates female coming, Barnes's *Almanack* implicitly confirms Dame Musset's view that "Love of Woman for Woman should increase Terror."

   In the *Ladies Almanack*, as in *Nightwood* (1936), Barnes managed to delineate the unique problems and passions of both the lesbian community and the lesbian couple. In part she suggests, as ⟨Radclyffe⟩ Hall does, that the lesbian-expatriate coterie is a menagerie of eccentrics, some of whom are wealthy voyeurs seeking to buy or steal the love they cannot otherwise attain. Like the lesbian community, moreover, the female couple suffers the same consequences of promiscuity detailed in *The Well of Loneliness. Nightwood* records Nora Flood's anguished reaction to her lover Robin Vote's sexual flings, an anguish explained by Nora's claim that if "A man is another person—a woman is yourself." Thus, the loss of the beloved is experienced as a loss of self, a point in *Nightwood* which reflects Barnes's own tortured erotic relationship with the sculptor Thelma Wood. Yet to the extent that Barnes attributes wisdom and creativity to Natalie Barney's circle and to the lesbian couple, she challenges assumptions about the autonomy of the author and the singularity of the subject.

Throughout *Nightwood*, in particular, lesbian desire educates the soul through a visionary breakdown of the self that illuminates the imperatives of the collaborative stance we have been tracing here: "She is myself," the lover exclaims about her beloved, the character modeled on Thelma Wood; "What am I to do?" Indeed, *Nightwood* can be read as an anxious meditation on the problem of identity in a lesbian relationship. When, early in their life together, Nora realizes that she cannot keep Robin from wandering to other lovers, her pain feels like self-division: "As an amputated hand cannot be disowned . . . so Robin was an amputation that Nora could not renounce." For all of her altruistic devotion to the other, Nora's unnerving dependency on her beloved sometimes feels like selfishness: "I thought I loved her for her sake, and I found it was for my own." The question Barnes poses is thus the query Nora puts to her spiritual adviser, the transvestite Dr. O'Connor: "have you ever loved someone and it became yourself?" Viewing the lesbian couple as a modern equivalent of Emily Bronte's passionately bonded Catherine Earnshaw and Heathcliff—"I can't live without my heart," Nora exclaims—Barnes delineates lesbianism as offering an almost mythic plenitude of being from which her characters, destined to fall, discover the knowledge of their perpetual exile.

—Sandra M. Gilbert and Susan Gubar, *No Man's Land: The Place of the Woman Writer in the Twentieth Century*, vol. 2: Sexchanges (New Haven: Yale University Press, 1989), 236–37

Lillian Faderman

⟨Djuna Barnes'⟩ biographer, Louis Kannenstine, observes in much of her early work "the art-for-art sake detachment of *The Yellow Book*, the mode of the decadents that would render aesthetic all emotions, appearances, and matters of life, including death," but this pose can be found in her later work too. In a 1923 poem, "Six Songs of Khalidine," the beloved's red hair flames and crawls and creeps, as in Verlaine's lesbian poems. Her fallen lids are stained with ebony, she and the speaker are in darkness, there is a thread of fear between them, and they hear a lost bird cry. The speaker exclaims, "It is not gentleness but mad despair/ That sets us kissing mouths, O Khalidine." In "A Little Girl Tells a Story to a Lady" (1929), the setting comes directly out of nineteenth-century French novels of decadence. Inevitably "the room was dark excepting for the moon, and two thin candles. . . . The curtains over the bed were red velvet, very Italian, and with gold fringes."

Barnes's major work, *Nightwood* (1936), was astutely characterized by Theodore Purdy in a 1937 review. He pointed out that the early chapters recall Wilde and Pater, and the rest of the book produces an atmosphere of decay which, despite its Elizabethan pretensions, "stems from the fin-de-siècle Frenchmen." Love of woman for woman in this novel is described as "insane passion for unmitigated anguish." Nora, Robin Vote's lover, says of her love for the other woman, "There's something evil in me that loves evil and degradation." The nineteenth-century views of lesbian narcissism and frustration are delivered up whole here: "A man is another person—a woman is yourself, caught as you turn in panic; on her mouth you kiss your own. If she is taken you cry that you have been robbed of yourself." Faithful to Louys's poem "The Doll," Nora observed, "When a woman gives [a doll] to a woman, it is the life they cannot have, it is their child, sacred and profane." But the nineteenth-century sexologists also make an appearance in this novel: Robin is the true born invert, a member of the third sex, who is distinguished from her lovers, the normal women that fall in love with the invert.

Barnes knew most intimately many lesbians, such as the subjects of her in-joke satire, *Ladies Almanack*, including Natalie Barney, Janet Flanner, and Dolly Wilde, who had absolutely no relationship to the women she described in *Nightwood*. Insane passion and degradation and doll games and roles had nothing to do with those women's conceptions of lesbianism. Barnes also knew enough to agree with Natalie Barney that Proust's treatment of flighty lesbians who follow gay male patterns of cruising and sexual contacts in *Remembrance of Things Past* was "improbable." Yet Barnes's treatment in her own novel was not much different. It attests to the power of literary images over lesbian writers that, even after criticizing Proust's lies, Barnes called on her knowledge of lesbians in literature rather than in life in order to write her own novel.

—Lillian Faderman, *Surpassing the Love of Men: Romantic Friendship and Love Between Women from the Renaissance to the Present* (New York: Quality Paperback Book Club, 1994), 364–65

B I B L I O G R A P H Y

The Book of Repulsive Women: 8 Rhythms and 5 Drawings. 1915.

A Book. 1923.

Ladies Almanack. 1928.

Ryder. 1928.

A Night Among the Horses. 1929.

Nightwood. 1936.

The Antiphon. 1958.

Selected Works. 1962.

Spillway. 1962.

Creatures in an Alphabet. 1982.

Smoke and Other Early Stories. Ed. Douglas Messerli. 1982.

Interviews. Ed. Alyce Barry. 1985.

RITA MAE BROWN

b. 1944

RITA MAE BROWN was adopted shortly after her birth on
November 28, 1944, by Ralph and Julia Brown of Hanover,
Pennsylvania. As a teenager, Brown began experimenting sexually
with males and females and was "exposed" as a lesbian at age 16. In
1964, Brown's academic scholarship to the University of Florida was
revoked because of her involvement in the civil rights movement and
her open lesbianism. She hitchhiked to New York City, where in 1967
she formed the Student Homophile League at New York University
and Columbia University.

Brown was active in several feminist and gay rights groups, including the National Organization for Women (N.O.W.) and the radical
group Gay Liberation, but left because she found them intolerant and
indifferent to the needs of lesbians. In 1971 she helped organize the
Furies Collective, a lesbian-feminist separatist group, in Washington,
D.C., but was voted out the following year. She was also one of the
founding editors of *Quest*, a feminist research journal.

Brown began her writing career with collections of poetry (*The
Hand that Cradles the Rock*, 1971; *Songs to a Handsome Woman*, 1973) and
essays (*A Plain Brown Rapper*, 1976). Her first novel, *Rubyfruit Jungle*, was
published by the feminist Daughters Press in 1973 and won immediate acclaim as a lesbian "cult" novel (she made the transition to mainstream press when Bantam Books purchased the novel in 1977).
Unquestionably her most renowned work, the picaresque *Rubyfruit
Jungle* has been compared to Twain's *The Adventures of Huckleberry Finn* in
its treatment of a lesbian protagonist struggling for her identity amid
hostile social forces.

Brown has continued to explore her themes of identity, sexuality,
family, home, and race in her novels, *Southern Discomfort* (1982), *Sudden
Death* (1983), *High Hearts* (1986), and *Venus Envy* (1992). She has occasionally shifted genres, with *Starting from Scratch: A Different Kind of
Writer's Manual* (1988), several murder mysteries, and a number of
screenplays. Though she has been criticized for abandoning her earlier radical feminist stance since attaining literary success, Brown
remains active in women's political issues. Nonetheless, she rejects
being categorized as a feminist or lesbian writer, saying simply, "I'm a
writer and I'm a woman and I'm from the South and I'm alive."

C R I T I C A L   E X T R A C T S

JANE RULE

The existence of the women's movement and of new women's presses puts pressure on establishment publishers who are forced to become aware of the wide audience there is for fiction which projects positive images of lesbians. Daughters Inc. brought out Rita Mae Brown's *Rubyfruit Jungle* in 1973. Already well known in the movement for the part she played in forcing the New York chapter of N.O.W. to face their hypocrisy about lesbians, for her article "Take a Lesbian to Lunch" and other position papers, Rita Mae Brown has written a novel which is also a lesbian/feminist manifesto. For those who think fiction is not the place to sermonize, *Rubyfruit Jungle* is often too blatantly preachy. Molly, the main character, has been a radical lesbian from birth, refusing all the conventional limitations of being a girl. In play she says, "I got to be the doctor because I'm the smart one and being a girl don't matter." Faced with the requirement to please others, she counters with, "I care if I like me, that's what I really care about." These assertions are the sort also to be found in the new, right-minded literature for children being published by feminist presses. There is nothing wrong with them. Nor is there anything wrong with Molly's ser-monizing to a friend who feels limited by her background in what she can do with her life. "It's always hard no matter who you are, where you come from or what sex you got stuck with—it's the hardest decision every individual has to make in their life, probably." But the earnestness would weigh heavily if the book were not lifted by arrogant humor, never-mind-the-consequences fury, and the transcending tenderness. The kid who won't be put down by being a bastard, poor, and a girl grows into a young woman who would lose her schol-arship and be expelled from college rather than deny her joyful sexual plea-sure with her roommate, who would work at the lousiest sort of job in order to have money to continue her education, and battle the male chauvinism of the university where she is constantly frustrated in her attempts to get materi-als and equipment so easily available to men in the film department. She is perhaps even harder in her judgments on other women than she is on men, for she encounters as much hypocrisy among the women she tries to love as she does among the men with whom she is forced to work. The dean who expels her is obviously a lesbian herself, and Molly does not hesitate to confront her with her own self-protective motives. Nor has Molly any patience with the lovers who refuse to call themselves lesbian while giving her that label. She has a fine satirical time with the sexual fantasies required for the middle-aged

to free themselves from either guilt or reality in bed. The film Molly makes of her adopted mother as a thesis for her degree is the device by which Molly transcends the bitterness she might otherwise have fixed on, for the film is the real portrait of a woman who did what she could in a narrow, prejudice-ridden world from which she had no way of escape. At the same time, it underlines the remarkable gifts of defiance and intelligence which have marked Molly for freedom. *Rubyfruit Jungle* is a far shout from the maimed religious and psychological apology of *The Well of Loneliness* and, as propaganda, healthier, for protest is a more accurate weapon against bigotry than special pleading. Rita Mae Brown is ready to play without a handicap.
    —Jane Rule, "Four Decades of Fiction," *Lesbian Images* (New York: Doubleday & Company, Inc., 1975), 194–95

MAB SEGREST

Rita Mae Brown's *Rubyfruit Jungle,* a much-loved lesbian novel of the early 1970s, traces the archetypal journey from the deep South to New York. The departure is precipitated by the "apple-cheeked, ex-marine sergeant" dean of women at Florida State, who accuses the first year woman of seducing "numerous innocents in the dorms," various Black women and men, and the president of Tri-Delta sorority. When Brown pointed out indignantly that the dean was a dyke also, she was put under house arrest.

    In the cities to which they migrated—especially New York and San Francisco—Southern lesbians such as Ti-Grace Atkinson, Rita Mae Brown, and Pat Parker benefitted from and helped give birth to the emerging movement. In New York, Atkinson and Brown both bolted from the local National Organization for Women. 〈. . .〉

    When Brown left New York NOW, the issue was its treatment of lesbians, and she went on with others in New York and Washington to articulate why lesbianism is a feminist issue and why feminists cannot exclude lesbians from the women's movement. Brown, Barbara Love, Sidney Abbott, and March Hoffman wrote in *The Woman-Identified Woman:*

> "What is a lesbian? A lesbian is the rage of all women condensed to
> the point of explosion. She is the woman who, often beginning at an
> extremely early age, acts in accordance with her inner compulsion to
> be a more complete and freer human being than her society—per-
> haps then, but certainly later—cares to allow her. . . . It is the pri-
> macy of women relating to women, of women creating a new
> consciousness of and with each other, which is at the heart of
> women's liberation, and the basis for the cultural revolution."

That women can and do love each other, that this love is an extension of loving self-respect, should not be so revolutionary an idea. But in patriarchal society it is. Brown and others went on to put the manifesto into practice. She moved to Washington and formed the Furies collective with eleven other lesbians. It was a "bolshevik cell" working together for revolutionary change—living together, sharing chores equally, sleeping on mattresses on the floor in the same room. In the first issue of *The Furies* newsletter, Ginny Bernson announced the group's intentions: "We want to build a movement in this country which can effectively stop the violent, sick, oppressive acts of male supremacy. We want to build a movement which can make all people free."

It was a decade of manifestoes, of huge intentions. Within two years the Furies had dissolved, split internally by class differences, but also by the magnitude of the problems they had taken on. "Change," Brown reflected later, "is not a convulsion of history but the slow, steady push of people over decades." When the Furies disbanded, many of its members went on to contribute to the growing network of lesbian presses, newsletters, and journals that I stumbled across in 1977. This lesbian-feminist cultural revolution was the slow, steady push that survived the convulsions of the late sixties and early seventies.

—Mab Segrest, *My Mama's Dead Squirrel: Lesbian Essays on Southern Culture* (Ithaca, NY: Firebrand Books, 1985), 121–22

BONNIE ZIMMERMAN

In Her Day ⟨. . .⟩ concerns a love affair that, despite its failure, symbolizes the creation of community out of difference. The characters of Ilse and of Carole are, for this reason, drawn quite differently. Ilse is young, political, upper class, an out and active lesbian. She embodies the future—the brash, forward-looking mover and shaker. Carole is in early middle-age, an academic, working class in origin, and closeted. She represents the past, in that she lives a traditional lesbian life and is a historian who appreciates roots and origins. As an art historian, she also represents culture in the relationship: Ilse represents politics. Carole lacks Ilse's energy and direction, Ilse needs Carole's perspective and wisdom. The novel is virtually an allegory of the early lesbian feminist movement (although the Ilses far outnumbered the Caroles). Through their love affair they attempt to bridge the differences between them and between the different characteristics necessary to a successful movement.

To an extent, the two women succeed. Carole comes out to her co-workers and discovers the necessity of political change. She plans, at the conclusion of the novel, to write a book on medieval women, her way of putting culture and history at the service of present-day politics. Influenced by Ilse, Carole also becomes more self-conscious and aware of her identity (foreshadowing the direction taken by the lesbian feminist community). At the end of the novel, Carole ⟨. . .⟩ thinks of returning to her southern roots. Ilse has changed Carole considerably, making her a fuller, more complete person.

Ilse in her turn is changed by Carole, although her change is more ideological, in keeping with her character. Whereas Ilse saw herself and the movement as cut off from the past—"reborn" into a new world free from original sin—she now begins to appreciate the longer view of history, the inherited experience of the past. She also understands that if we are to be born again, we need new language, new images, and new concepts—in short, we need artists. In this way, both women (and perhaps the author) reconcile politics and culture. They also reconcile history and vision, past and future, through their present-day love affair. Although Carole and Ilse don't survive as a couple, they have their moment, and each "in her day" moves herself and, symbolically, the women's movement, closer to the reconciliation of opposition and difference.

—Bonnie Zimmerman, *The Safe Sea of Women: Lesbian Fiction 1969-1989* (Boston: Beacon Press, 1990), 115–16

NICKIE HASTIE

The first 'authoritative' piece of critical writing I read on the lesbian coming out story as a re-vision of the *Bildungsroman* was Bonnie Zimmerman's 1983 essay 'Exiting from patriarchy: the lesbian novel of development' which provided the phrase 'myth of origins'. In that essay, Zimmerman surveys literature published in the late 1960s and during the 1970s, literature which seems to point either to a tragic end for the lesbian or to a completely idealised future. Zimmerman examines *Rubyfruit Jungle* in her essay, grouping it with the idealised texts. In them, lesbian heroes are imagined escaping from all patriarchal constraints, leaving behind the territory of patriarchy much as the traditional *Bildungsheld* or hero of the *Bildungsroman* leaves the intellectually and socially restrictive life in the provinces to make his way in the city. ⟨. . .⟩ What the lesbian hero escapes to, or into, is the 'Lesbian Nation': an utopian political separatism within a lesbian community far enough removed from patriarchal territory to mean 'male cultures, male law, and male power can no longer touch [her]' (Zimmerman, 1983, p 256). The myth of exit from patriarchy and entry into 'Lesbian Nation' is a symbolic return journey to a 'homeland' that is the mythologised reincarnation of the island of Lesbos. ⟨. . .⟩

I find I have a less-easily defined relationship with *Rubyfruit Jungle* than with Radclyffe Hall's *The Well of Loneliness*, even though Molly Bolt, the hero of *Rubyfruit Jungle*, insists on a positive self-defined sexuality. I don't think lesbian critical writing has yet had a chance properly to stand at a distance from Rita Mae Brown's 'pioneering' novel. *Rubyfruit Jungle* has certainly added a powerful example to the lesbian mythical 'hall of fame'. It has gone through many reprints and is marketed by its mainstream publisher as 'the ultimate word-of-mouth best-seller ... about growing up lesbian in America—and living happily ever after.' Does today's reader feel cheated by this claim? I did, finally succumbing to the 'Molly Myth' in 1990, and seeking out my own copy for a first reading. Molly Bolt has been 'hyped'—mythologised—right out of her context within the novel. She explodes from the pages, uncontainable, and also unknowable. Mythologising Molly reinforces her position in 'Lesbian Nation', for when her historical grounding is removed she seems to enter an imaginative 'cultural space', but equally it reveals 'Lesbian Nation' as myth or fantasy. I don't know any lesbians who could follow Molly there.

It is important to understand that, although mythologies can sometimes offer a point of reference and encourage our existence, at other times myth turns into the oppressor.

—Nicki Hastie, "Lesbian Bibliomythography," in *Outwrite: Lesbianism and Popular Culture*, ed. Gabriele Griffin (London: Pluto Press, 1993), 75–77

Louise Kawada

Rubyfruit Jungle is an important pioneer text in women's comedy because it begins to break down so many of the old myths and stereotypes. Most obviously, the novel does away with the myth of the maladjusted homosexual. Molly is attractive, athletic, popular—and, with some help from the high school principal and the dean of women whom she discovers having an extramarital affair, she is also class president. Hardly a scenario from *The Well of Loneliness*.

Amid all the pranks, the sometimes bawdy humor, and the ribald language, *Rubyfruit Jungle* offers some strong commentary on the arbitrary definition of normalcy and its ways of subverting and twisting those who do not meet the definition. Throughout the novel, Brown shows us figures such as Leroy, Molly's early childhood friend, and Carolyn, a high-school companion, who resist and suppress their own homosexual leanings because of social pressure. In this novel, too, the myth of first-night heterosexual ecstasy suffers, as does that of marital bliss. Molly sees her old friend and onetime lover Leota Phantom (née Bisland) now married with two children: "Same cat eyes, same languid body, but oh god, she looked forty-five years old and she had two brats hanging on her like possums" (216).

The world in *Rubyfruit Jungle* is an upside-down carnivalesque upheaval. The down and outs, like Chris, who befriended Molly, receive high scores for their humaneness; while those who are accepted as authority figures (the dean of women, probably herself gay, who dismissed Molly from college on the basis of homosexuality) often fail. Bakhtin praised madness as a way of seeing the possible and new in a tired system. At one point in *Rubyfruit Jungle*, a character calls Molly "lunatic" (301) when Molly suggests that love between women is beautiful. Just before, Molly had described to this woman how advertising and its hawking of the "good life" ultimately exploit women and condone violence. Molly adds:

> "You don't see ads of women kissing to get you to buy Salem ciga-
> rettes, do you?" She laughed. "That's funny, that's truly funny. Why
> the entire world must look different to you." (199)

Indeed it does, and the Lesbian writer seizes upon this anomalous perspective, this crack in the system, to try to change the system. The radical quality of the image presented here—two women kissing in a Salem ad—is so preposterous, so askew from Madison Avenue cool, that it amuses and prompts reflection. What are the constructs in our society that order and hierarchize sexual relations, that also sell violence and domination? And why is one image labeled as acceptable and the other as morally wrong?

Rubyfruit Jungle consistently seems to ask questions that too often go unframed and to voice (at least implicitly) answers to those questions. Making sense of the world (even if one has to turn it upside down), finding and affirming meaning, are important aspects of the novel's program. But to what extent is this epistemological quest a gender-related issue; does meaning matter more to women than it does to men?

Brown seems to structure the novel to point up differences in male and female sensibilities. At important moments, Molly is connected with the image of a raft and the implied notion of Huck Finn. Even Molly's Aunt Florence sounds like a recreation of the Widow Douglas and her "sivilizing" ways. Molly bemoans her situation:

> She ran on and she got me for this offense and that offense as well as
> one hundred trespasses. She's gonna make a lady out of me that sum-
> mer, a crash program. She was going to keep me in the house to
> teach me to act right, cook, clean, and sew and that scared me. (33)

On the one hand, the Huck comparison reflects Molly's role as *picaro*, but it also forces a subtle measuring of the two protagonists. Although Molly's future is uncertain at the close of the novel, her direction and accomplishments are clear. Huck, on the other hand, seems committed more to action than direction, and his tale finds closure in the maelstrom of pranks and

Missouri voodoo played on hapless Jim. Brown offers a more explicit reading of male/female perception in her comparison between Molly's retrospective of Carrie's life and the films made by the other (male) students, who focused their artistic energies on gang rapes, Martian attacks, and nuclear destruction in a hail of tinfoil balls. The rhetorical point of Molly's film is the discovery of meaning, while the message of the others' "works" is to insist on the absence of meaning, the violent and violated strata of contemporary existence.

—Louise Kawada, "Liberating Laughter: Comedic Form in Some Lesbian Novels," in *Sexual Practice/Textual Theory: Lesbian Cultural Criticism*, ed. Susan J. Wolfe and Julia Penelope (Cambridge, MA: Blackwell Publishers, 1993), 256–58

PAULINA PALMER

One of the earliest and best-known examples of lesbian comic fiction is Rita Mae Brown's *Rubyfruit Jungle* (1973). A *bildungsroman* written in the confessional style popular in the 1970s, it recounts in a breezy, colloquial tone the adventures of the narrator Molly Bolt. Focus is placed on Molly's childhood in Pennsylvania, her years at college and, most important of all, her discovery of her lesbian orientation. *Rubyfruit Jungle* achieved the status of a cult work in the newly-formed lesbian groups of the period and is generally remembered for its exuberantly frank celebration of lesbian sex. However, in the heterosexist climate of the early 1970s, this celebration could not take place without careful preparation on the author's part. In order to make a space for it and render it convincing, Brown first has to problematize heterosexual attitudes and values. She carries out this task with wit and panache.

A key feature of *Rubyfruit Jungle* is the humorous critique which it gives of romantic love and the importance which society attaches to heterosexual relations. Brown's treatment of these topics agrees with the radical feminist perspectives of Koedt and Millett, theorists who interrogate codes of romantic love and criticize society's fetishing of sexual intercourse. Brown treats these issues in a manner which is playfully iconoclastic. Teenager Connie, regaling Molly and her other girl friends with an account of her first experience of sex with a man, rejects the romantic notion that intercourse is 'a beautiful experience . . .the most intimate experience a human being can have'. Concentrating instead on its mundane and ridiculous aspects, she describes the prelude to the sex act as 'a half hour of dry humping and rolling all over the bed'. (Brown 1978: 79) As for the act itself, she laconically remarks that it is 'okay, but I can't believe that they write songs about first times and people kill themselves over it. I mean really!' (p. 80) Other episodes in the novel develop this critique. The female characters complain about the 'messy' and uncomfortable aspects of hetero sex (p. 100) and ridicule male sexual inhibitions. (p. 70) One of them discovers to her astonishment that she prefers sex with women to sex with men—and insists on giving Molly what she calls 'kissing lessons' to demonstrate the fact! (p. 102)

Episodes such as this, which problematize heterosexual practice and its supposed pleasures, are interspersed with others which expose the oppressive effects of gender stereotyping and inequalities between the sexes. Young Molly's announcement that she intends to be a doctor when she grows up is greeted with ridicule by the other children: 'You can't be a doctor. Only boys can be doctors'. (p. 34) Confusions and non sequiturs about sexual identity and gender difference are also subjected to playful scrutiny. Leroy, one of Molly's male friends, interprets her decision to purchase a motor bike as evidence that she is 'queer'. Revealing his insecurities about his masculinity, he plaintively protests, 'If you're doing what you please out there riding around on your motor-cycles, then what am I supposed to do? I mean how do I know how to act if you act the same way?' (p. 63) The humour of these gender-bending episodes is enhanced by the fact that both Molly and Leroy turn out to be gay.

—Paulina Palmer, in *Contemporary Lesbian Writing: Dreams, Desire, Difference* (Buckingham, UK: Open University Press, 1993), 81–82

CAROL M. WARD

"Dedicated to women everywhere," *The Hand That Cradles the Rock* conveys in its very title the issues of radical feminism and women's social role in contemporary society that Brown will explore in her later fiction. Instead of the traditional female role as mother, ruling the world through procreation, modern woman must gain political power through activism or even through violence, if necessary. Brown's poetry, like that of many feminist poets of the early seventies, expresses her radical social views. She criticizes the patriarchal system of institutionalized sexism for its oppression of the human spirit. Only after the destruction of that civilization can a new world be born, one that is modeled on the female principle. In this first volume of poetry, women are identified with nature, while men are defined by images of death, decay, and destruction. Brown seems to be searching for the common bonds between herself as a woman and the female of all species in her quest to reclaim women's history. As she writes in her introduction to the reprint edition of her two poetry volumes, "we must struggle for justice for ourselves and for others. Poetry is part of that struggle." Part of this revolutionary function entails evolving a new language to express the love that dares not speak its name, the love between women. ⟨. . .⟩

After this diverse volume of political diatribes, feminist anger, and Latin satirical influence (Brown was studying Latin and acknowledges the strong influence of Horace on her work during this period), Brown's second volume of poetry explores the dimensions of romantic love. Because it was inspired by Brown's relationship with a specific woman, the actress Alexis Smith, *Songs to a Handsome Woman* is more personal and intimate than *The Hand That Cradles the Rock*, which was dedicated to all women. But Brown refuses to separate the personal and the political. In her opening note to the reader, she knows that she cannot explain love although she is "fool enough to be open about [her] feelings" (*Songs*). The only certainty that she can express about love is that "it deepens experience, making all life exquisite and valuable" (*Songs*). When one individual loves another, then racism, classism, sexism are "doubly repulsive" (*Songs*). Love humanizes and calls one to action against the forces that would deny love and life. Written when she was also working on *Rubyfruit Jungle*, these love poems celebrate romantic love, a type of youthful adoration that Brown admits no longer interests her: "My typical preoccupation with romantic love has given way to a focusing on the love that lasts, or marathon love" ("Another Time," *Poems*). ⟨. . .⟩

Brown admits as she looks back on these early poems from the perspective of age and literary experience that she sees the volumes as the record of a brash young person, a recapturing of the spirit and events of those years in her life. Though some of the poems call to mind Wallace Stevens in the use of Floridean imagery or Stephen Crane in the use of the brief epigraph, or even William Butler Yeats in the use of apocalyptic landscape, the main merits of these poems are not literary. The significance of these works lies in their nonapologetic political stance and their unabashed celebration of women. Because of Brown's open politics, expressed vividly in her essays, and her vibrant lesbian sexuality, readers do not have to read between the lines to see what impact Brown's lifestyle had upon her artistic creations. The connections are clear, her sincerity unquestioned. The works were important, not only for their contribution to the feminist literary movement with its new emphasis on honesty, but also for their impact on Brown's perception of herself as a writer.

—Carol M. Ward, *Rita Mae Brown* (New York: Twayne Publishers, 1993), 27, 33–34, 37

LILLIAN FADERMAN

In lesbian-feminist journals and in many novels, the "given" is that lesbian-feminism is the norm, not an abnormality—and that other sociosexual orientations are indicative of a neurotic view of one's womanhood. Lesbian-feminist readers of the 1970's did not demand that all literature written for them reflect a utopian lesbian society. But they wanted and needed depictions of revolutionary cultures, lesbian heroes, and lesbian lives lived outside of the stereotypes.

Lesbian-feminist prose style is often nonlinear, but not for Gertrude Stein's reasons of obscuring the meaning. Many lesbian-feminist writers have rejected a traditional style as being an arbitrary invention of the patriarchal culture. Since they refuse the other limits of patriarchy, they see no reason to accept its narrow literary forms. Having no vested interest in the literary establishment, and little hope of becoming part of that male-dominated institution, many of them feel free to create their own stylistic experiments.

Earlier writing, if it treated lesbianism openly, focused on explaining the "problem" to heterosexuals, or it showed the lesbian characters trying to adjust, with varying degrees of success, to the demands of the straight world. Lesbianism was the major conflict of the story. In the writing which began to emerge with the lesbian-feminist movement, the "problem" is never one's lesbianism but it might be the stupidity of a society that can react to lesbianism only through prejudices. The lesbian hero's task is generally not to adjust to the heterosexual world, but to create herself in her lesbian world.

The most popular of the lesbian-feminist novels, Rita Mae Brown's *Rubyfruit Jungle* (1973), presents the central character, Molly Bolt, as a combination female Tom Jones and a crusader for justice. She is in all ways outstanding—a straight A student, a fine athlete, an effective leader, and absolutely beautiful. But unlike the polished, superior women of the antilesbian novels of earlier decades, Molly's perfection is just that. And it is connected with her lesbianism because she is much too good to form a subservient alliance with any of the males around her. The villain of this piece is never of course the central lesbian character, but rather heterosexually identified females who experiment with lesbianism, lesbians who hide their lesbianism, the rich who use their money to buy the poor, the straights who relate to lesbians through stereotypes. Molly battles their ignorance and hypocrisy, knowing always that she has truth and justice on her side. She goes through one picaresque adventure after another; she always comes out on top, always maintains her essential innocence, and always sees herself and demands that the reader see her as a hero. Unlike the one earlier comic novel about lesbians, Compton Mackenzie's *Extraordinary Women*, it is never Molly the lesbian who is laughable but rather all the fools she meets on her odyssey. The novel is so popular among lesbian-feminists because it gives them what they have long awaited: a character with whom they can identify, who is bold, brave, always in the right, an avenger of all the wrongs done to lesbians in the twentieth-century life and literature.

—Lillian Faderman, *Surpassing the Love of Men: Romantic Friendship and Love Between Women from the Renaissance to the Present* (New York: Quality Paperback Book Club, 1994), 406–7

B I B L I O G R A P H Y

The Hand that Cradles the Rock. 1971.

Hrotsvitra: Six Medieval Latin Plays (translator). 1971.

Rubyfruit Jungle. 1973.

Songs to a Handsome Woman. 1973.

In Her Day. 1976.

A Plain Brown Rapper. 1976.

Six of One. 1978.

Southern Discomfort. 1982.

Sudden Death. 1983.

High Hearts. 1986.

The Poems of Rita Mae Brown. 1987.

Bingo. 1988.

Starting from Scratch: A Different Kind of Writer's Manual. 1988.

Wish You Were Here. 1990.

Rest in Pieces. 1991.

Venus Envy. 1992.

Murder at Monticello. 1994.

Dolley: A Novel of Dolley Madison in Love & War. 1994.

Pay Dirt. 1995.

Riding Shotgun. 1996.

WILLA CATHER

1873–1947

WILLA CATHER was born in Gore, Virginia, on December 7, 1873, but moved with her family to Nebraska when she was nine years old. She received a B.A. from the University of Nebraska in 1895 and then worked for six years as a drama critic and telegraph editor for the Pittsburgh *Daily Leader*.

Cather published her first two books—a volume of poetry, *April Twilights* (1903), and a collection of short stories, *The Troll Garden* (1905)—while teaching high school English. Her work attracted the attention of S. S. McClure of *McClure's Magazine* in New York, and she became managing editor of the magazine from 1906 to 1912, when she published her first novel, *Alexander's Bridge*.

Cather achieved critical success with her second novel, *O Pioneers!* (1913). Based on her childhood memories of Nebraska, the book was written in the evocative, "unfurnished" prose that became her trademark. After ghostwriting an autobiography of S. S. McClure and completing a third novel, *The Song of the Lark* (1915), Cather returned to a Nebraska setting in what is widely considered her greatest novel, *My Ántonia* (1918).

Cather's next novel, *One of Ours* (1922), a bitter tale of World War I, received mixed critical reviews but became a best-seller and was awarded a Pulitzer Prize. The following year, Cather continued in the vein of *My Ántonia* with another story of Nebraska, *A Lost Lady*.

Cather's later novels are set in the Southwest, in a bleak landscape that suited the depression she felt throughout the 1920s. During this period she produced her most famous work, *Death Comes for the Archbishop* (1927), a fictionalized tale of the first bishop of New Mexico. Cather also produced dozens of short stories, several books of essays, and many poems.

From an early age, Cather preferred to dress in men's clothing. As a teenager she began signing her name "William Cather, Jr." and later "Dr. Will." She was an amateur actor and participated in community theater productions, where she often took male roles.

In 1901 Willa Cather met Isabelle McClung in Pittsburgh; the two became close companions and lived together until 1915. She had already met Edith Lewis while traveling to New York during this period, and when McClung married in 1915, Cather moved to New York to live with Lewis. The two were lifetime companions until Cather's death on April 24, 1947.

Though none of Cather's works deals specifically with lesbianism, many critics point out that her male characters often seem more like women in their interests, experiences, and attitudes. Many note that Cather's "gender switching" may have been the author's way of encoding what she did not feel free to write about explicitly. Indeed, in 1908 her friend and mentor Sarah Orne Jewett criticized Cather's delineation of the male protagonist in one of her early stories; Jewett advised her to avoid the inevitable "masquerade" and make the character female.

Whatever else they may be, Willa Cather's protagonists are pioneers in the broadest sense. They share a "spontaneous energy," in the words of one of her critics: the drive to overcome, with passion and self-confidence, "the obstacles offered by circumstance."

C R I T I C A L   E X T R A C T S

LLOYD MORRIS

From *Alexander's Bridge* to *A Lost Lady* Miss Cather's books reveal her explicit concentration upon a single theme. That theme is the effort of the individual to overcome the obstacles offered by circumstance and to control or dominate environment. She has been chiefly concerned with pioneers and with artists who, as she conceives them, bring to this effort similar propensities toward action and similar attitudes toward life. Both types, as Miss Cather has portrayed them, are driven forward by a spontaneous energy which they exercise without clearly understanding; they are passionate rather than intelligent, feeling life deeply, though seldom reflecting upon it profoundly; they are superbly self-confident though spiritually isolated; their abundant vitality nourishes the stubborn will which secures for them the prizes of intelligence in the absence of its possession. In a group of her novels, Miss Cather has dealt with the effort of the individual to subdue his physical environment to his own uses, revealing the warping contest between primitive human nature and the defiant soil of the frontier. Out of them arises her now considerable gallery of portraits of pioneers; the characters of *O Pioneers!* and *My Ántonia*, the elder generation of *One of Ours*, Captain Forrester and several of his lightly sketched associates in *A Lost Lady*. These are figures in the sunset of an epoch, and almost before the final accomplishment of their purposes they become picturesque survivors in a new order. The recalcitrant soil is finally tamed, the empty spaces of the frontier fill up, the era of rapid communication and mechanical agriculture sets in, and there are no frontiers left to conquer. There are none, at least, on the land.

The new frontier, Miss Cather suggests, occurs within the imagination. In the arts there are always unbroken lands open for settlement, and her pioneers of yesterday become the artists of today, turning from the conquest of the land to a fresh contest with an equally obdurate spiritual environment. In default, perhaps, of any ideal sufficiently comprehensive to claim an undivided loyalty, the undisciplined and unemployed spiritual energy of the race is pushing forward its discoveries in the creative life of the arts. Perceiving this, Miss Cather has chronicled the inception of a new age of pioneering in her portraits of arts; the figures who move through her stories in *Youth and the Bright Medusa*, Thea Kronborg in *The Song of the Lark*, the violinist in *One of Ours*.

Although Miss Cather responds vigorously to the heroism called forth by these two aspects of individual experience and indispensable to success in either, there is seldom absent from her work a recognition of its accompanying pathos. She reveals the beauty of wide horizons and open spaces and untamed solitude, but she does not fail to indicate that her prairies are more propitious to the ripening of wheat than to that of the human spirit. A group of characters intervenes between her pioneers and her artists, those who, unable to dominate their environment, have succumbed to it and are thereby defeated. ⟨. . .⟩

⟨. . .⟩ The total absence from Miss Cather's work of an epic outlook upon American life is nowhere more strikingly revealed than in the concluding section of *One of Ours*. It is perhaps not without significance that Miss Cather, who is among the most thoughtful of our contemporary novelists, has failed to isolate in our national life any ideal faith or noble purpose deserving the allegiance that awaits its discovery. So remote is she from that discovery that she intimates the futility of the quest.

—Lloyd Morris, "Willa Cather," *North American Review* (April 1924), in *The Chelsea House Library of Literary Criticism: Twentieth-Century American Literature*, vol. 2, ed. Harold Bloom (New York: Chelsea House Publishers, 1986), 693

REBECCA WEST

The most sensuous of writers, Willa Cather builds her imagined world almost as solidly as our five senses build the universe around us. This account of the activities of a French priest who was given a diocese in the southwest during the late 'forties, impresses one first of all by its amazing sensory achievements. She has within herself a sensitivity that constantly presents her with a body of material which would overwhelm most of us, so that we would give up all idea of transmitting it and would sink into a state of passivity; and she has also a quality of mountain-pony sturdiness that makes her push on unfatigued under her load and give an accurate account of every part of it. So it is that one is not quite sure whether it is one of the earlier pages in *Death Comes for the Archbishop* or a desert in central New Mexico, that is heaped up with small conical hills, red as brick-dust, a landscape of which the human aspect is thirst and confusion of the retina at seeing the earth itself veritably presenting such re-duplications of an image as one could conceive only as consequences of a visual disorder. When the young bishop on his mule finds this thirst smouldering up to flame in his throat and his confusion whirling faster and faster into vertigo, he blots out his own pain in meditating on the Passion of our Lord; he does not deny to consciousness that it is in a state of suffering, but leads it inward from the surface of being where it feebly feels itself contending with innumerable purposeless irritations to a place within the heart where suffering is held to have been proved of greater value than anything else in the world, the one coin sufficient to buy man's salvation; this, perhaps the most delicate legerdemain man has ever practised on his senses, falls into our comprehension as lightly as a snowflake into the hand, because of her complete mastery of every phase of the process. But she becomes committed to no degree of complication as her special field. A page later she writes of the moment when the priest and his horses come on water, in language simple as if she were writing a book for boys, in language exquisitely appropriate for the expression of a joy that must have been intensest in the youth of races.

—Rebecca West, *The Strange Necessity* (1928), in *The Chelsea House Library of Literary Criticism: Twentieth-Century American Literature*, vol. 2, ed. Harold Bloom (New York: Chelsea House Publishers, 1986), 698–99

T.K. WHIPPLE

The plains and prairies, friendly or hostile, are always present—often terrible but always beautiful, most terrible and most beautiful in winter. The sense of space which they add is all important in lending an effect of greatness to the novels, an epic scope which would have been denied by a more restricted background.

In all the novels from *O Pioneers!* to *One of Ours*, the human life which is set in this country is closely related to it either by sympathy or by contrast. Among Miss Cather's protagonists, the women have a peculiar kinship with the land: they are simple, primeval, robust with a strain of hardness, heroic. Alexandra is a heroine of the Sagas, Thea Kronborg in *The Song of the Lark* has the integrity of a single driving force, Ántonia is elemental motherhood. ⟨. . .⟩

⟨. . .⟩ On the other hand, the young men in the early books, including Claude Wheeler of *One of Ours* and Neil Herbert of *A Lost Lady*, are antipathetic to the environment; they are sensitive, artistic, idealistic, deficient in force if not weaklings, fitted to thrive in favorable conditions but unable to conquer difficulties. A more complicated social picture is presented by *One of Ours*, *A Lost Lady*, and their successors, a wider range and greater diversity of character, and less typical, more sharply individualized portraits. The Wheeler household and Claude's friends, Mrs. Forrester and her husband, the old railroad pioneer, Professor St. Peter and all his family and in-laws, Tom Outland and Rodney Blake, even the seamstress Augusta; above all Myra and Oswald Henshawe, and not only the Bishop and his friend, but the minor characters such as Señora Olivares—they have the variety and the separate uniqueness of life itself. Humanly speaking, Miss Cather's world is not made to fit a plan or theory and it is growing constantly richer in its multiplicity.

Yet her favorite theme persists throughout: the conflict of the superior individual with an unworthy society. And since this society is her version of the world in which she has lived—of the West primarily, and incidentally of the United States—it may be taken to embody implicitly her conception of American life. Her view is that the pioneers in general were folk largely endowed with creative power and imagination, but that the second generation, except for a few artists who have inherited the spirit of the fathers, has degenerated and succumbed to the tyranny of ease and money and things. ⟨. . .⟩

Yet the upshot of Miss Cather's tragedy is not a meaningless futility, for there is compensation in the very fineness which separates her characters from their neighbors. Theirs is not a tragedy of frustration, for even at the worst they have been true to themselves and maintained their own integrity. Besides, one infers from Miss Cather's work, the only real failure is indifference, tepidity, timidity, the fear which shrinks from encountering experience and possible unhappiness, for the reason that to have lived so, without passion and without valor, is not to have lived at all. To have cared intensely about anything, even if one has not gained it, is to have lived not altogether in vain; mere living, living as ardently, as wholeheartedly as possible, is an end that justifies itself. Miss Cather always tacitly champions the poetic temper and the life of realization against practicality. The quarrel between the two furnishes the theme of *The Song of the Lark* and *One of Ours*, and is prominent in *Oh Pioneers!* and *My Ántonia*, as well as in most of her short stories. All her chief characters have the poetic point of view, and are forced by their viewpoint into conflict with their families and neighbors. ⟨. . .⟩

⟨. . .⟩ Had she been born into any happier clime or age, I doubt whether, save for rendering more abundant social relationships, she would have done notably better. Though she began by largely subordinating herself to her subject-matter, she has ended complete mistress of the situation and produced books which enlist interest not as social documents but as fine art. She proves that the rule that American writers must be partially incapacitated by their environment has conspicuous exceptions—and she also proves the rule that they succeed in spite of their environment.

—T. K. Whipple, "Willa Cather," *Spokesmen* (1928), in *The Chelsea House Library of Literary Criticism: Twentieth-Century American Literature*, vol. 2, ed. Harold Bloom (New York: Chelsea House Publishers, 1986), 708–9

KATHERINE ANNE PORTER

Joyce had happened: or perhaps we should say, *Ulysses*, for the work has now fairly absorbed the man we knew. I believe that this is true of all artists of the first order. They are not magnified in their work, they disappear in it, consumed by it. That subterranean upheaval of language caused not even the barest tremor in Miss Cather's firm, lucid sentences. There is good internal evidence that she read a great deal of contemporary literature, contemporary over a stretch of fifty years, and think what contemporaries they were—from Tolstoy and Hardy and James and Chekhov to Gide and Proust and Joyce and Lawrence and Virginia Woolf, to Sherwood Anderson and Theodore Dreiser: the first names that come to mind. There was a regiment of them; it was as rich and fruitfully disturbing a period as literature has to show for several centuries. And it did make an enormous change. Miss Cather held firmly to what she had found for herself, did her own work in her own way, and did help greatly to save and reassert and illustrate the validity of certain great and dangerously threatened principles of art. Without too much fuss, too—and is quietly disappearing into her work altogether, as we might expect.

Mr. Maxwell Geismar wrote a book about her and some others, called *The Last of the Provincials*. Not having read it I do not know his argument; but he has a case: she is a provincial; and I hope not the last. She was a good artist, and all true art is provincial in the most realistic sense: of the very time and place of its making, out of human beings who are so particularly limited by their situation, whose faces and names are real and whose lives begin each one at an individual unique center. Indeed, Willa Cather was as provincial as Hawthorne or Flaubert or Turgenev, as little concerned with aesthetics and as much with morals as Tolstoy, as obstinately reserved as Melville. In fact she always reminds me of very good literary company, of the particularly admirable masters who formed her youthful tastes, her thinking and feeling.

She is a curiously immovable shape, monumental, virtue itself in her art and a symbol of virtue—like certain churches, in fact, or exemplary women, revered and neglected. Yet like these again, she has her faithful friends and true believers, even so to speak her lovers, and they last a lifetime, and after: the only kind of bond she would recognize or require or respect.

—Katherine Anne Porter, "Reflections on Willa Cather," *The Days Before* (1952), in *The Chelsea House Library of Literary Criticism: Twentieth-Century American Literature*, vol. 2, ed. Harold Bloom (New York: Chelsea House Publishers, 1986), 695–96

MORTON DAUWEN ZABEL

It was in young artists—the dreaming, headstrong, fractious, or unstable young, fated to defeat or bad ends by the materialism and ugliness of their sur-roundings—that ⟨Cather⟩ first envisaged the heroic ideal. Paul, Katharine Gaylord, Harvey Merrick, and Don Hedger are the defeated or dishonored "cases" that foreshadow the triumphant lives of Alexandra Bergson, Thea Kronborg, Ántonia Shimerda, Archbishop Machebeuf, and Nancy Till, and that lend their note of desire or vision to the middle terms of Miss Cather's argument—the inspired spirits who do not succeed but who, by some force of character or apartness of nature, lend significance to the faceless anonymity around them. These characters—the "lost lady" Marian Forrester, Myra Henshawe, Tom Outland, Professor St. Peter, even the slighter Lucy Gayheart in a later novel—are the most persuasive of Miss Cather's creations, her near-est claims to skill in a field where she was admittedly and obviously incompe-tent—complex and credible psychology. But somehow she could never bring her opposites into full play in a novel. They remained irreconcilably differen-tiated, dramatically hostile, morally and socially incapable of true complexity.

The full-bodied and heavily documented novel was never congenial to Miss Cather; she rightly understood her art to be one of elimination and selec-tion, which eventually meant that it was an art of simplification and didactic idealization. *The Song of the Lark* and *One of Ours* drag with detail. *My Ántonia* and *A Lost Lady* are her finest successes because there her selection defines, sug-gests, and evokes without falsely idealizing. When she seized a theme of gen-uine social and moral potentiality in *The Professor's House* or *My Mortal Enemy*, she pared away its substance until she produced what must always be, to her admirers, disappointingly frugal and bodiless sketches of two of the most interesting subjects in the America of her time. And when she decided to model *Death Comes for the Archbishop* on the pallid two-dimensional murals of Puvis de Chavannes, she prepared the way for the disembodied idealization, making for inertness and passivity, that overtook her in *Shadows on the Rock*, weakest of her books and portent of the thinness of her final volumes.

What overtook her plots and characters is the same thing that overtook her version of American life and history. She could not bring her early criti-cism into effective combination with her later nostalgic sentiment. ⟨. . .⟩ Miss

Cather, having never mastered the problem of desire in its full social and moral conditioning, passed from her tales of ambitious artists and defeated dreamers, worsted by provincial mediocrity or careerism, to versions of American idealism and its defeat that never come to satisfactory grips with the conditions of society and personal morality. As her lovers, her artists, her pioneers, and her visionary Titans become disembodied of complex emotion or thought, so her America itself became disembodied of its principles of growth, conflict, and historical maturity. There obviously worked in her nature that "poetic romanticism" to which Lionel Trilling has referred her case: what Parrington called "the inferiority complex of the frontier mind before the old and established"; the pioneer's fear of failure but greater fear of the success which comes "when an idea becomes an actuality"; the doctrine of American individualism to which F. J. Turner credited the pioneer's failure to "understand the richness and complexity of life as a whole." So to Willa Cather's early veneration for the distant goals and shining trophies of desire, ambition, and art, there succeeded a veneration for lost or distant sanctities which gradually spelled her diminution as a dramatic and poetic craftsman.

—Morton Dauwen Zabel, "Willa Cather: The Tone of Time," *Craft and Character in Fiction* (1957), in *The Chelsea House Library of Literary Criticism: Twentieth-Century American Literature*, vol. 2, ed. Harold Bloom (New York: Chelsea House Publishers, 1986), 696

BLANCHE H. GELFANT

Jim Burden belongs to a remarkable gallery of characters for whom Cather consistently invalidates sex. Her priests, pioneers, and artists invest all energy elsewhere. Her idealistic young men die prematurely; her bachelors, children, and old folk remain "neutral" observers. Since she wrote within a prohibitive genteel tradition, this reluctance to portray sexuality is hardly surprising. What should intrigue us is the strange involuted nature of her avoidance. She masks sexual ambivalence by certainty of manner, and displays sexual disturbance, even the macabre, with peculiar insouciance. Though the tenor of her writing is normality, normal sex stands barred from her fictional world. Her characters avoid sexual union with significant and sometimes bizarre ingenuity, or achieve it only in dreams. Alexandra Bergson, the heroine of *O Pioneers!*, finds in recurrent reveries the strong transporting arms of a lover; and Jim Burden in *My Ántonia* allows a half-nude woman to smother him with kisses only in unguarded moments of fantasy. Their dreams suggest the typical solipsism of Cather's heroes, who yield to a lover when they are most solitary, most inverted, encaptured by their own imaginations. As Alexandra dispels such reveries by a brisk cold shower, their inferential meaning becomes almost comically clear. Whenever sex enters the real world (as for Emil and Marie in

O Pioneers!), it becomes destructive, leading almost axiomatically to death. No wonder, then, that Cather's heroes have a strong intuitive aversion to sex which they reveal furtively through enigmatic gestures. ⟨. . .⟩

In *My Ántonia*, Jim Burden grows up with an intuitive fear of sex, never acknowledged, and in fact, denied: yet it is a determining force in his story. By deflecting attention from himself to Ántonia, of whom he can speak with utter assurance, he manages to conceal his muddied sexual attitudes. His narrative voice, reinforced by Cather's, emerges firm and certain; and it convinces. We tend to believe with Jim that his authoritative recitation of childhood memories validates the past and gives meaning to the present even though his mature years stream before him emptied of love, intimacy, and purpose. Memory transports him to richer and happier days spent with Ántonia, the young Bohemian girl who signifies "the country, the conditions, the whole adventure . . . childhood." Because a changing landscape brilliantly illumines his childhood—with copper-red prairies transformed to rich wheatfields and corn—his personal story seems to epitomize this larger historical drama. Jim uses the coincidence of his life-span with a historical era to imply that as the country changed and grew, so did he, and moreover, as his memoirs contained historical facts, so did they hold the truth about himself. Critics support Jim's bid for validity, pointing out that "*My Ántonia* exemplifies superbly [Frederick Jackson] Turner's concept of the recurring cultural evolution on the frontier."

Jim's account of both history and himself seems to me disingenuous, indeed, suspect; yet it is for this very reason highly pertinent to an understanding of our own uses of the past. ⟨. . .⟩ Ultimately, Jim forgets as much as he remembers, as his mind sifts through the years to retrieve what he most needs—a purified past in which he can find safety from sex and disorder. Of "a romantic disposition," Jim substitutes wish for reality in celebrating the past. His flight from sexuality parallels a flight from historical truth, and in this respect, he becomes an emblematic American figure, like Jay Gatsby and Clyde Griffiths.

—Blanche H. Gelfant, "The Forgotten Reaping-Hook: Sex in *My Ántonia*," *American Literature* 43, no. 1 (March 1971). © 1971 by Duke University Press, in *Willa Cather*, ed. Harold Bloom (New York: Chelsea House Publishers, 1985), 104–5

JANE RULE

Most interpreters of Willa Cather's work sooner or later remark on her "masculine sensibility" either in noting her preference for male narrators or her realistic and therefore not flattering explorations of heterosexual relationships. For some it is a virtue which places her above the more delicate and limited talents of other women writers. Others, like John H. Randall III, make personal accusations: "she could accept fertility in crops more easily than in human beings, the reason being her fear of physical passion and the dependence on others which it entails." ⟨. . .⟩

What actually characterizes Willa Cather's mind is not a masculine sensibility at all but a capacity to transcend the conventions of what is masculine and what is feminine to see the more complex humanity in her characters. Antonia, the character who so richly fulfills "the usual instinctive woman's lot" in a remarkably happy marriage and fine, loving sons, has physical strength and vitality as well as warmth, tenderness, and compassion. "Oh, better I like to work out of doors than in the house . . . I not care that your grandmother says it makes me like a man. I like to be like a man." In the frontier of Nebraska only those with such strength and pleasure in it can survive. Antonia's father, a frail, gentle artist, commits suicide in despair at crop failures and harsh winters. Willa Cather does not judge him. And she understands, too, Lena Lingard, who chooses to go to Lincoln and run a dress shop rather than marry. "She remembered home as a place where there were always too many children, a cross man, and work piling up around a sick woman."

Willa Cather's method of creating character is to submerge herself in that character, to achieve a total sympathy which will render the character authentically, inevitably, past judgment. Even the morally most objectionable of her characters, by this method, commands compassion and even at times admiration. ⟨. . .⟩

⟨. . .⟩ Willa Cather's literary mentor was Henry James, and, though she learned early not to imitate him, to find her own subject matter, her own style, her own creed of art as simplification, she shared his ability to create an enormous range of characters in accurate, limiting, and illuminating environments. Her sexual tastes, like his, extended rather than limited her sensibilities, whatever social and private burden they may sometimes have been to her. Her only "dangerous idiosyncrasy" is her great gift of perception and craft, which has always made those who are fearful of the truth uncomfortable before it.

—Jane Rule, *Lesbian Images* (New York: Doubleday & Company, Inc., 1975), 79–80, 87

EUDORA WELTY

The emotions of ⟨Willa Cather's⟩ characters ⟨. . .⟩ have deep roots in the physical world—in that actual physical land to which they were born. In such a land, how clear it is from the start that identity—self-identity—is hard to seize, hard to claim, and hard to hold on to.

Another of the touchstones of Willa Cather's work, I think, is her feeling for the young. "There is no work of art so big or so beautiful," she writes, "that it was not once all contained in some youthful body, like this one [it is Thea's] which lay on the floor in the moonlight, pulsing with ardour and anticipation." The burning drive of the young, the desire to live, to do, to make, to achieve, no matter what the sacrifice, is the feeling most surpassingly alive to the author, most moving to us. Life had made her terribly certain that being young in the world is not easy. "If youth did not matter so much to itself, it would never have the heart to go on," she says as Thea starts from home. And Dr. Archie, old friend and traveling companion, "knew that the splendid things of life are few, after all, and so very easy to miss." In O Pioneers! we read that "There is often a good deal of the child left in people who have had to grow up too soon." Miss Cather has a number of ways to tell us that life is most passionate in the promise, not in the fulfillment.

A strenuous physical life is lived throughout every novel, whether it is the struggle for survival or the keen experience of joy in simple physical well-being; it may reach in some characters the point of total identification with the living world around. It is a form of the passion that is all through Willa Cather's work; her work is written out of it. We see it in many modulations: desire—often exalted as ambition; devotion; loyalty; fidelity; physical nearness and kindness and comfort when it lies at rest. Love? It is affection that warms the life in her stories and hate that chills it. There is reconcilement, and there is pity. There is obsession here too, and so is the hunger for something impossible: all of these are forms of love. And there is marriage, though the marriages that occur along the way of the novels are milestones, hardly destinations; as required in the careful building of her plots, they are inclined to be unavailing. Sexual love is not often present in the here and now; we more often learn of it after it is over, or see it in its results. My own feeling is that along with her other superior gifts Willa Cather had a rare sureness as to her subject matter, the knowledge of just what to touch and what not to touch in the best interests of her story.

What her characters are most truly meant for, it seems to me, is to rebel. For her heroines in particular, rebelling is much easier than not rebelling, and we may include love, too, in "not rebelling." It is the strong, clear impulse in Willa Cather's stories. It is the real springwater. It is rebelling, we should always add, not for its own sake as much as for the sake of something a great deal bigger—that of integrity, of truth, of art. It is the other face of aspiration. Willa Cather used her own terms; and she left nothing out. What other honorable way is there for an artist to have her say?

—Eudora Welty, "The House of Willa Cather," The Eye of the Story: Selected Essays and Reviews (New York: Random House, 1977), 52–54

DEBORAH G. LAMBERT

Cather never adequately dealt with her homosexuality in her fiction. In two early novels, the question of sexuality is peripheral: *Alexander's Bridge* (1912) and *The Song of the Lark* ⟨1915⟩ concern the integration of identity, and the expression of sexuality is limited and unobtrusive. Yet Cather began to approach the issue of homosexuality obliquely in subsequent novels. Many, although not all, of the later novels include homosexual relationships concealed in heterosexual guises. Joanna Russ points out that these disguised relationships are characterized by an irrational, hopeless quality and by the fact that the male member of the couple, who is also the central consciousness of the novel, is unconvincingly male—is, in fact, female and a lesbian. ⟨. . .⟩

The original of Ántonia was Annie Sadilek Pavelka, a Bohemian woman whom Cather had loved and admired from childhood, and with whom she maintained a lifelong, affectionate friendship. In 1921, after completion of the novel, Cather wrote of her feeling for Annie and her decision to use the male point of view:

> Of the people who interested me most as a child was the Bohemian
> hired girl of one of our neighbors, who was so good to me. . . . Annie
> fascinated me and I always had it in mind to write a story about
> her. . . . Finally, I concluded that I would write from the point of view
> of the detached observer, because that was what I had always been.
> Then I noticed that much of what I knew about Annie came from the
> talks I had with young men. She had a fascination for them, and they
> used to be with her whenever they could. They had to manage it on
> the sly, because she was only a hired girl. But they respected her, and
> she meant a good deal to some of them. So I decided to make my
> observer a young man.

Here Cather suggests the long genesis of this tale and, significantly, her own replication of the "male" response to Annie, reflected in the language of the passage: "Annie fascinated me"/"She had a fascination for them." The fascination here seems to imply not only a romantic and sexual attraction, but also horror at the attraction. Cather suggests that the young men's response to Ántonia is ambivalent because Annie is forbidden; she is a hired girl, with all of that phrase's various suggestions, and so they see her "on the sly." For Cather that fascination is more complex. Identifying with the young men in their forbidden response to Annie, her impulse is that of the lesbian. Yet, when she wrote the novel and transposed to Jim her own strong attraction to Annie/Ántonia, she also transposed her restrictions on its erotic content. Although she adopts the male persona, she cannot allow him full expression of her feelings. Thus, what would seem to be Jim's legitimate response to Ántonia is prohibited and omitted: its homosexual threat is, evidently, too great, and so we find at the heart of the novel that emptiness ⟨. . . .⟩

The avoidance of sexuality (which does not extend beyond the Jim-Ántonia relationship, however) must be seen in connection with McClung's desertion of Cather, which occurred after she had composed the first two or three chapters of *My Ántonia*. During this time of grieving, she seemed not to trust herself to write of her own experience of love and sex. For the Cather persona and the beloved woman are not only separated, both are actually denied sexuality, although sexuality arises in distorted, grotesque forms throughout the novel.

During the writing of *My Ántonia*, Cather's grief coincided with the already great burden of anxiety of the woman who is a writer. After this time, her heroic stance in her fiction could not continue, and she abandons the creation of strong fictional women. In *My Ántonia* she denies Jim's erotic impulses and Ántonia's sexuality as well; and she retreats into the safety of convention by ensconcing Ántonia in marriage and rendering her apotheosis as earth mother. She abandons Ántonia's selfhood along with her sexuality: as Mrs. Cuzak, Ántonia is "a battered woman," and a "rich mine of life, like the founders of early races." Interestingly, critics have recognized the absence of sexuality in Jim, although not in Ántonia, and focus their analyses on the male in the case, as though the novel had been written about a male character by a male author—or, as if the male experience were always central.

—Deborah G. Lambert, "The Defeat of the Hero: Autonomy and Sexuality in *My Ántonia*," *American Literature* 53, no. 4 (January 1982). © 1982 by Duke University Press, in *Willa Cather's My Ántonia*, ed. Harold Bloom (New York: Chelsea House Publishers, 1987), 124–26

PHYLLIS ROSE

In the 1950s David Daiches cannily predicted that literary historians would have difficulty placing Willa Cather. He did not foresee that Cather's work would be underrated because it was hard to place, but such may have been the case. It could be said that Cather has been ignored because she was a woman, but that would not explain why her rediscovery has taken ten years longer than Virginia Woolf's. Generally perceived as a traditionalist, Cather has been patronized. Many people read her for pleasure, but for the past twenty years few have taught her works or written about them. The novels seem curiously self-evident. They are defiantly smooth and elegant, lacking the rough edges that so often provide convenient starting points for literary analysis. To a critical tradition that has valued complexity, ambiguity, even obscurity, the hard-won simplicities of Cather's art seem merely simple. Her lucidity can be read as shallowness; her massive, abstract forms can be—and have been—viewed as naively traditional, the appropriate vehicle for an art essentially nostalgic and elegaic.

Although I am deeply distrustful of the way in which, for twentieth-century writers, the term "modernist" is not merely an honorific but the precondition of attention from literary critics and scholars, I will nonetheless try to show ways in which Willa Cather's work is allied to modernism. I do this by way of redressing a balance. Her public stance was so belligerently reactionary (perhaps in order to mask the radically unacceptable nature of her private life) that she herself encouraged the flattening of her work into a glorification of the past, a lament for the shabbiness of the present, which has persisted for decades. The writer who titled a collection of essays *Not Under Forty* would have been the last person to feel congratulated at being called a modernist. But it is time to risk her wrath. In part because of her defensive self-presentation, in part because her fiction so perfectly embodies certain aesthetic ideals of modernism—monumentality, functionalism, anonymity—we have overlooked its innovative nature. To see its modernist elements is to readjust and enrich our response to her work—and also to widen our notions of modernism. If Cather is a modernist, she is a tempered, transitional modernist closer to Hardy than to Pound. Nonetheless, her work is moved in important ways by a modernist urge to simplify and to suggest the eternal through the particular. Because we have paid more attention to other aspects of literary modernism—the overtly experimental, the representation of subjectivity, the literary analogues of cubist collage—we react to Cather's novels as though we have stumbled across some giant work of nature, a boulder, something so massive that it seems inhuman, uncrafted. But I would suggest that what we have stumbled upon in fact is something like the literary equivalent of an Arp, a Brancusi, a Moore.

I would point first of all to her scale. I do not mean, of course, the size of her books, for they are conspicuously slender, little masterpieces of economy; I mean the size of the subjects to which her imagination responds. In her strongest work, the land is as much a presence as the human characters, and the landscapes that move her imagination are large and unbroken ones, the plains and fields of the American Midwest, the canyonlands and deserts of the Southwest. Reading *O Pioneers!, My Ántonia,* or *Death Comes for the Archbishop,* we experience the exhilarating potential of clear blank spaces. Few novels I can think of are less cluttered than these; they offer the breathing space of all outdoors, and one feels that Cather may be describing herself when she says of Alexandra Bergson, the Swedish immigrant farmer who is her first great female protagonist, that she was uncertain in her indoor tastes and expressed herself best in her fields, that properly speaking her house was the out-of-doors. ⟨. . .⟩

Visual analogues for Cather's modernism are many. The determining fac-
tor, as in so much modernist painting which exploded out of the confines of
easel-sized canvases, is scale. One thinks of the wall-sized works of Picasso
and Matisse, such as *Guernica* and *The Dance of Life;* one thinks of the giant canvases of Jackson Pollock and the vast areas, made to seem even vaster by their
minimalist treatment, of works by Rothko, Frankenthaler, Barnett Newman;
one thinks of the murals of Orozsco and Thomas Hart Benton. To work on
that scale involves simplification. The reduction to essential forms, which
began in the visual arts with Cézanne, finds a literary analogue in Cather's
insistence that the cone, the circle, and the square are at the basis of everything we see. If her novels seem consequently simple, their simplicity has the
same aim as Klee's figures, Matisse's late abstract cutouts, or Picasso's consciously childlike drawings. It is a simplicity that aims to capture the elemental and enduring and that requires the greatest art to produce.

    —Phyllis Rose, "Modernism: The Case of Willa Cather," *Modernism Reconsidered* (Harvard
University Press, 1983), in *American Fiction 1914 to 1945*, ed. Harold Bloom (New York:
Chelsea House Publishers, 1987), 61–62, 75

JUDITH FETTERLEY

In revising the "Introduction" Cather removed all references to herself.
Dramatized in the act of revision and embedded thus in the revision itself,
palimpsest sub-text informing the super-imposed surface text, is the renunciation of Cather's own point of view and of the story that could be told from that
point of view. To return to the motif of Camille, I would suggest that the
renunciation at issue is Cather's own. In *My Ántonia* Cather renounces the possibility of writing directly in her own voice, telling her own story, and imag-
ining herself in the pages of her text. Obviously autobiographical, the obvious
narrator for *My Ántonia* would be Cather herself. Yet for Cather to write in a
female voice about Ántonia as an object of intense and powerful feelings
would require that she acknowledge a lesbian sensibility and feel comfortable
with such a self-presentation—a task only slightly easier to do now than then.
Indeed, in the context of early 20th century self-consciousness of sexual
"deviance" and thus of the potentially sexual content of "female friendships,"
Jewett's directive to Cather to avoid the "masquerade" of masculine impersonation and write openly in her own voice of women's love for women—("a
woman could love her in that same protecting way—a woman could even care
enough to wish to take her away from such a life, by some means or other"
⟨*The Letters of Sarah Orne Jewett*, ed. Annie Fields, 1911, 246⟩)—seems faintly spe-
cious. In fact, it was not "safer" for Cather to write "about him as you did about
the others, and not try to be he!" ⟨Jewett, 247⟩ Her "safety" lay precisely in her
masquerade.

Yet *My Ántonia* is not simply "safe." Choosing to transpose her own experience into a masculine key, Cather nonetheless confronts us with a transposition which is radically incomplete. At the end of Book IV, Jim confesses to Ántonia, "I'd have liked to have you for a sweetheart, or a wife, or my mother or my sister—anything that a woman can be to a man" (p. 321). Why, then, does he not so have her? No reader of *My Ántonia* can avoid asking this question because Cather makes no attempt to answer it and thus prevent us. For the contradiction between speech and act cracks open the text and reveals the story within the story, the story which can't be told directly, the essence of whose meaning is the fact that it can't be told.

Though nominally male, Jim behaves in ways that mark him as female. From the start he is anomalous. On the farm, he rarely leaves the kitchen; he inhabits women's space: "When grandmother and I went into the Shimerda's house, we found the women-folk alone. . . . The cold drove the women into the cave-house, and it was soon crowded" (pp. 114, 115). Yet Cather can't have him doing women's work; thus Jim does virtually nothing, a fact which at once contributes to his insubstantiality and provides a context for understanding its source. Jim's most active moment comes, not surprisingly, when he is left alone. With no one to observe him and with responsibility for all tasks of both sexes, he throws himself into housework and barn work with equal vigor. ⟨. . .⟩

In the "Introduction" to *My Ántonia*, we hear a voice that is marked as neither male nor female. This voice recurs throughout the text. Often we forget that we are listening to Jim Burden—his masculinity, as suggested above, has been made easy to forget—and we assume instead that we are hearing the voice of Willa Cather. This slippage occurs most frequently and most easily when the subject of contemplation is the landscape. A woman's voice making love to a feminine landscape—here, I would suggest, is the key to Cather's genius and achievement. Unable to write directly of her own experience and to tell her own story in her own voice, and thus baffled and inhibited in the development of character and plot, Cather turned her attention elsewhere, bringing the force of her talent to bear on the creation of the land, her country, her *matria*. In the land, Cather created a female figure of heroic proportions, proportions adequate to both her lived experience as a woman and her imaginative reach as a woman writer. In the land, Cather successfully imagined herself; in the land, she imagined a woman who could be safely eroticized and safely loved. Thus the story she could not tell in terms of character and character is told in terms of narrator and country, and the flattening and foreshortening of personality which is the consequence of her renunciation of her own voice has as its corollary a complementary lengthening and enriching of landscape. Cather made her mark in the territory of American literature with her landscape; we remember her *matria* long after we have forgotten her masquerade. Though she may have sold her birthright, the price she got for it was gold.

—Judith Fetterley, "*My Ántonia,* Jim Burden and the Dilemma of the Lesbian Writer," *Gender Studies: New Directions in Feminist Criticism,* ed. Judith Spector (Bowling Green, OH: Bowling Green State University Popular Press, 1986), in *Ántonia,* ed. Harold Bloom (New York: Chelsea House Publishers, 1991), 140–41, 145–46

SHARON O'BRIEN

Cather's projection of self into male characters, her portrayal of romantic love as heterosexual, and her occasional creation of unconvincing male masks whose gender seems indeterminate or female raise another interpretive difficulty for the reader of her fiction. Those critics who view Cather's portrayal of heterosexual passion as an encoded transcription of lesbian love assume that the overt text conceals a covert text which is the "real" story Cather would have written had she been able. But assuming that all Cather's heterosexual plots are cover stories for homosexual ones and that her male lovers are invariably masks for women simplifies both text and writer. To argue that most of her male characters engaged in love affairs are not male at all is to question the writer's ability to transcend self, gender, and sexuality to adopt other selves; it is also to assume that whenever Cather wrote of heterosexual love she was encoding a lesbian attachment, a reductive view of her fiction as well as of her imagination. ⟨. . .⟩

In stories where textual clues direct us to consider the male characters as masks for a female perceiver, the heterosexual "cover" story functions simultaneously as disguise and defense and serves a social as well as a psychological function. Of course this does not mean that Cather was not invested in the surface story: like the costumes she chose to wear in life, her literary disguises revealed as well as concealed the self. Hence Cather's early stories call for the same interpretive strategy required by most of her fiction. Since at times she was writing two stories at once, a heterosexual and a homosexual one, just as she projected herself into both male and female characters, we are frequently faced with indeterminate meaning rather than with a clearly encoded subtext that constitutes the "real" message of the text. The heterosexual "cover" story, although socially necessary as a way of naming indirectly the "thing not named," is not invariably the false one, the hidden lesbian story the real. Instead, meaning and authorial intention oscillate back and forth between the two. The spatial metaphor that best captures this pattern is the continual interplay between figure and ground rather than hierarchical opposition between surface and hidden, overt and covert meaning.

Cather's need to imply the presence of the "not named" may also have contributed to her fiction the allusive, suggestive qualities we associate with modernism. The aesthetic of indirection she espoused in "The Novel Démeublé" evokes at once the lesbian writer forced to conceal and the twentieth-century writer aware both of the inadequacies and the possibilities of language. Even though she was not a self-conscious modernist and in fact espoused an antimodernist rhetoric, because Cather could not tell the truth directly she was, at times, forced to tell it slant, and the resulting creative tension between expression and suppression produced novels that are subtle, richly symbolic, and ambiguous, enriched by the repressed, the hidden, and the covert. Ultimately her need both to disclose and to conceal lesbianism—one of the conflicts that threatened to silence the beginning writer—contributed to the pleasure she found in the creative process.

Unlike her novels, however, Cather's first stories are weakened rather than enriched by the "inexplicable presence" of the unnamed. The young writer did not possess enough control over the psychological and emotional conflicts revealed in the unassimilated subtexts. As a result, unlike her novels the short stories are not separate enough from their unconscious sources to be fictions that both draw upon the self and exist apart from it. Although there are occasionally powerful moments that anticipate the later fiction—her understated description of Peter's suicide, for example—the technical flaws reflect not only the inexperienced writer's failure to command the tools of the trade, but also the young woman's failure to control and shape her recurrent psychological preoccupations. Indeed, these two failures were connected. Cather could not master either her craft or the psychic material from which her fiction sprang until she could momentarily abandon control and make the artist's closed secret open. When she could, the reworked story of the child's search for the mother became *My Ántonia*. Hence, Cather's twenty-year journey from her first short stories to her novels reveals psychological as well as technical growth.

—Sharon O'Brien, "Disclosure and Concealment: The First Stories," *Willa Cather: The Emerging Voice* (New York: Oxford University Press, 1987), 217–18

B I B L I O G R A P H Y

April Twilights. 1903.

The Troll Garden. 1905.

The Life of Mary Baker Eddy and the History of Christian Science, by Georgine Milmine (editor). 1909.

Alexander's Bridge. 1912.

O Pioneers! 1913.

My Autobiography, by S. S. McClure (ghostwriter). 1914.

The Song of the Lark. 1915.

My Ántonia. 1918.

Youth and the Bright Medusa. 1920.

One of Ours. 1922.

Verse. 1922.

A Lost Lady. 1923.

April Twilights and Other Poems. 1923.

The Professor's House. 1925.

My Mortal Enemy. 1926.

Death Comes for the Archbishop. 1927.

Shadows on the Rock. 1931.

The Fear That Walks by Noonday. 1931.

Obscure Destinies. 1932.

December Night. 1933.

Lucy Gayheart. 1935.

Not under Forty. 1936.

Novels and Stories (13 vols.). 1937-41.

Sapphira and the Slave Girl. 1940.

The Old Beauty and Others. 1948.

On Writing: Critical Studies on Writing as an Art. 1949.

Writings from Willa Cather's Campus Years. Ed. James R. Shively. 1950.

Father Juniper's Holy Family. 1955.

Five Stories. 1956.

Willa Cather in Europe: Her Own Story of the First Journey. Ed. George N. Kates. 1956.

Early Stories. Ed. Mildred R. Bennet. 1957.

Collected Short Fiction 1892-1912. Ed. Virginia Faulkner. 1965.

The Kingdom of Art: Willa Cather's First Principles and Critical Principles 1893-1896. Ed. Bernice Slote. 1966.

The World and the Parish: Willa Cather's Articles and Reviews 1893-1902. Ed. Willam M. Curtin (2 vols.). 1970.

Uncle Valentine and Other Stories: Uncollected Fiction 1915-1929. Ed. Bernice Slote. 1973.

Friend of My Springtime: A Classic Story of Friendship. 1974.

The Troll Garden; Obscure Destinies. 1981.

Neighbor Rosicky. 1986.

RADCLYFFE HALL

1886–1943

MARGUERITE RADCLYFFE-HALL was born in 1886 in Bournemouth, Hampshire, England. She was raised by her mother and her Italian stepfather, who were by turns indifferent and emotionally and physically abusive. From her maternal grandmother, who was affectionate and encouraging, she developed lifelong interests in nature, animals, music, and fine arts.

When she was 17, Hall inherited a considerable fortune from her natural father, whom she had met only twice. She purchased a house for herself and her grandmother and traveled extensively throughout Europe, where she discovered a supportive lesbian community. She attended King's College in London and later studied in Germany.

An accomplished pianist, Hall was encouraged by her grandmother to publish the poetry she had written as lyrics to her piano compositions. *'Twixt Earth and Stars*, her first book of poetry, appeared in 1903; in the next 12 years Hall would publish three more volumes of poetry.

Around this time Hall met Lady Mabel Batten, who became her lover and adviser. In an effort to further Hall's career, Batten introduced her to members of London's literary circles and urged her to write fiction as a further outlet for her increasingly autobiographical and erotically explicit poetry. In 1915, Hall met Lady Una Troubridge, Batten's cousin; Troubridge would become her lifelong companion and eventual biographer.

Hall published two novels in 1924, *The Forge* and *The Unlit Lamp*. She earned critical respect with the prizewinning *Adam's Breed* (1926), an autobiographical novel—with a male protagonist—about the struggle for acceptance by others.

Hall consulted Una Troubridge before beginning work on her most famous and most heavily autobiographical novel, *The Well of Loneliness* (1928). The only novel in which Hall dealt explicitly with lesbianism, *The Well* was banned as obscene in England and in the United States. Among the members of the literary community who supported her during the obscenity trial were Leonard and Virginia Woolf, Bernard Shaw, H. G. Wells, Aldous Huxley, and Hugh Walpole; others feared being associated with such a controversial subject. The novel was eventually cleared by a United States court and has since become a classic of lesbian fiction.

Hall, who frequently dressed in men's clothing and referred to herself as "John," continued to write with compassion about nonconforming individuals. Her devout Catholicism and her belief in psychic phenomena are reflected in such novels as *The Master of the House* (1932), *The Sixth Beatitude* (1936), and *The Well of Loneliness*. After years of illness and repeated surgery, Hall died of cancer on October 7, 1943. She was buried according to her wishes in a plot between Batten and Troubridge, believing they would all be reunited after death.

CRITICAL EXTRACTS

HAVELOCK ELLIS

I have read *The Well of Loneliness* with great interest because—apart from its fine qualities as a novel by a writer of accomplished art—it possesses a notable psychological and sociological significance. So far as I know, it is the first English novel which presents, in a completely faithful and uncompromising form, one particular aspect of sexual life as it exists among us to-day. The relation of certain people—who, while different from their fellow human beings are sometimes of the highest character and the finest aptitudes—to the often hostile society in which they move, presents difficult and still unsolved problems. The poignant situations which thus arise here set forth so vividly, and yet with such complete absence of offence, that we must place Radclyffe Hall's book on a high level of distinction.

    —Havelock Ellis, "Commentary," *The Well of Loneliness* (New York: Anchor Books Doubleday, 1956, orig. pub. 1928), 6

CYRIL CONNOLLY

The Well of Loneliness is a serious novel on the theme of homosexuality in women. It is a long, tedious and absolutely humourless book. There is a very simple literary rule in dealing with this kind of subject. What the author takes for granted, the reader will take for granted, what the author makes a fuss about the reader will fuss about too. A very easy instance of this is the fact that no reader of Sherlock Holmes questions his right to inject himself freely with cocaine—a slight twist in the author's sense of values would have altered this into a terrible weakness which would in its turn have shocked and grieved the reader. Similarly one of the most successful novels of the last few years described an episode as typical as any in *The Well of Loneliness*, but because it was described without flourish or comment it was quite quietly received. It is just this rule which Miss Hall failed to keep. *The Well of Loneliness* is a melodramatic description of a subject which has nothing melodramatic about it. What literary interest it has, and it might have a great deal, is obscured by the constant stream of propaganda of every kind, and the author's perpetual insistence that the invert is a great tragic figure, branded with the mark of Cain, set apart from her kind as the victim of the injustice of God and the persecution of the world. The book is really a chronicle of the misfortunes of the invert, but since it assumes the invert to be born an invert and condemned beyond all hope of cure to remain one, it can hardly be said to point a moral of any kind. It is presumably a plea for greater tolerance, but the world is perfectly prepared to tolerate the invert, if the invert will only make concessions to the world. Most of us are resigned to the doctrine of homosexuals, that they alone possess all the greatest heroes and all the finer feelings, but it is surely preposterous that they should claim a right, not only to the mark of Cain, but to the martyr's crown. The tragedy of Stephen Gordon, the heroine of this book, is not really that of inversion but of genius; but if of genius, it is that of any sensitive, artistic, religious and uncompromising human being who refuses to adapt herself to the conditions of life. ⟨. . .⟩

The Well of Loneliness may be a brave book to have written, but let us hope it will pave the way for someone to write a better. Homosexuality is, after all, as rich in comedy as in tragedy, and it is time it was emancipated from the aura of distinguished damnation and religious martyrdom which surrounds its so fiercely aggressive apologists. Stephen Gordon is a Victorian character, an *âme damnée*; once we are reconciled to her position, we are distressed by her lack of spirit, her failure to revenge herself on her tormentors. Sappho had never heard of the mark of Cain, she was also well able to look after herself, but never did she possess a disciple so conscious of her inferiority as Stephen Gordon, or so lacking—for 15s.!—in the rudiments of charm.

   —Cyril Connolly, "New Novels," *New Statesman* (25 Aug. 1928), in *The Chelsea House Library of Literary Criticism: Twentieth-Century British Literature*, vol. 2, ed. Harold Bloom (New York: Chelsea House Publishers, 1986), 1032–33

UNA, LADY TROUBRIDGE

It was after the success of *Adam's Breed* that John came to me one day with unusual gravity and asked for my decision in a serious matter: she had long wanted to write a book on sexual inversion, a novel that would be accessible to the general public who did not have access to technical treatises. At one time she had thought of making it a 'period' book, built round an actual personality of the early nineteenth century. But her instinct had told her that in any case she must postpone such a book until her name was made; until her unusual theme would get a hearing as being the work of an established writer.

It was her absolute conviction that such a book could only be written by a sexual invert, who alone could be qualified by personal knowledge and experience to speak on behalf of a misunderstood and misjudged minority.

It was with this conviction that she came to me, telling me that in her view the time was ripe, and that although the publication of such a book might mean the shipwreck of her whole career, she was fully prepared to make any sacrifice except—the sacrifice of my peace of mind.

She pointed out that in view of our union and of all the years that we had shared a home, what affected her must also affect me and that I would be included in any condemnation. Therefore she placed the decision in my hands and would write or refrain as I should decide.

I am glad to remember that my reply was made without so much as an instant's hesitation: I told her to write what was in her heart, that so far as any effect upon myself was concerned, I was sick to death of ambiguities, and only wished to be known for what I was and to dwell with her in the palace of truth.

Then and there she set to work on *The Well of Loneliness*.

—Una, Lady Troubridge, *The Life and Death of Radclyffe Hall* (1961), in *The Chelsea House Library of Literary Criticism: Twentieth-Century British Literature*, vol. 2, ed. Harold Bloom (New York: Chelsea House Publishers, 1986), 1031

MARGARET LAWRENCE

Radclyffe Hall suggests without actually declaring it that the women of the Lesbian group with which she deals in one section of the book are women of out-and-out muscularity of brain. It leaves the reader with still another question in mind, and that is the possibility of mental muscularity presupposing a definite amount of masculine content in a woman; and the corollary that the woman who uses her brain in the struggle of accomplishment becomes more and more masculine with time. And that question also has to be left unanswered inasmuch as the history of feminism is still too young to indicate any reliable answer.

Apart altogether from its psychiatric implications, *The Well of Loneliness* produces an artistic impression which is somewhat similar to the artistic impression of the Greek tragedies. The Greeks accepted inversion in all its variations as being of excellent dramatic substance. The Greeks were able to separate their intellectual curiosity from their instinctive regard for the preservation of the normal, which fact alone makes them stand out in history a superior people. Radclyffe Hall set herself the mission of portraying to the normal the sufferings of the invert in society. She pleads for pity and for understanding. She says that mankind, having only just begun to find the laws relating to sex, may in a relatively short time discover that there are biological accidents producing inversion. Her heroine she presents as a victim for our sympathy. The pity note in the book is pity that goes out to all creatures who are not able, through her theory of biological accident, or through the psychiatric theory of trauma, to partake of normal experience.

There is pity also for the race which, through its terror of the abnormal, punishes the victims, and may thereby lose valuable services in the fields that are other than racial. She believes that these people, because of their peculiarity, have something else to do for the race than to continue it. She stresses their acutely sensitized nerves—the nerves that always go with beings of high capacity. She dwells upon the invert's susceptibility to sound. Radclyffe Hall herself writes with mystical sensitivity to tone. Her phrasing shows it. Her words are put down in relation to their sounds set against other sounds. She produces by this means a disturbing emotional effect.

The importance of her fictional comment upon the situation of the invert lies in this—that inasmuch as inversion, by reason of its distortion of nerves, can at least be tentatively held to be a nervous disorder, the invert should not be treated as a pariah, but rather as a person who through no fault of his or her own is suffering from nervous excitement coming from the kinetic response of the whole human fabric to change. It can be drawn from her story that only the highly sensitized members of society take shock acutely enough to be disorganized away from the normal, and that in the long run it is only the highly sensitized members of society who are in the spiritual sense valuable. The race goes on. The normal people see to that. But art and religion and thought and science have always been maintained in the race by the variously abnormal, and meanwhile they suffer tortures through being unable to adjust themselves to normality.

—Margaret Lawrence, "Priestesses," *The School of Femininity* (1936), in *The Chelsea House Library of Literary Criticism: Twentieth-Century British Literature*, vol. 2, ed. Harold Bloom (New York: Chelsea House Publishers, 1986), 1033

JANE RULE

The Well of Loneliness by Radclyffe Hall, published in 1928, remains *the* lesbian novel, a title familiar to most readers of fiction, either a bible or a horror story for any lesbian who reads at all. There have been other books published since, better written, more accurate according to recent moral and psychological speculation, but none of them has seriously challenged the position of *The Well of Loneliness*. Often a book finds momentary identity only by negative comparison with that "noble, tragic tract about the love that cannot speak its name." Along with the teachings of the church and the moral translations of those teachings by psychologists, *The Well of Loneliness* has influenced millions of readers in their attitudes toward lesbians.

Radclyffe Hall's intention was to write a sympathetic and accurate book about inversion. She was already a novelist and poet of some reputation, and, if she had neither the craft nor the power of insight of her contemporary D. H. Lawrence, she shared his zeal for educating the public. Scientific books were not at that time generally available. Krafft-Ebing's famous *Psychopathia Sexualis* was directed at the medical profession, and details of case studies, like the title, were written in Latin lest the book fall into the wrong hands and corrupt the naive reader. Radclyffe Hall had read Krafft-Ebing, as well as the less well-known studies of Karl Heinrich Ulrichs, himself a homosexual trying to prove that inversion was as natural an orientation as left-handedness. She obviously read not only with a scholar's interest but with a desire to understand herself, a congenital invert in her own eyes whose sexual appetites were satisfied exclusively by women. *The Well of Loneliness* was, therefore, not only a novel intended to give insight into the experience of inverts but also to justify Radclyffe Hall's own life. She must have been the more pressed to defend the innocence of her nature because she was a Catholic, apparently thoughtfully and deeply committed to most of the doctrines of the Church. She died, after a long struggle with cancer, serene in her belief that she would be only temporarily separated from Una, Lady Troubridge, the woman with whom she had lived for some years. She did not expect that reunion to take place in the appropriate circle of Dante's hell, for, if there was anyone responsible for her nature, it was God, Who "in a thoughtless moment had created in His turn, those pitiful thousands who must stand forever outside His blessing." Outside His blessing on earth, she must have rationalized. Or in some way she singled herself out, redeemed by the book she had written in which her last plea is "Acknowledge us, o God, before the whole world. Give us also the right to our existence." There is no final evidence for how she reconciled her sexual life with her faith. There is only the testimony of those closest to her that she had resolved the conflict for herself. ⟨. . .⟩

Though *The Well of Loneliness* was viciously attacked for its sympathetic idealizing of the invert, giving it greater importance at the time than it deserved, its survival as the single authoritative novel on lesbian love depends on its misconceptions. It supports the view that men are naturally superior, that, given a choice, any woman would prefer a real man unless she herself is a congenital freak. Though inept and feminine men are criticized, though some are seen to abuse the power they have, their right to that power is never questioned. Stephen does not defy the social structure she was born into. Male domination is intolerable to her only when she can't assert it for herself. Women are inferior. Loving relationships must be between superior and inferior persons. Stephen's sexual rejection of Martin, though it is offered as conclusive proof of her irreversible inversion, is basically a rejection of being the inferior partner in a relationship. Her reaction is one of "repulsion—terror and repulsion . . . a look of outrage." In her relationship with Mary, Stephen is "all things to Mary; father, mother, friend and lover, all things, and Mary is all things to her—the child, the friend, the beloved, all things." The repetition of "all things" is not persuasive enough to cover the inequality of the categories. When Stephen decides not to fight for Mary, she gives her to Martin much as one would give any other thing one owns. And though her altruism is sometimes associated with her female gender, it is more often likened to the virtues of Christ. It is courageous or foolhardy for a woman to behave like a man, but, since she accepts herself as a freak, since in fiction if not in life she is made to give up the ultimate prize, she is no political threat to anyone. The natural order of things is reasserted, and she is left on the outside, calling to God and to society for recognition. ⟨. . .⟩

Radclyffe Hall was a courageous woman, and *The Well of Loneliness* is an important book because it does so carefully reveal the honest misconceptions about women's nature and experience which have limited and crippled so many people. Radclyffe Hall did think of herself as a freak, but emotionally and intellectually she was far more a "womanly woman" than many of her literary contemporaries. She worshiped the very institutions which oppressed her, the Church and the patriarchy, which have taught women there are only two choices, inferiority or perversion. Inside that framework, she made and tried to redefine the only proud choice she had. The "bible" she offered is really no better for women than the Bible she would not reject.

—Jane Rule, *Lesbian Images* (1975), in *The Chelsea House Library of Literary Criticism: Twentieth-Century British Literature*, vol. 2, ed. Harold Bloom (New York: Chelsea House Publishers, 1986), 1035, 1038

LOUISE BERNIKOW

The Well of Loneliness is about exile. Its mood is apologetic; it is meant as a plea for tolerance (of "inversion") and it is dense with self-hate . . .

Shadow and sunlight, clouded and free, victimized and defiant, these are the terms that come to mind as *The Well of Loneliness* is placed beside *Orlando* and both placed in historical context. Shadow, clouds, victimization, emanating from self-hate, which itself emanates from the contagion of homophobia in the surrounding culture. This characterizes not only Radclyffe Hall's novel, but the diary that Vita Sackville-West kept about her affair with Violet Trefusis. This is "monster" literature—the lesbian as deviant, deformed, sick—in which ethics require her defeat. Most masculine literature about love is in this vein. The woman must be vanquished; the man in the story triumphs.

The context is homophobia. Opposition comes from all quarters. Definitions are made—heterosexuality is the norm in language and culture—

applied and, often, internalized. Whatever the core of the love experience, its encounter with the world ends in devastation. Shakespeare showed this in Romeo and Juliet, and those lovers remain in readers' minds with benign grace and the youthful aura of tragedy. Not so lesbian lovers, who, like Radclyffe Hall's protagonist, must parade their pain, express anger at heterosexual tyranny by passivity: look what you have done to me.

Opposition comes from all quarters, even in the period under considera-tion, the only time in history, except, perhaps, for Sappho's, when a culture to support the literature thrived. E. M. Forster, for example, indignant as he became at the suppression of *The Well of Loneliness*, told Virginia Woolf that he did not, in fact, approve of lesbians because he "disliked the idea of women being independent of men." . . .

Opposition comes also, and perhaps more painfully, from women. In *The Well of Loneliness*, it is Stephen's mother who reviles her and sends her into exile. In their confrontation, the mother begins with her own physical revulsion— "a desire not to touch or be touched by you—a terrible thing for a mother to feel"—and moves, as tyrants always do, from the personal to the universal with no thought or feeling in between. The mother, enforcer, in this novel of patri-archal values, says easily that Stephen is "unnatural" a "sin against creation," but especially "a sin against the father who bred you." Stephen defends herself against her mother and against the world by accepting their terms and trying to put herself into the existing scheme of things. "As a man loves a woman," she says, "that was how I loved."

—Louise Bernikow, "Lovers," *Among Women* (1980), in *The Chelsea House Library of Literary Criticism: Twentieth-Century British Literature*, vol. 2, ed. Harold Bloom (New York: Chelsea House Publishers, 1986), 1034–35

CLAUDIA STILLMAN FRANKS

I have called this study 'Beyond *The Well of Loneliness*' because I have wanted to dispel the misconception that Radclyffe Hall was a one-book thesis novelist, and because I believe that she should finally be acknowledged as a writer who successfully employed a variety of fictional themes, personality types, and nar-rative tones in her work. Indeed, one of the most striking features of her fic-tion, when it is viewed in its entirety, is the large panorama of characters who inhabit her world. They come from all walks of life, all social classes, and all age groups; they also vary widely in intellectual capability, creative capacity, and sexual inclination. Many are conventional, and many are unconventional; some melt into the crowd, and others are loners or eccentrics. Once it is rec-ognized, however, that *The Well of Loneliness* represents merely one part of Radclyffe Hall's total achievement, it is worth asking to what extent the book is representative of all her writing; in other words, to what extent is Stephen Gordon a kind of paradigm of the alienated individual within the context of Radclyffe Hall's universe? And how does Radclyffe Hall characteristically order her fictional world?

At the centre of each of Radclyffe Hall's seven novels and five short stories stands a character who is marked by unusual sensitivity, by vague or concrete longings or ambitions, and by a tendency to reject the limitations of his or her environment. Joan Ogden of *The Unlit Lamp*, Susan Brent of *The Forge*, Sidonia Shore of *A Saturday Life*, and Stephen Gordon of *The Well of Loneliness*, all temporarily or permanently refuse to accept a woman's traditional role: Gian-Luca of *Adam's Breed*, Christophe Bénédit of *The Master of the House*, and Hannah Bullen of *The Sixth Beatitude* reject the purely materialistic orientation of their milieu and perish in the attempt to incorporate spiritual reality into the context of mundane experience; and the protagonists of *Miss Ogilvy Finds Herself* are isolated by self-deception, by contingencies of time and place, or by a value system which is incomprehensible to other people. Stephen Gordon, then, is far from an unusual character in the Radclyffe Hall canon, and, although the problems she faces as a lesbian in society are painfully real, I do not think that it is an exaggeration to say that her lesbianism also serves as a type of metaphor for the alienation that Radclyffe Hall saw at the root of human existence, just as racial and ethnic characteristics have been used partially as metaphors for alienation in modern literature.

Despite the sense of personal alienation which dominates her fiction, however, Radclyffe Hall's world is not a uniformly bleak one, for it does contain sources of joy. Among these are human love, community feeling, apprehension of divinity, and receptivity to natural beauty. Except in her two comedies, though, none of these sources of fulfilment proves permanently sustaining for the central characters, at least not within the context of their ordinary lives. ⟨. . .⟩

The basic theme of the individual's ultimate isolation, whether it is socially-imposed, self-imposed, or the result of impersonal natural laws, dominates Radclyffe Hall's writing. There is no development of this concept throughout her fiction; rather, it is a given condition of the world she creates. Only in her comedies does she make exceptions, but even there, the feeling of isolation is evoked by important secondary characters—Venetia Ford in *The Forge*, and Frances Reide in *A Saturday Life*. In view of the most crucial episodes in Radclyffe Hall's life, her fictional emphasis is hardly surprising. When one considers her major biographical events and circumstances up to 1916—her lonely childhood, her unsympathetic mother and step-father, her longing for her real father, her subservient devotion to Agnes Nichols, her frustrating affairs with women, her almost unavoidable sense of inferiority in her relationship with Mabel Batten, then finally Ladye's tragic death—one sees that the underlying tone of Radclyffe Hall's life quite naturally manifested itself in her fiction. Her happiness with Una Troubridge may have freed her to realize her creative potential, but it could hardly have been expected to wipe out the effects of her first thirty-five years.

And so all of Radclyffe Hall's writing is partially autobiographical in that it reflects a vision of the world in which the individual is necessarily thwarted—if not by sexual nature, then by some other condition of life. It is in this wider context that *The Well of Loneliness* should be seen; Stephen Gordon is not merely the somewhat masochistic outcast who cries to an unlistening god for the right to existence; instead, in her sensitivity, her struggle for happiness, and her inevitable failure, she is typical of Radclyffe Hall's major protagonists, like them embodying aspects of her creator, and like them reflecting parts of her rich and complex personality.

—Claudia Stillman Franks, "Conclusion," *Beyond "The Well of Loneliness"* (1982), in *The Chelsea House Library of Literary Criticism: Twentieth-Century British Literature*, vol. 2, ed. Harold Bloom (New York: Chelsea House Publishers, 1986), 1038–40

INEZ MARTINEZ

I believe that Hall's rendering of the psyche in her two lesbian novels has little to do with what she read or what she had her characters read, and I believe the power of her portrait of the lesbian hero in love with the beautiful woman accounts for the continued meaningfulness of the novels, even to "hip" readers. Modern readers persist through her prose (written appropriately enough in the mode of heroic elaboration rather than, say, ironic or elliptical terseness) because Hall wrote of the failure of hero-beauty eros, and because she grounded this failure in the hero's worship of a consuming mother.

Eros based on opposition involves an attempt to unite with what one is not. The hero-beauty opposition poses strength or feats at one pole and beauty or being at the other. Historically, of course, strength and doing have been associated with the male hero, and beauty and being with the adored female. The terms in which Hall rendered the basic emotional dynamic between these two poles are conventional enough: her heroes have to struggle against fear, draw upon personal resources, and be endlessly protective in order to offer feats to the worshiped woman; the female is charged with so valuing her beautiful being that she is willing to be worshiped, gratefully accept protection from her hero, and bestow on her hero approval, admiration, and her self. The hero does not consciously identify as the beautiful flower who needs protection and whose life purpose is fulfilled simply through being—even if to be so serves her. In turn, the worshiped female—even if controlling events herself—

does not identify with the competitor triumphing through personal strength and gaining life's purpose by winning a flower to protect.

Hall departed from convention by simply removing the sex-linking from these two poles. In Joan Ogden, hero of *The Unlit Lamp*, and in Stephen Gordon, hero of *The Well of Loneliness*, but particularly in Stephen, Hall created female protagonists who naturally and utterly identify with the heroic position. These characterizations imply that the hero-beauty dynamic is archetypal, i.e., a way of manifesting a human potential (in this case erotic attraction) inherent in the human psyche.

Although Hall created lovers for her heroes, lovers who identify with the worshiped female, the women who possess the power of approval for Joan and Stephen are their mothers. In most respects no two women could be more different than Mrs. Ogden and Anna Gordon, but the two of them are identical in refusing to affirm the maturation of their daughters and in assuming that absolute service from them is their due. Ultimately, it is in the struggle against the values of their mothers that Joan and Stephen must choose between self-affirmation and self-sacrifice.

This dilemma led Hall to an uncharacteristic critique of self-sacrifice. In her other novels Hall idealized characters capable of total self-abnegation in the service of others. In Madalena of *Adam's Breed*, in Hannah of *The Sixth Beatitude*, and in Christophe of *Master of the House* Hall seemed to think the Christian cross, the nailing together of love and death, a vindication of human suffering. Because Hall's attitude in these novels is passionately orthodox, her description of the destructiveness of self-sacrifice in her lesbian heroes is particularly arresting. As she has plotted their lives, maturation demands self-affirmation at the cost of pain to the beloved.

At this point a wary reader might think I am writing in support of the commonplace idea that lesbian love is a substitute mother-daughter relationship. 〈. . .〉

The pattern in Hall's novels at once resembles the commonplace idea about lesbian love and differs essentially from it. In Hall's rendering, both heroes have mothers who are intensely selfish and do not want their daughters to be themselves. But the solution for the daughters does not lie in a substitute mother-daughter relationship; rather, Joan and Stephen are tasked to wrest the affirming power from their mothers and assume it themselves. In Hall's novels, such self-affirmation is a condition for successful lesbian love; unfortunately, it is by definition inaccessible to the heroic attitude.

—Inez Martinez, "The Lesbian Hero Bound: Radclyffe Hall's Portrait of Sapphic Daughters and Their Mothers," *Literary Visions of Homosexuality* (1983), in *The Chelsea House Library of Literary Criticism: Twentieth-Century British Literature*, vol. 2, ed. Harold Bloom (New York: Chelsea House Publishers, 1986), 1040–41

CATHARINE R. STIMPSON

Lesbian novels in English have responded judgementally to the perversion that has made homosexuality perverse by developing two repetitive patterns: the dying fall, a narrative of damnation, of the lesbian's suffering as a lonely outcast attracted to a psychological lower caste; and the enabling escape, a narrative of the reversal of such descending trajectories, of the lesbian's rebellion against social stigma and self-contempt. Because the first has been dominant during the twentieth century, the second has had to flee from the imaginative grip of that tradition as well. 〈. . .〉

If the lesbian writer wished to name her experience but still feared plain speech, she could encrypt her text in another sense and use codes. 〈. . .〉 In some lesbian fiction, the encoding is allegorical, a straightforward shift from one set of terms to another, from a clitoris to a cow. Other acts are more resistant to any reading that might wholly reveal, or wholly deny, lesbian eroticism. 〈. . .〉

〈. . .〉 As if making an implicit, perhaps unconscious pact with her culture, the lesbian writer who rejects both silence and excessive coding can claim the right to write for the public in exchange for adopting the narrative of damnation. The paradigm of this narrative is Radclyffe Hall's *The Well of Loneliness*— published, banned in England, and quickly issued elsewhere in 1928, by which time scorn for lesbianism had hardened into orthodoxy. Novelist as well as novel have entered minor mythology. Hall represents the lesbian as scandal and the lesbian as woman-who-is-man, who proves "her" masculinity through taking a feminine woman-who-is-woman as "her" lover. In a baroque and savage satire published after *The Well of Loneliness*, Wyndham Lewis excoriates a den of dykes in which a woman artist in "a stiff Radcliffe-Hall collar, of antique masculine cut" torments a heterosexual fellow and dabbles with a voluptuous mate. He is too jealous and enraged to recognize either the sadness of costume and role reversal (the stigmatized seeking to erase the mark through aping the stigmatizers) or the courage of the masquerade (the emblazoning of defiance and jaunty play). Be it mimicry or bravery, the woman who would be man reaches for status and for freedom. The man who would be woman, because of the devaluation of the female and feminine, participates, in part, in a ritual of degradation.

Comparing *The Well of Loneliness* to Hall's life reveals a discrepancy between the pleasures she seems to have found with her lover, Una Taylor, Lady Troubridge, and the sorrows of her hero, Stephen Gordon. Hall offers a parallel to the phenomenon of the woman novelist who creates women characters less accomplished and successful than she. In addition, the novel is more pessimistic about the threat of homosexuality as such to happiness than Hall's earlier novel, *The Unlit Lamp* (1924). 〈. . .〉

⟨. . .⟩ In brief, *The Well of Loneliness* tends to ignore the more benign possibilities of lesbianism. Hall projects homosexuality as a sickness. To deepen the horror, the abnormal illness is inescapable, preordained; an ascribed, not an achieved, status. For Stephen is a "congenital invert," the term John Addington Symonds probably coined around 1883. ⟨. . .⟩

The congenital female invert has male physical traits—narrow hips, wide shoulders—as "part of an organic instinct." Stephen also has a livid scar on her cheek. Literally, it is a war wound; socially, a mark of the stigmatized individual who may blame the self for a lack of acceptability; mythically, the mark of Cain. *The Well of Loneliness* stresses the morbidity of a stigma that the politics of heaven, not of earth, must first relieve.

Yet Hall planned an explicit protest against that morbidity. Indeed, having Stephen Gordon be a congenital invert who has no choice about her condition strengthens Hall's argument about the unfairness of equating homosexuality with punishable deviancy. The novel claims that God created homosexuals. If they are good enough for Him, they ought to be good enough for us. Hall cries out for sacred and social toleration, for an end to the cruelties of alienation. In the novel's famous last paragraph, Stephen gasps, "God . . . we believe; we have told You we believe. . . . We have not denied You, then rise up and defend us. Acknowledge us, oh God, before the whole world. Give us the right to our existence." Ironically, the very explicitness of that cry in a climate increasingly harsh for lesbians, combined with the vividness of Hall's description of homosexual subworlds, propelled *The Well of Loneliness* into scandal while the far more subversive, if subtle *Unlit Lamp* was a success. To double the irony, Hall's strategies of protest against damnation so entangle her in damnation that they intensify the sense of its inevitability and power. The novel's attack on homophobia becomes particularly self-defeating. The text is, then, like a Janus with one face looming larger than the other. It gives the heterosexual a voyeuristic tour and the vicarious comfort of reading about an enforced stigma—in greater measure than it provokes guilt. It gives the homosexual, particularly the lesbian, riddling images of pity, self-pity, and terror—in greater measure than it consoles.

—Catharine R. Stimpson, "Zero Degree Deviancy: The Lesbian Novel in English," in *Feminisms: An Anthology of Literary Theory and Criticism*, ed. Robyn R. Warhol and Diane Price Herndl (New Brunswick: Rutgers University Press, 1992), 301–5

LILLIAN FADERMAN

Hall believed that her novel would provide lesbians with a moral and medical defense against a society which viewed same-sex love as immoral or curable. If a female argued that she chose to center her life on another female, she laid herself open to accusations of immorality, she willfully flew in the face of the conventions of her day. If she accepted the psychoanalytical theory that something had happened to her in childhood to cause her aberration, she had no excuse not to seek a cure which would undo the trauma and set her straight. But if she maintained that she was born with her "condition," although some might consider her a freak she could insist, as Hall actually did, that God created her that way, that she had a purpose in God's scheme of things even if she was a freak. Unless a lesbian accepted the congenitalists' theories, her grounds for not changing were indefensible if she did not live in a society totally committed to the principle of free choice—and Hall knew that her barely post-Victorian society had no such commitment. ⟨. . .⟩

There was probably no lesbian in the four decades between 1928 and the late 1960's capable of reading English or any of the eleven languages into which the book was translated who was unfamiliar with *The Well of Loneliness*. Del Martin, co-author of *Lesbian/Woman*, has called it a "Lesbian Bible." It was widely used in college abnormal psychology classes, and was the only lesbian novel known to the masses. But many lesbians who read the book during Hall's day and after felt angered and betrayed by it. An American Sociological study of lesbians in the 1920's and 1930's indicated that "almost to a woman, they decried its publication." They believed that if the novel did not actually do harm to their cause, at the least it "put homosexuality in the wrong light." The responses of individual lesbians were similar. The artist Romaine Brooks, for example, called *The Well* "a ridiculous book, trite, superficial" and Hall "a digger up of worms with the pretention of a distinguished archaeologist." Violet Trefusis in a letter to her lover, Vita Sackville-West, declared the book a "loathesome example," and said she longed herself to write a story of same-sex love in response that would be very different.

Nor has the novel brought much satisfaction or joy to women in more recent times. It has often served to label for a woman what her love for another female has meant to society in the twentieth century, and it plays a sad, prominent part in many an individual lesbian history. ⟨. . .⟩

The Well has had generally such a devastating effect on female same-sex love not only because its central character ends in loneliness but—and much more significantly—because its writer fell into the congenitalist trap. She believed that if she argued that some women were born different, society would free them to pursue their independence; instead, her popular rendition of "congenital inversion" further morbidified the most natural impulses and healthy views. It reinforced the notion that some women would not marry not because the institution was often unjust, that they sought independence not because they believed it would make them whole people, that they loved other women not because such love was natural—but instead because they were born into the wrong body. To be born into the wrong body was freakish. Many a woman must have decided to tolerate even the worst heterosexual inequities rather than to view herself in such a way.

—Lillian Faderman, *Surpassing the Love of Men: Romantic Friendship and Love Between Women from the Renaissance to the Present* (New York: Quality Paperback Book Club, 1994), 317–18, 322–23

BIBLIOGRAPHY

'Twixt Earth and Stars. 1903.
A Sheaf of Verses. 1908.
Poems of the Past and Present. 1910.
Songs of Three Counties, and Other Poems. 1913.
The Forgotten Island. 1915.
The Forge. 1924.
The Unlit Lamp. 1924.
A Saturday Life. 1925.
Adam's Breed. 1926.
The Well of Loneliness. 1928.
The Master of the House. 1932.
Miss Ogilvy Finds Herself. 1934.
The Sixth Beatitude. 1936.

PATRICIA HIGHSMITH

1921–1995

MARY PATRICIA HIGHSMITH was born in Fort Worth, Texas, on January 19, 1921, and grew up in New York. Her parents, who separated before she was born, were both commercial artists, as was her stepfather, whose name she adopted after her mother's remarriage. Highsmith herself drew and painted before devoting herself to writing. After receiving a B.A. from Barnard College in 1942, she worked as a freelance comic-book writer while publishing occasional short stories. Her first novel, a thriller called *Strangers on a Train* (1950), provided the basis for one of Alfred Hitchcock's finest films.

Highsmith's second novel, *The Price of Salt*, is the tale of a lesbian love affair, published in 1952 under the pseudonym Claire Morgan. Though the book received only fair reviews, it sold one million paperback copies and Highsmith was deluged with fan mail. In 1984, *The Price of Salt* was reissued under her own name with a new afterword by the author; it was published in England six years later as *Carol*.

Highsmith returned to the thriller genre in 1955 with *The Talented Mr. Ripley*, which became a film under the title *Purple Noon*. A clumsy but likable murderer, Tom Ripley became Highsmith's most enduring character, appearing in several sequels, among them *Ripley Under Ground* (1970), *Ripley's Game* (1974), and *Ripley Under Water* (1991). But Highsmith's Ripley novels are not entirely representative of her work, which is largely grim, cheerless, and tautly written. The psychology of guilt and the effects of crime upon individuals in society inform much of her work. She has described her theories and practice of suspense writing in *Plotting and Writing Suspense Fiction* (1966).

Highsmith was less widely recognized in America than in Europe, where she lived after the 1950s. She was awarded the Grand Prix de Littérature Policière for *The Talented Mr. Ripley* and in 1964 won the Crime Writers Association of England Silver Dagger Award for *The Two Faces of January*.

Highsmith produced several volumes of short stories, including *The Snail-Watcher and Other Stories* (1970), *Little Tales of Misogyny* (1977), and *Tales of Natural and Unnatural Catastrophes* (1987). Many of her stories are tales of fantasy, horror, or comedy rather than crime or suspense.

Patricia Highsmith died in Switzerland on February 5, 1995.

C R I T I C A L   E X T R A C T S

FRANCIS WYNDHAM

Miss Highsmith writes murder stories which are literally that: stories about murder. They are about what drives people to kill and about what the event of murder is like for the killer and for the people connected with him and his victim. It is rare for death to occur in a Highsmith novel until at least a third of the book is past; often it is reserved for the very end. When it takes place, her readers are made aware not only of the horror, but also of the embarrassment following an act of destructive violence; it is as if a person one knows quite well were suddenly killed by somebody else one knows quite well. And although Miss Highsmith makes the most scrupulous psychological preparation for her murders, so that their eruption is never unconvincing, yet the effect on her readers is shocking in the same kind of way as the experience of murder would be in life. For very rarely, in life, can murder be expected: yet it happens.

Guilt is her theme, and she approaches it through two contrasting heroes. These may be simplified as the guilty man who has justified his guilt and the innocent man who feels himself to be guilty. Both appeared in her first and most famous novel, *Strangers on a Train*: the soft, plausible charmer who is really a psychopath and the shy bungler who allows himself to be engulfed in a nightmare from which he is too ineffectual (and perhaps basically unwilling) to extricate himself. Variations on one or other of these mutually attractive figures dominate her later books: *The Blunderer, A Game for the Living* and *The Cry of the Owl* concentrate on the victim of malign events who is hypnotised into immobility by the horror of his situation; while *The Talented Mr. Ripley, Deep Water* and *This Sweet Sickness* provide full-length portraits of the well-spoken young man, somehow incomplete and yet not apparently sinister, who slithers into mania and murder. The books in the first group also contain a detective whose behaviour is capricious, irrational yet depressingly dogged; this figure is the more menacing because he is invariably wrong. Miss Highsmith specialises in male characters, but two types of women recur throughout her work: the bitch and the nice girl. The bitch (Melinda in *Deep Water*, Nickie in *The Cry of the Owl*) can be a creature of Strindbergian venom, compensating for some mysterious sexual outrage or disappointment by the total destruction of a man. The nice girl (Marge in *Mr. Ripley*, Effie in *This Sweet Sickness*, Jenny in *The Cry of the Owl*) is intense, affectionate, rather arty, and fatally unsuspicious. ⟨. . .⟩

⟨. . .⟩ Miss Highsmith's plots are often praised for being ingenious, but they are never tidy; chance, coincidence, silly misunderstandings play their part, as they do in life. She knows that people do not always act in their own best interests, and that their motives are more obscure than psychological novelists often care to admit. Her peculiar brand of horror comes less from the inevitability of disaster, than from the ease with which it might have been avoided. The evil of her agents is answered by the impotence of her patients—this is not the attraction of opposites, but in some subtle way the call of like to like. When they finally clash in climactic catastrophe, the reader's sense of satisfaction may derive from sources as dark as those which motivate Patricia Highsmith's destroyers and their fascinated victims.

    —Francis Wyndham, "Miss Highsmith," *New Statesman* (31 May 1963), in *The Chelsea House Library of Literary Criticism: Twentieth-Century American Literature*, vol. 1, ed. Harold Bloom (New York: Chelsea House Publishers, 1985), 1884

GRAHAM GREENE

Miss Highsmith is a crime novelist whose books one can reread many times. There are very few of whom one can say that. She is a writer who has created a world of her own—a world claustrophobic and irrational which we enter each time with a sense of personal danger, with the head half turned over the shoulder, even with a certain reluctance, for these are cruel pleasures we are going to experience, until somewhere about the third chapter the frontier is closed behind us, we cannot retreat, we are doomed to live till the story's end with another of her long series of wanted men.

It makes the tension worse that we are never sure whether even the worst of them, like the talented Mr. Ripley, won't get away with it or that the relatively innocent won't suffer like the blunderer Walter or the relatively guilty escape altogether like Sydney Bartleby in *The Story-Teller*. This is a world without moral endings. It has nothing in common with the heroic world of her peers, Hammett and Chandler, and her detectives (sometimes monsters of cruelty like the American Lieutenant Corby of *The Blunderer* or dull sympathetic rational characters like the British Inspector Brockway) have nothing in common with the romantic and disillusioned private eyes who will always, we know, triumph finally over evil and see that justice is done, even though they may have to send a mistress to the chair.

Nothing is certain when we have crossed *this* frontier. It is not the world as we once believed we knew it, but it is frighteningly more real to us than the house next door. Actions are sudden and impromptu and the motives sometimes so inexplicable that we simply have to accept them on trust. I believe because it is impossible. Her characters are irrational, and they leap to life in their very lack of reason; suddenly we realise how unbelievably rational most fictional characters are as they lead their lives from A to Z, like commuters always taking the same train. The motives of these are never inexplicable because they are so drearily obvious. The characters are as flat as a mathematical symbol. We accepted them as real once, but when we look back at them from Miss Highsmith's side of the frontier, we realise that our world was not really as rational as all that. Suddenly with a sense of fear we think, "Perhaps I really belong *here*," and going out into the familiar street we pass with a shiver of apprehension the offices of the American Express, the centre, for so many of Miss Highsmith's dubious men, of their rootless European experience, where letters are to be picked up (though the name on the envelope is probably false) and travellers' cheques are to be cashed (with a forged signature).

—Graham Greene, "Introduction" to *The Snail-Watcher and Other Stories* (1970), in *The Chelsea House Library of Literary Criticism: Twentieth-Century American Literature*, vol. 1, ed. Harold Bloom (New York: Chelsea House Publishers, 1985), 1886–87

BRIGID BROPHY

Taken (which it could but I don't think it should be) purely as a novel of suspense, *A Dog's Ransom* is a virtuoso piece. Miss Highsmith is in such command that she can actually do without mystery and still compel you to read urgently on. ⟨. . .⟩

What *A Dog's Ransom* counts on, to carry the reader, is the soundness of its construction. Before quite renouncing mystery by entering the psychopath's mind, it establishes the strategic centres from which it is going to explore the responses forced from the sane by erratic and lunatic acts of violence. Ed Reynolds is at first unambivalent, concerned simply and reasonably for the safety of his dog. The narrative builds up his plausibility by an engaging circumstantialness about his actions; and by the same token it evokes, without needing to describe, the physical grittiness and social unease of New York: 'He had just come from the office, and as he let the water rinse away the soap, he thought: "I'm washing my hands of the subway and also of that damned letter." '

Ed's quasi-parental responsibility for his dog is reinforced by the fact that, a year before the story opens, his grown-up daughter has died by violence. This looks like an item of merely worldly-wise plotting, a device to hook the sympathy even of readers cold towards dogs. But it turns out to be a structural necessity in the design, carrying the book deeper into its theme and also creating a contrasting link between Ed and the narrative's other chief centre of consciousness, which resides in Patrolman Clarence Duhamell.

Duhamell is a realistically elastic and amorphous personality. He aspires to be good, and has indeed chosen deliberately to be a 'good cop' in the sense of eschewing the corruption practised by his colleagues. Impressed by the patent fact that Ed, in the altruism of his immediate relationships, simply is good, Duhamell involves himself in the case of the poodle, to which he is not assigned. He wants to help Ed and, in doing so, to act out his own large but unshaped aspirations towards being a parent and protector of society as a whole. But Duhamell traps himself into making an attack on violence that is itself violent. Ed is riven by moral ambivalence towards the 'help' Duhamell affords him. And Duhamell fails to get away with committing evil for the ironic reason that he is, precisely, not one of the bad cops. ⟨. . .⟩

The intellectual effort that goes into (and the intellectual profit that a reader can take from) a novel lies not in the overt statements of the narrative and dialogue but in the power of the thought incarnated in the design. No more than it describes New York does *A Dog's Ransom* make statements about society and violence. Yet it is a profound act of thought on the theme of violence seducing its opponents into violence. Statistics might affirm that the problem is most acute in New York: *A Dog's Ransom* can achieve the imaginative rightness of being set there. Sociology and reporting, with their wide scatter, can set out contradictions in moral attitudes: *A Dog's Ransom* performs the indispensable function of fiction by taking the reader deep into the ironies of his own ambivalence.

—Brigid Brophy, "Poodle," *Listener* (11 May 1972), in *The Chelsea House Library of Literary Criticism: Twentieth-Century American Literature*, vol. 1, ed. Harold Bloom (New York: Chelsea House Publishers, 1985), 1887–88.

PATRICIA HIGHSMITH

The suspense writer can improve his lot and the reputation of the suspense novel by putting into his books the qualities that have always made books good—insight, character, an opening of new horizons for the imagination of the reader. I do not speak, in this paragraph, about mystery books, because they are out of my line, and it is a characteristic of them that the identity of the murderer is not deeply explored, if at all. If a suspense writer is going to write about murderers and victims, about people in the vortex of this awful whirl of events, he should do more than describe brutality and gore and the gooseflesh in the night. He should throw some light on his characters' minds; he should be interested in justice or the absence of it in the world we live in; he should be interested in the morality, good and bad, that exists today; he should be interested in human cowardice or courage, and not merely as forces to push his plot this way and that. In a word, his people should be real. This seriousness may sound at variance with the element of playing that I mentioned in regard to plot, but it is not, since I am talking of another matter. The spirit of playing is necessary in plotting to permit freedom of the imagination. It is also necessary in inventing characters. But once one has the characters in mind, and the plot, the characters should be given most serious consideration, and one should pay attention to what they are doing and why, and if one does not explain it—and it may be artistically bad to explain too much—then a writer should know why his characters behave as they do and should be able to answer this question to himself. It is by this that insight is born, by this that the book acquires value. Insight is not something found in psychology books; it is in every creative person. And—see Dostoyevsky—writers are decades ahead of the textbooks, anyway.

It often happens that a writer has a theme or a pattern in his books, and he should be aware of this, though again not in a hampering way. He should be aware of it so as to exploit it well, and so as not to repeat it without realizing it. Some writers' themes may be a quest for something—a father one never knew, the pot of gold which does not exist at the foot of the rainbow. Others may have a recurrent girl-in-distress motif, which starts them off plotting, and without which they are not exactly comfortable writing. Another is a doomed love or a doomed marriage. Mine is the relationship between two men, usually quite different in make-up, sometimes obviously the good and the evil, sometimes merely ill-matched friends. I might have realized this theme in myself at least by the middle of *Strangers on a Train*, but it was a friend, a newspaperman, who pointed it out to me when I was twenty-six and just beginning *Strangers*, a man who had seen the manuscript of my first effort at twenty-two that I have already mentioned, the book that was never finished. This was about a rich, spoiled boy, and a poor boy who wanted to be a painter. They were fifteen years old in the book. As if that weren't enough, there were two minor characters, a tough athletic boy who seldom attended school (and then only to shock the school with things like the bloated corpse of a drowned dog he had found on the banks of the East River) and a puny, clever boy who giggled a great deal and adored him and was always in his company. The two-men theme turned up also in *The Blunderer*, *The Talented Mr. Ripley*, in *A Game for the Living*, and *The Two Faces of January*, and raises its head a little in *The Glass Cell* in the curious comrades-in-social-defiance attitude between Carter and Gawill. So in six books out of ten it has turned up, certainly in my "best" books in public opinion. Unless one is in danger of repeating oneself, they should be used to the fullest, because a writer will write better making use of what is, for some strange reason, innate.

—Patricia Highsmith, "Some Notes on Suspense in General," *Plotting and Writing Suspense Fiction* (1972), in *The Chelsea House Library of Literary Criticism: Twentieth-Century American Literature*, vol. 1, ed. Harold Bloom (New York: Chelsea House Publishers, 1985), 1884–85

LOUIS FINGER

Up to now, Miss Highsmith has chosen to alert us by exhibiting the spirals of frightful and outlandish consequence that it's possible to get caught up in, and—with Ripley—how it's all too easy to be awful. In *Edith's Diary*, the matter is approached from, as it were, the far end of the tunnel. Instead of moving outwards from the banal to the spectacular, we are led deeper and deeper into the heart of the banal, to where the real horror is of what's utterly familiar. Miss Highsmith employs her dead-pan suspense techniques to unfold the day-to-day, year-to-year, minutiae of a life that's almost wholly passive, a life that is defined in nearly every detail by its obligations, its rituals, its chores, its ever-darkening banality.

Edith is a well-off, Left-progressive, middle-middle-class housewife, a busy and capable manager, a loyal wife, and a genial and tolerant mother to her only child. When the book opens, the family is packing to leave for a new house in the country, where Brett's salary will be lower but the air less polluted, where there will be space for the boy to grow up in and opportunity for her and Brett to start their own Left-progressive town newspaper and in their small way maybe do some good. It sounds a reliable recipe for a distinctive type of American good life. Edith writes optimistically about the move in the diary she's been keeping for some years.

It's a fairly typical Highsmith opening, so when the packing is interrupted briefly by the sound of the boy Cliffie tormenting the cat, or when Edith reflects idly on an ugly dream she's had a few nights earlier, we settle down to wait for the menace to start building up. And this is more or less where we stay throughout the book. Things happen: Brett's old uncle is moved into the house and proves demanding and irritating. Cliffie grows more and more sullen and disaffected; Brett falls in love with his secretary and goes off with her; there are deaths in the family and quarrels with neighbors; there are the impinging political upheavals of Vietnam, Watergate, and so on.

Summed up, it's a fairly ordinary sequence of events; and, although the neutral, itemising clarity of Highsmith's prose hints all the time that an eruption is just around the corner, the book's real shock effect is registered precisely through the steady lifelessness of the lives it so inertly charts. Gradually we are made aware that there are two ways of describing Edith's life, and that the second way—the way that sees it as horribly devoured by odious dependents—is the way Edith can't afford to contemplate. Hence her diary, in which she invents a successful career for her son, arranges a satisfactory marriage, two fine children, frequent loving visits to the old homestead. The keeping of the diary and the clinging to the last meticulous, desperate detail of her imprisoning routine is what she hopes will keep her sane; and, of course, if that effort fails, she'll be the last to know. As the pressure intensifies, the most mundane domestic function is made to seem like an icy little melodrama. It's not going to be easy from now on for Miss Highsmith to scare us with mere murder.

—Louis Finger, "Mere Murder," *New Statesman* (1 July 1977), in *The Chelsea House Library of Literary Criticism: Twentieth-Century American Literature*, vol. 1, ed. Harold Bloom (New York: Chelsea House Publishers, 1985), 1886

ERLENE HUBLY

Patricia Highsmith's artists, those characters who create works of art and often themselves in the process, form, even when compared to some of her other protagonists, a unique group of characters. There is Sydney Bartleby, the writer-hero of *A Suspension of Mercy*, who in order to stimulate his imagination, plans the imaginary murder of his wife, an endeavor which he then proceeds to act out as though it were so. His ruse is so successful that both his friends and the authorities think he has murdered his wife, as does he himself at times. There is Howard Ingham, the writer-hero of *The Tremor of Forgery*, who, again, in order to excite his imagination, deliberately lives in a dangerous place, Tunisia, in order to undergo new and dark passions, committing, possibly, even a murder, so that he can write about his experiences. And there is, above all others, the character of Tom Ripley, who if he is not a writer, is an actor, a master of the art of impersonation. It is this art, when coupled with the act of murder, that enables Ripley not only to kill a wealthy young American, Dickie Greenleaf, and then to pose as him, but also to provide for his own future security as well, Ripley producing, after Dickie's death, a will, forged, of course, by him, in which Dickie Greenleaf leaves all his money to his good friend, Tom Ripley. Indeed, Highsmith's artists display her ingenuity at its best, allowing her to fashion plots that dazzle the reader with their inventiveness. In addition, Highsmith's artists get the reader closer to the heart of her fictional world perhaps better than any other of her characters. For by examining her artists, we explore some of her major themes: the nature of identity; homosexuality; the real versus the imagined world; the effect of a foreign country on the Americans who live there. ⟨. . .⟩

If murder stimulates Highsmith's writers' imaginations, it can do so because of their peculiar view of reality. For Highsmith's artists, having manipulated reality for so long through the act of writing, masters at turning the real into fiction, live in a fluid world where few things are clearly defined. Sydney Bartleby, for example, often has difficulty distinguishing the real from the imagined and at times thinks that real conversations he is having with real people are imaginary ones, the words being spoken sounding "like lines in a play they were performing." His efforts at creating fiction, of acting out and experiencing the murder of Alicia, are so successful that he convinces himself that she is dead. And at the height of his difficulties with the police, when asked by Inspector Brockway if he did kill his wife, Bartleby can barely answer "no," feels as if his imagined murder of her is real, that he has "only hours more of freedom" before he is arrested for the crime of murder. The line between the real and the imagined becomes so blurred in Bartleby's mind that later, when he commits a real murder, that of Edward Tilbury, the man with whom Alicia had lived while she was at Brighton, he does so with less effort and with fewer feelings of guilt than he experienced when he committed the imaginary murder of Alicia. Indeed, it is his imagined murder that affects him most deeply.

—Erlene Hubly, "A Portrait of the Artist: The Novels of Patricia Highsmith," *Clues* 5, no. 1 (Spring-Summer 1984), in *Modern Crime and Suspense Writers*, ed. Harold Bloom (New York: Chelsea House Publishers, 1995), 94–95

KATHLEEN GREGORY KLEIN

A key to both *Strangers* ⟨*on a Train*⟩ and Highsmith's inversion of the standard techniques of the genre can be found in Guy Haines' profession. As an architect he is concerned with design, order, harmony and honesty. When he rejects a beach club commission because of Miriam's new entanglement in his life, Guy is genuinely pained to think of the imitation Frank Lloyd Wright building which will replace his perfect conception; in designing his own Y-shaped house, he refused necessary economies which would truncate the building. His work is, for him, a spiritual act, defined by unity and wholeness; it rejects disorder, fragmentation and shallowness. Contrasted in the two sections of the book are his description of the bridge he hopes to build as the climax of his career and his inability to accept the commission when telegraphed an offer. His dream of a great white bridge with a span like angels' wings is shattered when his feeling of corruption keeps him from his talent.

In Highsmith's fictional world, issues of order, harmony or civilization—whatever it is called—are seldom so simple and traditional. Contrasted with the more stereotyped perspective which Guy accepts is her series character Tom Ripley. His notions of order are equally predictable; Bach, or classical music in general, provides the right stimuli to focus his attention, distill and concentrate his mind. Ripley uses these devices, however sincerely he may value them as entities in themselves, as personal preparations for crime: fraud, theft, murder. Not so amoral, Guy uses them as avoidance mechanisms; he refuses to consider trying to create perfect order out of his own disordered mind. These attitudes toward order mark Highsmith's vacillating and threatening challenge to oversimplified theories of order and disorder, harmony and chaos. Never committing her fiction to either the triumph of order or the inevitability of chaos, she creates worlds which misuse both, locations in which both are equally and simultaneously present; in fact, she suggests that they may be indistinguishable. Highsmith's manipulation of these dualities suggests closer parallels with contemporary absurdists and existentialists than with her colleagues in crime or suspense fiction. Challenging the either/or structure of human thinking in a work ostensibly about a pair of murders and murderers is part of Highsmith's conscious expansion of an established genre into a new and provocative form.

> —Kathleen Gregory Klein, "Patricia Highsmith," *And Then There Were Nine . . .: More Women of Mystery*, ed. Jane S. Bakerman (Bowling Green, OH: Bowling Green State University Popular Press, 1985), in *Modern Crime and Suspense Writers*, ed. Harold Bloom (New York: Chelsea House Publishers, 1995), 95–96

SUSANNAH CLAPP

Carol is a novel about a lesbian love-affair and was written shortly after *Strangers on a Train*, which was branded by Harper as 'A Harper Novel of Suspense.' Anxious not to be relabelled as 'a lesbian-book writer,' Highsmith submitted the manuscript under a pseudonym: Harper turned it down. She changed publishers, and the book appeared in 1952. It was called 'The Price of Salt' and was said to be by Claire Morgan; it received 'respectable' reviews, piles of fan mail, and sold a million copies in paperback. It is a romance which reads almost exactly like a Patricia Highsmith thriller.

Highsmith got the idea for *Carol* in 1948 when she was 27. She had finished her first novel, was broke and fed up, and had taken a job in a Manhattan department store. She was sent to work in the toy department, on the dolls' counter—where all those floppy or morbidly stiff little limbs and those rows of glassy eyeballs must have appealed to her. One day a blonde woman in a mink coat came into the store. She was elegant and a little uncertain. She bought a doll, gave a delivery name and address, and left. 'It was a routine transaction . . . But I felt cold and swimmy in the head, near to fainting, yet at the same time uplifted, as if I had seen a vision.' Highsmith went home and wrote out the entire plot of *Carol*, which begins with a meeting between a salesgirl and a glamorous older woman in the toy department of a large store, spills out across the North American continent, as the two women decide to go travelling together (at first simply as friends, later as lovers), and ends with the couple looking as if they will try to settle down together. ⟨. . .⟩

Like her murderers, Highsmith's lovers make their dreams come true. In *Strangers on a Train* Bruno imagines committing the perfect murder ('the idea of my life') and then does it. In *Carol* the 19-year-old shop assistant fantasises about kissing the beautiful older woman—who has money, a husband, a child and a huge house—and ends up running off with her. In many novels such success would be punished, but in Highsmith's fiction people get away with things. Tom Ripley begins a murderous career by drowning one acquaintance and battering another—and then swans off to a Greek island. Therese and Carol are vilified and threatened by husbands, lovers and lawyers, but finally decide they can manage a future together. It was this glimmer of a happy ending that attracted early readers of *Carol*. 'Prior to this book,' Highsmith reflects, 'homosexuals male and female in American novels had had to pay for their deviation by cutting their wrists, drowning themselves in a swimming-pool, or by switching to heterosexuality (so it was stated), or by collapsing—alone and miserable and shunned—into a depression equal to hell.'

    —Susannah Clapp, "Lovers on a Train," *London Review of Books* (10 January 1991), in *Modern Crime and Suspense Writers*, ed. Harold Bloom (New York: Chelsea House Publishers, 1995), 96–97

B I B L I O G R A P H Y

Strangers on a Train. 1950.
The Price of Salt (Carol). 1952.
The Blunderer. 1954.
The Talented Mr. Ripley. 1955.
Deep Water. 1957.
A Game for the Living. 1958.
Miranda, the Panda, Is on the Veranda (with Doris Sanders). 1958.
This Sweet Sickness. 1960.
The Cry of the Owl. 1962.
The Two Faces of January. 1964.
The Glass Cell. 1964.
The Story-Teller (A Suspension of Mercy). 1965.
Plotting and Writing Suspense Fiction. 1966, 1981.
Those Who Walk Away. 1967.
The Tremor of Forgery. 1969.
The Snail-Watcher and Other Stories (Eleven). 1970.
Ripley Under Ground. 1970.
A Dog's Ransom. 1972.
Ripley's Game. 1974.
The Animal Lover's Book of Beastly Murder. 1975.

Edith's Diary. 1977.

Little Tales of Misogyny. 1977.

Slowly, Slowly in the Wind. 1979.

The Boy Who Followed Ripley. 1980.

The Black House. 1981.

People Who Knock on the Door. 1983.

The Mysterious Mr. Ripley (The Talented Mr. Ripley, Ripley Under Ground, Ripley's Game). 1985.

Mermaids on the Golf Course and Other Stories. 1985.

Found in the Street. 1986.

Tales of Natural and Unnatural Catastrophes. 1987.

Folie à Deux: Three Novels (Strangers on a Train, The Talented Mr. Ripley, This Sweet Sickness). 1988.

Ripley Under Water. 1991.

SARAH ORNE JEWETT

1849–1909

SARAH ORNE JEWETT was born on September 3, 1849, in South
Berwick, Maine, to a wealthy and established family. Though she
attended Berwick Academy until 1866, Jewett later claimed that her
real education came from her father, a country physician whom she
often accompanied on house calls. Her parents and grandparents
encouraged her to read classic authors such as Cervantes, Fielding,
Sterne, Austen, and George Eliot; much of her early work shows this
European influence.

In 1869 Jewett's first story, "Mr. Bruce," was published in the
Atlantic. Not until the September 1875 appearance of the first of the
"Deephaven" sketches in the same magazine, however, did Jewett find
her true subject—the people and landscape of Maine. She subsequently wrote a number of tales, novels, and sketches notable for their
sympathetic realism, including *A Country Doctor* (1884); *A Marsh Island*
(1885); *A White Heron and Other Stories* (1886); and her most critically
acclaimed work, *The Country of the Pointed Firs* (1896).

Jewett's early success allowed her entry into Boston's literary society, where she quickly befriended two of its chief forces: the prominent editor and publisher James T. Fields and his wife, Annie Adams
Fields. After James Fields died in 1881, Jewett's close friendship with
Annie deepened, and the two formed what was called a "Boston marriage": a lifetime monogamous partnership between women. Jewett
and Fields would spend about half of each year together in Boston or
at the Fields family's Massachusetts cottage. The rest of the year
Jewett would spend with her family in Maine, with occasional visits
by Fields.

Jewett often praised the "transfiguring" power of close friendship.
She was a member of a lively and successful circle of women artists
and writers, including the poet Celia Thaxter, the artist Sarah Wyman
Whitman (to whom Jewett dedicated *Strangers and Wayfarers* in 1890),
and the novelist Marie Thérèse Blanc, who translated Jewett's work
into French. In addition, she was acquainted with the writers Harriet
Beecher Stowe, Julia Ward Howe, and May Sinclair. The Fields' literary salon included regular visits from Matthew Arnold and Charles
Dickens, and in her trips to Europe Jewett met a number of celebrated
literary figures, including Lord Tennyson, Henry James, Mark Twain,
and Rudyard Kipling. Perhaps her most famous association was with

Willa Cather; the younger author records Jewett's influence on her writing in *Not Under Forty* (1936).

In 1902, Jewett was thrown from a carriage and sustained a concussion and extensive spinal injuries. In the spring of 1909, she had a stroke; she died in her South Berwick home on June 24, 1909. Two collections of her works were published posthumously: *Verses* (1916) and *The Best Short Stories of Sarah Orne Jewett* (1925), the latter edited by Willa Cather.

CRITICAL EXTRACTS

WARNER BERTHOFF

The superiority of Jewett's work in the local-color genre—and here, too *Pointed Firs* marks her for a distinct advance—appears in the combined bluntness and subtlety, the overwhelming indirection, with which she presents a norm of distorted, repressed, unfulfilled or transformed sexuality as an index to her essential story. When there is a marriage, it is like that of Ann Floyd and Jerry Lane—the weak boy marrying for protection and security the energetic spinster who has the competence and strength of a proper man; that the marriage is childless and ends in desertion does not come as a surprise. More usually there is no marriage at all, simply the desertion, as in "A Lost Lover": here the elderly heroine, whose lover was long ago supposed lost at sea but really has run away, has come to be regarded as a widow and, on the basis of this lie, a person of consequence in the village as well as in her own eyes; she has achieved position and respect, but at the cost of playing a woman's full part. The men do have the choice to go, though it may destroy them, and only the already defeated or crippled, the childish or woman-like, stay on. But for the women the only choice, the sacrifice required for survival, is to give up a woman's proper life and cover the default of the men, to be the guardians and preservers of a community with no other source of vitality and support. In a society without a future, the woman's instinct to carry on the life of the tribe can only be fulfilled by devotion to what remains, and her energies must go to preservation of the past, to intercourse with nature, to disguising and delaying the inevitable dissolution. This is the ambiance even of a story like "A White Heron," in which the heroine is only a little girl. In the presence of the hunter "the woman's heart, asleep in the child," stirs with a premonition of the power and release of love; but in defense of her mysterious sympathy with wild creatures and her secret knowledge of the heron's sanctuary, she refuses his appeal like a profaning courtship (in his offering her money there is again the imputation of grossness); and the suggestion is made that her whole life will turn on this renunciation.

The story of the region, we may say, would not be honestly told if the sexual warping were not brought into it, but it would not be fully told if that were made the main, the climactic, theme of it. Sexuality figures, rather, as one among several of the great natural contingencies determining the forms life must take in this life-abandoned society. Old age and death are another: it is with the aged that the pressure of decay is registered most vividly. External nature provides the others—thus, perhaps, in the final clarifying of her vision and refining of its expression, Jewett's choice of title; and thus, in *The Country of the Pointed Firs*, the constant counterpointing of personal and tribal histories by the invoked presence not only of the landscape but of season and weather, too, and the incessant audible movement of the sea in its storms and calms, its tidal rise and fall. Only society is dying, only human life: water, rock, woods, birds, vegetation are alive and—in the time we are allowed to look at them— surpassingly beautiful. The season is nearly always early or full summer, and rarely later than the first touch of fall; it is as though winter, reinforcing all too harshly the testimony of the region's economic life, were too terrible to contemplate.

Framed by the vitality of the landscape and the inanition of human affairs, a fight for life goes on through all Jewett's work. The sexual warping is subsumed by this more general tension between the signs of natural power and the signs of impotence and death.

—Warner Berthoff, "The Art of Jewett's *Pointed Firs*," *New England Quarterly* (March 1959), in *The Chelsea House Library of Literary Criticism: The Critical Perspective*, vol. 10, ed. Harold Bloom (New York: Chelsea House Publishers, 1989), 6176

JOSEPHINE DONOVAN

Jewett herself had treated relationships between women in her fiction from the beginning ⟨. . .⟩ but with more frequency by the mid-'80s. Perhaps *A Country Doctor* was a kind of turning point; or perhaps Jewett's own growing involvement with Annie Fields (and other women artists) is reflected in her fiction.

Two of the stories in *A White Heron and Other Stories* (1886) deal with women couples. One is a comic masterpiece, "The Dulham Ladies" (1886), and the other, "Mary and Martha" (1885), deals with the resourcefulness of two women in establishing their economic security.

Another story published at this time, but never collected, is "A Garden Story" (1886), a somewhat sentimental piece about an older woman who lives alone in the country and who is joined by a young orphan girl from the city through a social welfare program, and the growing intensity of their attach-ment. This theme is picked up later in "A Village Shop" (1888) where the younger woman eventually marries the brother of the older woman, much to the misery and jealousy of the latter.

In "Fair Day" (1888), a relatively unnoticed story, Jewett brings the theme of sisterhood to a level of significance not seen in earlier stories. It involves the re-establishment of a connection between two women in-laws who had been alienated for forty years due to a quarrel. The central episode is their decision to patch things up between them. This is a most positive step in Jewett's world, for community is a central value and women are its prime sustainers.

Several of Jewett's stories deal with pilgrimages made by women in quest of community and/or significance. These include "Miss Becky's Pilgrimage" (1881), "Going to Shrewsbury" (1889), "The Flight of Betsey Lane" (1893), and the pilgrimage of Mrs. Todd and her mother to a family reunion in *The Country of the Pointed Firs*.

While stories featuring women couples continue, including "Miss Tempy's Watchers" (1888), "The Town Poor" (1890), "The Guests of Mrs. Timms" (1894), and "The Green Bowl" (1901), the theme of woman love reaches its culmination in one of Jewett's greatest stories, "Martha's Lady" (1897). This piece, somewhat reminiscent of Flaubert's "Un Coeur simple," involves a ser-vant woman Martha, who develops an intense attachment to a young woman visitor who is kind to her. Promising soon to return, the visitor leaves and pro-ceeds through life, not coming back for twenty years. Throughout this period Martha worshipfully follows the events of her life, thinks of nothing but her, dreaming of her return. Finally, the woman does return and in a joyous moment of reunion realizes the devotion and love that Martha has bestowed upon her from afar through the years. Again, the tone is markedly elegiac for the waste of human emotion potential.

It is in stories like this that Jewett leaves the company of good storytellers like Daudet and Maupassant and enters the ranks of Flaubert, Turgenev and Tolstoi. Oddly enough, Jewett worried about the "dullness" of this story and revealingly commented that Martha was Jewett herself.

—Josephine Donovan, "A Woman's Vision of Transcendence: A New Interpretation of the Works of Sarah Orne Jewett," *Massachusetts Review* (Summer 1980), in *The Chelsea House Library of Literary Criticism: The Critical Perspective*, vol. 10, ed. Harold Bloom (New York: Chelsea House Publishers, 1989), 6183

ELIZABETH AMMONS

Jewett never did become skillful at conventional plotting. Her attempt to cre-ate an interesting historical novel in *The Tory Lover* (1901) is notably unsuc-cessful: her three novels for girls, while pleasant, are very ordinary. Probably because conventional, long, dramatic structures requiring exposition, complication, climax, and resolution—the standard protagonist/antagonist model—did not work well for her, she wrote few long works. The problem of how to sustain a long narrative without relying on stock dramatic architecture was not easy to solve. She could do a respectable job with conventional form if her subject matter was fairly predictable, as *A Country Doctor* demonstrates in 1884; but even this novel, interesting thematically, is not particularly exciting aesthetically. It remained for *The Country of the Pointed Firs* a dozen years later to reveal a solution to Jewett's problem of putting together a long piece of fiction that would not attempt to imitate conventional dramatic structure yet would be unified and exciting. To accomplish that end, Jewett structures the novel around two essentially female psychic patterns: one of web, the other of descent. ⟨. . .⟩

⟨. . .⟩ Instead of being linear, it is nuclear; the narrative moves out from one base to a given point and back again, out to another point, and back again, out again, back again, and so forth, like arteries on a spider's web. Instead of building to an asymmetric height, it collects weight at the middle: the most highly charged experience of the book, the visit to Green Island, comes at the center of the book (in the eighth through eleventh of twenty-one chapters), not toward the end. And instead of being relationally exclusive, it is inclusive and accumulative: relationships do not vie with but complement each other. The narrator does not go through a series of people; she adds new friendships onto her life multidirectionally. ⟨. . .⟩

Jewett makes the dramatic center of *The Country of the Pointed Firs* unmistakable. In the tenth of her twenty-one chapters, titled "Where Pennyroyal Grew," the narrator and Mrs. Todd descend together into a silent, sacred, lush, female space in nature where past and present, self and other, myth and reality merge. In journeying "down to the pennyroyal plot," a place Mrs. Todd explicitly calls "sainted," the two women leave behind "the plain every-day world" (78, 77) to come together in the presence of the sacred earth, the healing Mother, herself. As Marjorie Pryse says in an excellent Introduction to a recent edition of the book ⟨Norton, 1981⟩, "it is clear that Mrs. Todd, in her role as guide, herbalist, and priestess, is here helping her summer visitor to go directly to the source of all vision and inspiration." That source is primal, archetypal female love. ⟨. . .⟩

This descent into a sacred female space in nature, a grove, a cave ⟨. . .⟩ is the journey that the narrator and Mrs. Todd take to the sacred plot of pennyroyal on Green Island at the center of Jewett's *Country of the Pointed Firs*. Mrs. Todd shows the narrator a treasured picture of her mother and then bares her feelings, taking the narrator into her most intimate confidence. In so doing Almira Todd evokes the ancient, perhaps timeless, grief and courage of all women: "She might have been Antigone alone on the Theban plain. . . . An absolute, archaic grief possessed this countrywoman; she seemed like a renewal of some historic soul, with her sorrows and the remoteness of a daily life busied with rustic simplicities and the scents of primeval herbs" (78). Her "favorite," not surprisingly, is pennyroyal (211). ⟨. . .⟩

The artistic geography of *The Country of the Pointed Firs*, a book, as its title signals, about geography, is complex. Instead of relying on conventional inherited forms, at which she was not very good anyway, Jewett made a book that locates itself formally outside the masculine mainstream. Patterns of concentricity, net-work, web, and oscillation mold a narrative that does not know how to march and scale. Rather, it rocks, circles, ebbs, and swells. That Jewett never mastered conventional form is no loss at all.

—Elizabeth Ammons, "Going in Circles: The Female Geography of Jewett's *Country of the Pointed Firs*," *Studies in the Literary Imagination* (Fall 1983), in *The Chelsea House Library of Literary Criticism: The Critical Perspective*, vol. 10, ed. Harold Bloom (New York: Chelsea House Publishers, 1989), 6186–88

MARGARET ROMAN

With the knowledge that people are entombed in rigid gender roles, Jewett explores the idea of sexual transformation and role reversal. Several critics have noticed this phenomenon in Jewett. ⟨. . .⟩ Overwhelmingly, Jewett does not appear to view switching roles as an answer in itself; the change still results in a malformed, one-sided being.

This discussion is limited to the stories wherein specific characters are noticed by others in the story as dressing or acting like the opposite sex. Jewett handles the subject differently for men and for women. The men are depicted in a comical vein, almost as if Jewett acknowledges that it is more of a joke than a reality for a man to want to be like a woman. It is also an exterior change. Literally the men dress up as women; they are merely changing clothes, trying them on. They are, with the exception of Daniel Gunn in "An Autumn Holiday," not interested in experiencing what it feels like to be a woman, but how it looks. ⟨. . .⟩

The account of Daniel Gunn is a different story entirely. Beneath the surface of this seemingly comical tale, Jewett may be offering weighty comments about the necessity to experience both the masculine as well as the feminine modes of existence. Daniel Gunn is not intentionally masquerading. After having sunstroke, Gunn thinks he is his dead sister, Patience. He only semirecovers. During the morning, he is Daniel Gunn, who attends to all the manly jobs on the farm, and after his afternoon nap, he is transformed into his sister. Daniel dons Patience's clothes and sits and knits with a cat in his lap, just as his sister was wont to do. In his delirium, Daniel can learn what life was like for his sister, a diametrically opposite existence to his own. Daniel has been solidly masculine up until this point. Reflecting his last name of "gun," Daniel's occupation has been that of a captain in the militia. His neighbors remember him as being "dreadful precise." Now he must give up his chain of stern command, his life of action, and learn "patience" as he sits every afternoon. Daniel rarely leaves the house. ⟨. . .⟩ Jewett is having great fun, but it is fun with a purpose. Men should experience the passivity, the triviality, as well as the affectionate community of women. The lifestyles of men versus women, of "gun" versus "patience," need to be examined so an ameliorated, healthy version for both can be chosen.

There is nothing humorous in Jewett's stories of sexual transformation for women. Instead of masquerading, women deliberately assume male roles because of an inherent necessity to achieve, an achievement missing in the roles provided for them as women.

—Margaret Roman, *Sarah Orne Jewett: Reconstructing Gender* (Tuscaloosa, AL: University of Alabama Press, 1992), 135–37

MICHAEL DAVITT BELL

In Grant's *Memoirs*, ⟨W. R.⟩ Howells writes, "there is not a moment wasted in preening and prettifying, after the fashion of literary men; there is no thought of style, and so the style is good as it is in the Book of Chronicles, as it is in the Pilgrim's Progress, with a peculiar, almost plebeian, plainness at times." Here we see clearly the assumptions and values underlying Howell's thinking about literature, particularly the distinction, not between modes of literary representation ("realism," "romance," and the like), but between kinds of men. On the one side are artists, overwhelmed by "literary consciousness," concerned with "style"; on the other side are "real" men, "men whose lives have been passed in activities," and it is with this group that Howells seeks to ally himself. In an 1895 memoir, Howells describes his childhood recognition that "my reading gave me no standing among the boys, . . . with boys who were more valiant in fight or in play," and his subsequent discovery "that literature gives one no more certain station in the world of men's activities, either idle or useful." To put it bluntly and succinctly, literary realism mattered to Howells as an effort to suppress or overcome this discovery, to distinguish literary vocation, or at least realist literary vocation, from "criticism" and "style"—all this in order to present literature as part of the "world of men's activities" ⟨*Criticism and Fiction and Other Essays by W. R. Howells*, 1959, p. 26; *My Literary Passions*, 1895, 26⟩. ⟨. . .⟩

The heavily gendered assumptions at the heart of American realist thinking have surely had much to do with what official literary history has made of Jewett, but there may be a more interesting way to approach the relation of

American realism to *The Country of the Pointed Firs*. Instead of asking what American realism made of Jewett, we might ask what Jewett made of American realism—of the ideas of Howells and others about the "reality" of "men's activities." ⟨. . .⟩ The programs of Howells and ⟨Frank⟩ Norris endorse a movement from the less to the more "real," from the feminine world of "teacup tragedies" to the "marching world," the "world of men's activities." *The Country of the Pointed Firs* seems to reverse this movement while retaining the valuation; here it is a movement *out* of the "world of men's activities" that appears to lead into a more intense "reality." ⟨. . .⟩

When Captain Littlepage visits the narrator's schoolhouse, he tells her a story he heard from a man named Gaffett, whom he met when he was shipwrecked and stranded on the shores of Hudson's Bay with winter setting in. Gaffett claimed to be the sole survivor of a polar expedition (recalling the southern voyage in Poe's *Narrative of Arthur Gordon Pym*) that discovered "a strange sort of a country 'way up north beyond the ice, and strange folks living in it." From a distance the place looked like any other town, but it was inhabited by silent "blowing gray figures," "fog-shaped men" who vanished when approached "like a leaf the wind takes with it, or a piece of cobweb." The explorers believed this to be "a kind of waiting-place between this world an' the next" (pp. 24–6). The captain's story, with which he has become obsessed, is dismissed by his neighbors as the raving of an unbalanced mind, but this "waiting place" might strike one as a pertinent and somber analogue of Dunnet Landing itself, stranded in northern isolation, populated mainly by relics of its own lost past. ⟨. . .⟩

Still, what seems to matter most about Gaffett's "waiting-place" is that it is a community of fog-shaped men, an image of failed male power, and Dunnet Landing, by contrast, is a community of women, presided over by Almira Todd and her universally beloved mother. This is the reality Jewett seems to substitute for the compensatory masculinity of writers like Howells and Norris. ⟨. . .⟩

It is only fitting that the *female* "world beyond this," the world "where mother lives," be *Green* Island, its fertility standing in contrast to the polar grayness of Gaffett's realm of fog-shaped men. So, too, the true center of authority at the Bowden family reunion is not Sant Bowden—whose military posturing nicely deflates, for instance, Frank Norris's fantasy of the "marching world"—but Mrs. Blackett. As Mrs. Todd puts it, shortly after the crowd has been described as resembling "bees . . . swarming in the lilac bushes," "Mother's always the queen" (p. 98). In this matriarchal world, it would seem, the men can only be drones.

—Michael Davitt Bell, "Gender and American Realism in *The Country of the Pointed Firs*," in *New Essays on "The Country of the Pointed Firs"*, ed. June Howard (Cambridge: Cambridge University Press, 1994), 63, 66–70

Paula Blanchard

The main theme of Jewett's work after *Deephaven* continued to be the spiritual links uniting God, humanity, the natural world, the living and the dead, the past and the present. The typical Jewett plot revolves around the rupture and reconnection of those links as they are expressed in human sympathy: a protagonist is alienated from her or his fellows and then redeemed through an impulse of kindness. Or the protagonist may temporarily put ambition or pride ahead of community, but then has an epiphany of some kind that brings her or him back into harmony with others. The less successful stories are simplistic morality tales, very like her children's stories. More fully imagined but still insistently pedagogic is the early "Miss Sydney's Flowers," in which a rich, solitary old woman is taught to reach out to other people by means of the flowers in her own conservatory. In "The King of Folly Island" the theme is spun out into a long, fully developed story in which a wealthy city man who has allowed himself to drift away from human relationships is brought to a realization of his own failings through the example of another man for whom isolation has become a tragic obsession.

One of Jewett's finest tales about interdependence is "Miss Tempy's Watchers," published in 1888. Two women who scarcely know one another are brought together to watch in the kitchen of a dead friend, who lies in the bedchamber above them. Mrs. Crowe is the wife of a rich farmer, and though kindhearted is apt to be stingy in spite of herself. "It ain't so easy for me to give as it is for some," she confesses in some perplexity, as if she were talking about a physical handicap. (*The King of Folly Island*, p. 213) Her companion, Sarah Ann Binson, is a farmer, the family breadwinner for herself, her widowed sister, and "six unpromising and unwilling nieces and nephews." (p. 210) Her hard life has left her with a rather pinched and frugal look, "a little too sharp-set," to quote her neighbors (p. 209); but her spareness is all on the outside, while Mrs. Crowe's is all on the inside. In the course of reminiscing about their deceased friend Miss Tempy Dent, they exchange confidences they otherwise never would have shared, and through understanding one another's lives and remembering Miss Tempy's they become friends, and Mrs. Crowe's native kindliness expands into what one hopes is permanent bloom. The story is achieved with an impeccable blend of humor and psychological realism, and as readers we spend the night in that country kitchen, nibbling on the funeral cakes to keep up our strength and guiltily nodding off on our hard wooden chairs.

There is nothing fortuitous about the meeting of the two women. Tempy Dent had asked them to be her watchers, and throughout the story her lingering influence is felt, in the loud voice of the brook outside that seems "as if it tried to make the watchers understand something that related to the past," and in the wind that puffs companionably at the window crack. (p. 211) "The watchers could not rid their minds of the feeling that they were being watched themselves," the narrator says, and later on, when they have dozed off despite their best efforts, the narrator wonders if Tempy herself is the only watcher. (p. 212) But this benign manipulation is not, within the framework of Jewett's own belief, Tempy's own: the dead are agents, just as the natural voices of water and wind are agents. The author-narrator herself is an agent. Similarly, Frankfort in "The King of Folly Island," setting out for the islands in the boat of postmaster Jabez Pennell, idly wonders if he was "addressed by fate to some human being who expected him." (p. 6) Human events are helped along by unseen powers, as the writer's imagination is directed by forces beyond her. "Fate," or God, is the best storyteller of all.

—Paula Blanchard, *Sarah Orne Jewett: Her World and Her Work* (Reading, MA: Addison-Wesley Publishing Company, 1994), 235–36

LILLIAN FADERMAN

A model Boston marriage existed between the novelist Sarah Orne Jewett and Annie Fields, which lasted for almost three decades. For many years during that time the two women lived together a part of each year, separated for another part of the year so that they could devote complete attention to their work, traveled together frequently, shared interests in books and people, and provided each other with love and stability. ⟨. . .⟩

The letters ⟨. . .⟩ indicate that the two women had a support group of other couples who were engaged in "Boston marriages," both in Boston and elsewhere: Elizabeth McCracken, author of *The Women of America*, and her friend; two women with whom they went to Europe in 1892; the novelist Vernon Lee (Violet Paget) and Kit Anstruther-Thomson; Willa Cather and the woman with whom she lived for forty years, Edith Lewis.

It probably would have astonished Jewett that Mark Howe saw anything to censor in her letters to Annie Fields. In the context of her time, her love for Annie was very fine. But Willa Cather, who was almost twenty-five years her junior and came of age in a different environment, knew that what Jewett's generation would have seen as admirable, hers would consider abnormal. There is absolutely no suggestion of same-sex love in Cather's fiction. Perhaps she felt the need to be more reticent about love between women than even some of her patently heterosexual contemporaries because she bore a burden of guilt for what came to be labeled perversion. The Cather characters that are suspiciously autobiographical, such as the narrator in *My Antonia*, appear as male whenever they show love interest in females. Jewett, whose own writing Cather greatly admired, noted the falsity of this characterization, even in the younger woman's early fiction, and warned her against it. For example, after reading Cather's "On the Gull's Road," which appeared in *McClure's* in 1908, she wrote the younger writer, "The lover is as well done as he could be when a woman writes in the man's character,—it must always, I believe, be something of a masquerade . . . and you could almost have done it as yourself—a woman could love her in the same protecting way—a woman could even care enough to wish to take her away from such a life, by some means or other." The letter must have made Cather blush—but Jewett probably would not have known what she was blushing about.

In her own writing Jewett did not feel the need to use the word "man" when she meant "woman." Her story "Martha's Lady," which first appeared in *The Atlantic Monthly* in October 1897, could never have been written by Cather—not because Cather did not wholeheartedly believe in its basic premise about the redemptive power of love, but because the two principals were female. Jewett treats this fact entirely without self-consciousness. Her own Boston marriage confirmed her belief that love—perhaps any kind of love, but especially between women—had the power to foster the most praiseworthy ambition and to bestow the energy to carry that ambition out. The love described in "Martha's Lady" demands renunciation, but Martha anyway reaps those benefits of love which Jewett seems to have valued most in her "marriage."

 —Lillian Faderman, *Surpassing the Love of Men: Romantic Friendship and Love Between Women from the Renaissance to the Present* (New York: Quality Paperback Book Club, 1994), 197, 201–2

B I B L I O G R A P H Y

Deephaven. 1877.
Play Days: A Book of Stories for Children. 1878.
Old Friends and New. 1879.
Country By-Ways. 1881.
The Mate of the Daylight and Friends Ashore. 1884.
A Country Doctor. 1884.
A Marsh Island. 1885.
A White Heron and Other Stories. 1886.
The Story of the Normans Told Chiefly in Relation to Their Conquest of England. 1887.
The King of Folly Island and Other People. 1888.
Betty Leicester: A Story for Girls. 1890.
Strangers and Wayfarers. 1890.
A Memorial of the One Hundredth Anniversary of the Founding of Berwick Academy (editor). 1891.

A Native of Winby and Other Tales. 1893.
Betty Leicester's English Xmas: A New Chapter of an Old Story. 1894.
The Life of Nancy. 1895.
Stories and Poems for Children by Celia Thaxter (editor). 1895.
A Village Patriot. 1896.
The Poems of Celia Thaxter (editor). 1896.
The Country of the Pointed Firs. 1896.
The Queen's Twin and Other Stories. 1899.
The Tory Lover. 1901.
The Green Bowl. 1901.
An Empty Purse: A Christmas Story. 1905.
Letters of Sarah Wyman Whitman (editor). 1907.
Stories and Tales (7 vols.). 1910.
Letters. Ed. Annie Fields. 1911.
Verses. Ed. M.A. DeWolfe Howe. 1916.
The Best Short Stories of Sarah Orne Jewett. Ed. Willa Cather. 1925.
The Only Rose and Other Tales. 1937.

CARSON McCULLERS
1917–1967

LULA CARSON SMITH was born on February 19, 1917, in Colum-
bus, Georgia. During her youth she studied music intensively, but
after contracting rheumatic fever at 15 she turned to writing, completing several plays, a novel, and poetry "that nobody could make
out, including the author." In 1934 she went to New York, hoping to
continue her music studies at Juilliard, but her tuition money was "lost"
by a roommate who was holding the cash for her. She took a series of
day jobs and studied creative writing at Columbia University at night.
In 1937 she married a fellow southerner and aspiring writer, Reeves
McCullers; the two eventually settled in New York.

McCullers's first work of fiction, "Wunderkind," was published in
Story magazine in 1936. Her first novel, *The Heart Is a Lonely Hunter*,
appeared four years later. It was reviewed favorably and was followed
by another novel, *Reflections in a Golden Eye*, in 1941.

Though married to Reeves, Carson had long felt that her nature
also "demanded, craved, a reciprocal love relationship with a woman."
Her important female friends included Muriel Rukeyser, Isak Dinesen,
Elizabeth Bowen, and Edith Sitwell. Reeves too was bisexual, and by
1940 the emotional strain of their various sexual relationships became
overwhelming. Carson moved into February House, the famed
Brooklyn writers' enclave whose residents included W. H. Auden,
Christopher Isherwood, Hugh MacNiece, and later Salvador Dali and
Anaïs Nin. She divorced Reeves in 1942 and stayed in Brooklyn until
1945, spending summers at the Yaddo Colony writers' retreat in
Saratoga, New York. In 1945 she remarried Reeves and moved with
him to Nyack, New York.

McCullers continued to write throughout the 1940s, publishing
The Ballad of the Sad Café in 1943 and *The Member of the Wedding* in 1946;
both were great successes. At the suggestion of Tennessee Williams,
McCullers dramatized *The Member of the Wedding*, which began a long
Broadway run in 1950 and was awarded the New York Drama Critics
Circle and Donaldson prizes for best play of 1950.

Beginning in 1947, McCullers's health seriously deteriorated. She
suffered several bouts of pneumonia and two strokes, the second of
which left her partially blind and temporarily paralyzed. In 1948 she
attempted suicide after a brief separation from Reeves, but she refused
to participate in a double suicide as Reeves urged her to do before he
killed himself five years later. McCullers's mother died in 1955; the

loss sent her into prolonged grieving, which was complicated by further medical problems, including breast cancer.

McCullers's fiction is considered largely autobiographical, with its recurring themes of isolation, homosexuality (albeit primarily male), gender confusion, and unrequited love. Her characters are nearly always "freakish" in some way—the deaf-mute John Singer and the mentally handicapped Antonapoulos in *The Heart Is a Lonely Hunter*, for example; the strong, mannish, cross-eyed businesswoman Miss Amelia in *The Ballad of the Sad Café*; or the sadomasochistic and voyeuristic characters of *Reflections in a Golden Eye*. All are society's misfits, outsiders struggling to overcome isolation through love.

In the last ten years of her life, McCullers wrote *The Square Root of Wonderful* (1958), a story involving a premature death from leukemia, and *Clock Without Hands* (1961), her last novel; Edward Albee dramatized *The Ballad of the Sad Café* in 1963. She continued to travel and lecture as her health permitted, but by 1962 she was mostly confined to a wheelchair. When she died of complications from a stroke on September 29, 1967, she left unfinished a journal work, tentatively named *Illuminations and Night Glare*.

C R I T I C A L   E X T R A C T S

FRANK BALDANZA

The articulation of the truths about love and being which form the core of ⟨*The Member of the Wedding*⟩ comes out of a long twilit kitchen seminar, punctuated by the sounds of rats in the walls and the distant tuning of a piano, and culminating in tears on the parts of all three participants. Berenice reviews in her song-like chant her own erotic history, a direct duplication of the essentials of Aristophanes' speech in *Symposium*, but this time the theme is played in reverse, rather than "one octave lower" as in "A Tree . A Rock . A Cloud." It will be remembered that Aristophanes maintains that at one time each human being was a double creature with two heads, four arms and legs, and the like; and that Zeus, in a moment of fury, punished mankind by splitting each creature in two; Aristophanes interprets the frenzied search of humans for love simply as a pursuit of one's own other half-soul; as a consequence, obviously, success and failure in love are dependent on whether or not one actually finds the other half of his own soul in the beloved. Thus love is synonymous, almost mathematically, with wholeness. Berenice extols her ecstatic first marriage to

Ludie Freeman as a transfiguring experience. After his death, however, repeated attempts to duplicate the relation failed; she took up with Jamie Beale
because his thumb resembled Ludie's, and with Henry Johnson because he had
come into possession of Ludie's coat, and so on for a whole series of husbands.
She drives the lesson home to F. Jasmine thus: " 'It applies to everybody and it
is a warning. . . . Why don't you see what I was doing?' asked Berenice. 'I loved
Ludie and he was the first man I ever loved. Therefore, I had to go and copy
myself forever afterward. What I did was to marry off little pieces of Ludie
whenever I come across them. It was just my misfortune they all turned out to
be the wrong pieces. My intention was to repeat me and Ludie.' "

She was reversing the Platonic theory by continuing the search after
Ludie's death because supposedly once she had found the other half of her soul
in Ludie, there would be no second chance, short of his reincarnation. But
Berenice is very wise in the ways of love, and knows all about its power and
its variety: " 'I have knew mens to fall in love with girls so ugly that you wonder if their eyes is straight. I have seen some of the most peculiar weddings
anybody could conjecture. Once I knew a boy with his whole face burned off
so that—!' " After a bite of cornbread, she continues: " 'I have knew womens to
love veritable Satans and thank Jesus when they put their split hooves over the
threshold. I have knew boys to take it into their heads to fall in love with other
boys.' " But the aim of her whole exposition is the exclamation that despite all
her experience, she has never known someone to fall in love with a wedding.
She soberly warns F. Jasmine against the obsession. However, Berenice's commitment to sensual love puts her in a category of lesser beings, and the real
concern of the tale is with F. Jasmine's spiritual discoveries about love and
being. She realizes that she is no longer the child who was hustled out of a
movie for hooting at a showing of *Camille*, and now actually participates as an
equal in the kitchen discussion of love. Berenice's warning about the troubles
ahead for F. Jasmine may be well founded, to be sure, but it is the experience
of people like her, Carson McCullers means to say, that embodies the most
exquisite values.

What Frankie learns, and what Berenice knows only very fleetingly, is a
nearly mystical conviction of "connections" with all sorts of random people
seen casually on the street—precisely what Walt Whitman feels on the
Brooklyn ferry and what Virginia Woolf's Mrs. Dalloway feels in her mean-
derings on London streets. In Platonic terminology, she had begun to experience love as an absolute. She can now exclaim with the tramp in the short
story " 'All strangers and all loved!' "

      —Frank Baldanza, "Plato in Dixie," *Georgia Review* (Summer 1958), in *The Chelsea House Library
      of Literary Criticism: Twentieth-Century American Literature*, vol. 4, ed. Harold Bloom (New York:
      Chelsea House Publishers, 1986), 2386

CARSON McCULLERS

A writer's main asset is intuition; too many facts impede intuition. A writer needs to know so many things, but there are so many things he doesn't need to know—he needs to know human things even if they aren't "wholesome," as they call it.

Every day, I read the New York *Daily News*, and very soberly. It is interesting to know the name of the lover's lane where the stabbing took place, and the circumstances which the *New York Times* never reports. In that unsolved murder in Staten Island, it is interesting to know that the doctor and his wife, when they were stabbed, were wearing Mormon nightgowns, three-quarter length. Lizzie Borden's breakfast, on the sweltering summer day she killed her father, was mutton soup. Always details provoke more ideas than any generality could furnish. When Christ was pierced in His *left* side, it is more moving and evocative than if He were just pierced.

One cannot explain accusations of morbidity. A writer can only say he writes from the seed which flowers later in the subconscious. Nature is not abnormal, only lifelessness is abnormal. Anything that pulses and moves and walks around the room, no matter what thing it is doing, is natural and human to a writer. The fact that John Singer, in *The Heart Is a Lonely Hunter*, is a deaf-and-dumb man is a symbol, and the fact that Captain Penderton, in *Reflections in a Golden Eye*, is homosexual, is also a symbol, of handicap and impotence. The deaf mute, Singer, is a symbol of infirmity, and he loves a person who is incapable of receiving his love. Symbols suggest the story and theme and incident, and they are so interwoven that one cannot understand consciously where the suggestion begins. I become the characters I write about. I am so immersed in them that their motives are my own. When I write about a thief, I become one; when I write about Captain Penderton, I become a homosexual man; when I write about a deaf mute, I become dumb during the time of the story. I become the characters I write about and I bless the Latin poet Terence who said, "Nothing human is alien to me."

When I wrote the stage version of *The Member of the Wedding*, I was at the time paralyzed, and my outward situation was miserable indeed; but when I finished that script, I wrote to a friend of mine, "Oh, how wonderful it is to be a writer, I have never been so happy. . . . "

When work does not go well, no life is more miserable than that of a writer. But when it does go well, when the illumination has focused a work so that it goes limpidly and flows, there is no gladness like it. ⟨. . .⟩

The writer's work is predicated not only on his personality but by the region in which he was born. I wonder sometimes if what they call the "Gothic" school of Southern writing, in which the grotesque is paralleled with the sublime, is not due largely to the cheapness of human life in the South.

The Russians are like the Southern writers in that respect. In my childhood, the South was almost a feudal society. But the South is complicated by the racial problem more severely than the Russian society. To many a poor Southerner, the only pride that he has is the fact that he is white, and when one's self-pride is so pitiably debased, how can one learn to love? Above all, love is the main generator of all good writing. Love, passion, compassion are all welded together.

In any communication, a thing says to one person quite a different thing from what it says to another, but writing, in essence, is communication; and communication is the only access to love—to love, to conscience, to nature, to God, and to the dream. For myself, the further I go into my own work and the more I read of those I love, the more aware I am of the dream and the logic of God, which indeed is a Divine collusion.

—Carson McCullers, "The Flowering Dream: Notes on Writing," *Esquire* (December 1959), in *The Chelsea House Library of Literary Criticism: Twentieth-Century American Literature*, vol. 4, ed. Harold Bloom (New York: Chelsea House Publishers, 1986), 2381, 2383

JOHN B. VICKERY

Clearly Carson McCullers is primarily interested in the drama that is enacted within the soul of the lover and which finds its source in the painful discovery of the self as a sharply defined and limited ego. The very act of loving implies a desire for some vital and immediate contact and hence a separation. As Berenice explains to Frankie Addams, one becomes conscious of the fact that " 'me is me and you is you and he is he. We each one of us somehow caught all by ourself.' " The feeling of being trapped within one's own identity and unable to form a meaningful relationship with others leads to the idea of uniqueness and ultimately of freakishness. In its simplest form, this is apparent in the actual physical deformities of Amelia Evans and Cousin Lymon in *The Ballad of the Sad Café*. In subsequent books the freakishness is attributed to the characters either by the observers who see in Blount, for example, something deformed even though "when you looked at him closely each part of him was normal and as it ought to be" or by the characters themselves who, like Frankie, imagine and fear their own abnormality. ⟨. . .⟩

The archetypal pattern of love is presented in its clearest and simplest form in *The Ballad of the Sad Café*. For each of the three main characters is successively lover and beloved. Each, then, is in turn a slave and a tyrant, depending on whether he is loving or being loved. The refusal or inability of the characters to synchronize their changes of heart produces the interlocking romantic triangles which constitute the plot, while the grotesque comedy arises out of their each in turn conforming to a role they contemptuously rejected in another.

Chronologically Marvin Macy is the first to be subjected to the meta-morphosis of love. Without rhyme or reason, this man, handsome and virile though insolent and wild in nature, falls passionately in love with Amelia Evans of the Amazonian figure and crossed eyes. In the process he is trans-formed into a love-sick calf, shorn of his masculine pride and inherent vio-lence. As the villagers watch with malicious delight, he is unceremoniously ejected from the marriage bed and finally from the house itself. By refusing to accept him into her home and life, to call him by name, or even to speak of him save "with a terrible and spiteful bitterness," Amelia preserves her physi-cal and emotional inviolateness. Thus Marvin's love simply reinforces her in her chosen isolation and complete self-sufficiency.

She herself, however, is not invulnerable. That passion which she incon-gruously awakened in Marvin is evoked in her by a pompous little hunchback. Cousin Lymon becomes the focus of her life, providing her with a whole new world and whole new set of relationships. For to her he is simultaneously the lover-husband she has rejected and the child she will never have. Furthermore, through him she establishes a precarious contact with the rest of the village insofar as the cafe, formed for Lymon's entertainment, becomes a meeting place for all who seek "fellowship, the satisfactions of the belly, and a certain gaiety and grace of behavior." But even as she escapes from that constricting loneliness of which Cousin Lymon makes her aware, she loses her cherished independence. As in the case of Marvin, by loving she herself creates the beloved tyrant who eventually repudiates and destroys her.

Although Lymon, unlike Marvin, is courted and does not court, yet in his first meeting with Amelia he too begs wordlessly, like a child, for her com-passion. It is only later when this compassion has deepened into a grotesque love that he assumes his place as master and invites Marvin to stay in Amelia's house. Only when he becomes imbued with the masculinity which Marvin has regained in the world outside the town is he capable of straightforward self-assertion. Indeed he himself becomes a psychic projection of Marvin, and by stealing Amelia's love, he amply redresses the latter's failure. But if the hunch-back comes to love the power resident in that violence of which Marvin is the symbol, he, nevertheless, began as the child of Amelia's heart. In relation to her he is a homuncular incubus, the product of a nightmare marriage and the dark, secret perversion of her own soul. And it is only with the flight of the hunchback and the victorious Marvin, who wins revenge by publicly humili-ating her, that she grasps the solitary nature of love and accepts its suffering. It is this awareness which constitutes the first stage in the agon of experience which is human love.

—John B. Vickery, "Carson McCullers: A Map of Love," *Contemporary Literature* (Winter 1960), in *The Chelsea House Library of Literary Criticism: Twentieth-Century American Literature*, vol. 4, ed. Harold Bloom (New York: Chelsea House Publishers, 1986), 2376–77

IHAB HASSAN

In *The Member of the Wedding*, 1946, Carson McCullers exhibits the kind of formal unity which her first novel lacks. There is also a smarting sense of life in the work, a profound sense of change, and a quality of intense groping which the behavior of the central characters seeks continually to incarnate. The story is primarily that of Frankie Addams, a motherless, twelve-year-old girl engaged in a romance with the world. The agonies of growth, the search for identity, the paradoxical desire to escape, to experience, to belong, suddenly converge on Frankie on the occasion of her brother's wedding which becomes the intolerable symbol of all her longings and the focus of her perverse misunderstanding of the adult world. ⟨. . .⟩

Formally the novel is divided into three parts, each taking its character from the role Frankie assumes. We see her first as Frankie Addams, the tomboy, bored and restive. "Until the April of that year, and all the years of her life before, she had been like other people." Her actual world is defined by the kitchen which she shares with Berenice and John Henry. "The three of them sat at the kitchen table, saying the same things over and over, so that by August the words began to rhyme with each other and sound strange." The transformations begin when Frankie suddenly decides to become a member of the wedding: her heart divides like two wings. In the next section of the novel we see Frankie as the new, exotic personality, F. Jasmine, who is all pride and anticipation. Her flirtation with a soldier, her lengthy conversations with Berenice on the subject of love, her lone wanderings through town, reflect the mood of willfulness which is the prelude to disenchantment. It is in the last part of the novel that disenchantment—what else?—sets in. Mrs. McCullers beautifully disposes of the wedding itself in a few lines and devotes the rest of the book to convert the initial bitterness of, not Frankie or F. Jasmine, but Frances now, to a final affirmation of youth's resilience. Frances, entitled at last to her full name, outgrows the humiliation of her first defeat. Unlike Mick Kelly, she moves beyond the acrid feeling that the world has cheated her. And with the heedlessness of youth she takes up new friends and other illusions, remotely conscious of the death of John Henry and the separation from Berenice. There is change; there is really no knowledge or confirmation. Guilt and anxiety are equally forgotten, only pathos remains. As the identity of Frankie changes from part to part, so do her images of "the spinning world," now fractured, now whole; and the seasons, keeping richly in step, change from spring to fall. ⟨. . .⟩

The style of the novel presents the blossoming of human feelings no less aptly than it presents the varying moods of nature. But it is a style of confession, or rather manifestation sensitive to the sudden epiphanies of daily life. It is not dramatic despite the inimitable tang and humor of its dialogue, and despite the plasticity of character which allowed the novel to be made into a successful play.

What drama the novel contains, it draws from the juxtaposition of three characters to one another—not from their interactions. Thus is Frankie caught between the violated innocence of John Henry and the viable experience of Berenice. Berenice is indeed the rock on which the novel rests. She calls to mind both Portia and Brannon, and calls forth a quality of existence as wholesome as our daily bread and as enduring. To all of Frankie's wild dreams, she stands as a silent modifier—for she is too wise to rebuke. With three husbands behind her and a fourth in the offing, she speaks as one who has known love and experienced loneliness. Her understanding of life is as tragic as Frankie's misunderstanding is pathetic. Without her, the tortured sensitivity of Frankie—a sensitivity, after all, which has no correlative but the wistfulness of puberty—would seem pointless and contrived. But between innocence and experience only illusions can lie. And the illusions of Frankie disguise the hopes of all mankind even if her destiny falls short of what our moment fully requires.

—Ihab Hassan, "Carson McCullers: The Aesthetics of Love and Pain," *Radical Innocence* (1961), in *The Chelsea House Library of Literary Criticism: Twentieth-Century American Literature*, vol. 4, ed. Harold Bloom (New York: Chelsea House Publishers, 1986), 2378–79

LOUISE WESTLING

The sexual dynamics of *The Ballad of the Sad Café* are an inversion of traditional heterosexual patterns. ⟨. . .⟩ Rather than accepting her femininity by consummating her marriage to the aggressively masculine Marvin Macy, Miss Amelia focuses her affections on the little hunchback who seems to function simultaneously as child, pet, and rather feminine companion. But Cousin Lymon is much less devoted to Miss Amelia than she is to him, and this gives him an emotional advantage over her which proves ultimately disastrous. It seems inevitable that the foppish dwarf should fall helplessly in love with Marvin Macy, thus completing the destructive triangular relationship which McCullers used to develop her theory that "almost everyone wants to be the lover" and that "in a deep secret way, the state of being loved is intolerable to many." But this theory and McCuller's statement that *Ballad* was intended to show the inferiority of passionate individual love to *agape* fail to account for the individual peculiarities of her characters and for the sexual dimensions of their problems in love. The real force of *The Ballad of the Sad Café* lies in its depiction of a masculine amazon whose transgression of conventional sexual boundaries brings catastrophic male retribution. ⟨. . .⟩ McCullers sought to deny the feminine entirely and to allow a woman to function successfully as a man. She could not sustain her vision because she knew it was impossible. I believe that the consequences of her experiment in this novella play a part in determining the final form of *The Member of the Wedding*, which as I have argued elsewhere, inexorably moves Frankie toward an acceptance of conventional femininity. After writing *The Ballad of the Sad Café* in only a few months, when McCullers returned to her six-year struggle with the materials of *The Member of the Wedding*, she knew that Frankie would have to submit as Miss Amelia had not.

—Louise Westling, "Carson McCullers's Amazon Nightmare," *Modern Fiction Studies* 28, no. 3 (Autumn 1982), in *Carson McCullers*, ed. Harold Bloom (New York: Chelsea House Publishers, 1986), 115–16

BARBARA A. WHITE

Honey Brown, who "just can't breathe no more," is Frankie's double in ⟨*The Member of the Wedding*⟩. Frankie feels a kinship with him because she senses that he is in the same divided state that she is. On the one hand, Honey works hard studying music and French; on the other, he "suddenly run[s] hog-wild all over Sugarville and tear[s] around for several days, until his friends bring him home more dead than living." Although he can talk "like a white schoolteacher," he often adopts his expected role with a vengeance, speaking in a "colored jumble" that even his family cannot understand. Honey spends only part of his energy trying to overcome or protesting the limitations placed on him; the rest of the time he accepts society's label of "inferior" and punishes himself.

Frankie exhibits this same psychology. She frequently "hates herself," and her attempts at rebellion against the female role are mainly symbolic. As Simone de Beauvoir puts it, the young girl "is too much divided against herself to join battle with the world; she limits herself to a flight from reality or a symbolic struggle against it." De Beauvoir mentions four common forms of "symbolic struggle": odd eating habits, kleptomania, self-mutilation, and running away from home. While Frankie never carries these behaviors to extremes, she indulges in all four types. She eats "greedily," pilfers from the five-and-ten, hacks at her foot with a knife, and tries to run away. It is characteristic of these acts that, like Honey's rampages, they are ineffective—the young girl is "struggling in her cage rather than trying to get out of it." At the end of the novel we find Honey in an actual prison and Frankie in a jail of her own.

Frankie's principal "flight from reality" is her creation of a fantasy world. The adult Honey laughs at her solution to racism, that he go to Cuba and pass as a Cuban. But Frankie still deals with her feeling of being trapped by escaping to the haven of her dreams where she can fly airplanes and see the whole world. Her favorite pastime with Berenice and John Henry is their game of criticizing God and putting themselves in the position of creator. Frankie agrees with the basic modifications Berenice would make. The world would be "just and reasonable": there would be no separate colored people, no killed Jews, and no hunger. Frankie makes a major addition, however. "She planned it so that people could instantly change back and forth from boys to girls, whichever way they felt like and wanted." This plan provides a neat symbolic solution to Frankie's conflicts.

To many commentators on McCullers's work, however, Frankie's dream is an "abnormal" one; a product of the author's "homosexual sensibility." We saw earlier that Leslie Fiedler initiated discussion of gender in McCullers's fiction when he referred to Frankie and Mick as "boy-girl" characters. This point might have led to recognition of McCullers's portrayal of the conflict between a woman's humanity and her destiny as a woman; but Fiedler went on, in a dis-approving tone, to call the "tomboy image" "lesbian" and argue that McCullers is "projecting in her neo-tomboys, ambiguous and epicene, the homosexual's . . . uneasiness before heterosexual passion." Fiedler ends up in the absurd posi-tion of contending that Frankie and Berenice are having a "homosexual romance."

Some critics have tried to preserve Fiedler's basic argument by giving Frankie a more appropriate lover. They see her relationship at the end of the novel with her newfound friend, Mary Littlejohn, as "latently homosexual"; Mary's name fits conveniently with this theory—she is a "little John," a "surro-gate male lover." Other critics influenced by Fiedler take Frankie's refusal to recognize "the facts of life" as evidence of different sexual "abnormalities." Perhaps she wants to join her brother's wedding so that she can commit incest; perhaps she is really "asexual" (to Ihab Hassan, McCullers's "men-women freaks" are "all bi-sexual, which is to say a-sexual"). The critics who have fol-lowed Fiedler's lead leave as many questions unanswered as he does. We never learn what a "homosexual sensibility" might be and how it is "abnormal," what the "tomboy image" has to do with lesbianism, how "bisexual" and "a-sexual" are the same. Because so many terms remain undefined, discussion of sex and gender in McCullers's fiction has been hopelessly confused.

At issue seems to be McCullers's endorsement of androgyny in her fiction. Frankie and Mick are only two among many androgynous characters, includ-ing Singer and Biff Brannon in *The Heart Is a Lonely Hunter*, Captain Penderton in *Reflections in a Golden Eye* (1941), and Amelia in *Ballad of the Sad Café* (1943). These characters are McCullers's most sympathetic, and they often seem to speak for her. ⟨. . .⟩

⟨. . .⟩ If McCullers implies any solution besides racial equality to the social injustice and personal isolation and despair she portrays in her novels, it is a move toward the loosening of conventional gender roles, toward the more androgynous world Frankie envisions when she wishes people could "change back and forth from boys to girls."

—Barbara A. White, "Loss of Self in *The Member of the Wedding*," *Growing Up Female: Adolescent Girlhood in American Fiction* (Greenwood Press, 1985), in *Carson McCullers*, ed. Harold Bloom (New York: Chelsea House Publishers, 1986), 133–35

SANDRA M. GILBERT AND SUSAN GUBAR

Since the terms of the psychodrama unfolding in McCullers's sad cafe are so inexorable, Miss Amelia is doomed from the start to lose the physical battle with Macy which constitutes the novella's climax. Because she has given up her bed to Lymon (who has given up his to Marvin Macy), her only bed has been an uncomfortable sofa, and perhaps, we are told, "lack of sleep . . . clouded her wits." But in itself, as McCullers makes clear, neither sleeplessness nor the stress of having her house invaded would necessarily have been enough to guarantee Miss Amelia's defeat. "A fine fighter," this powerful woman "know[s] all manner of mean holds and squeezes," so that "the town [is] betting on" her victory, remembering "the great fight between Miss Amelia and a Fork Falls lawyer who had tried to cheat her . . . a huge strapping fellow [who] was left three quarters dead when she finished with him. And it was not only her talent as a boxer that had impressed everyone—she could demoralize her enemy by making terrifying faces and fierce noises" (61). In spite of Miss Amelia's unnatural strength, though, the sexual subtext represented by the grotesque triangle in which she is involved dooms her to defeat.

For as McCullers describes it, the spectacular fight in which Marvin Macy and Miss Amelia engage before a mass of spectators in the cleared cafe at seven P.M. on Ground Hog Day is not just a jealous struggle for power over Lymon, it is the primal scene of sexual consummation which did not take place on their wedding night. ⟨. . .⟩

Why is the hunchback the agent of Miss Amelia's symbolic defloration as well as her literal defeat and thus the instrument of Marvin Macy's sexual triumph? And why is his leap into the fray accompanied by a mysterious cry? McCullers's text is so complex that we have to read it as overdetermined. From one perspective, if we take the hunchback to represent the false phallus associated with Miss Amelia's presumptuous usurpation of masculine privilege—with, that is, what Freud would call her "penis envy" and her "masculinity complex"—then his intervention in the fight signals the moment when she must be forced to confront the delusional quality of her pseudo-virility. Deformed himself, Lymon lands on her back to dramatize the way in which his physical deformity echoes her sexual deformity. In this reading, then, as Miss Amelia is made to surrender her pretensions to power, true masculinity reasserts itself with a victorious war whoop that sends a shiver down the spines of the onlookers, who realize that they are present at a solemn cultural event.

From another perspective, if we see the hunchback as representing the "little man" that is the female clitoris or, in a more generalized sense, the authentic if truncated female libido that Miss Amelia has refused to acknowledge, then the intervention of the hunchback in the fight signals the moment when she has been forced to confront her desire for Marvin Macy. Certainly from the day Macy returned to town, her behavior has notably changed: abandoning overalls for a dress, feeding Macy at her table, and finally bedding him down in her private quarters, she might almost "[seem] to have lost her will" (53) because she is in a kind of erotic trance, and the hunchback's open flirtation with Marvin Macy might well express her own secret enthrallment. In this reading, therefore, the mysterious cry is a cry of female orgasmic surrender which sends a shiver down the spine of onlookers because they realize that they are voyeurs witnessing a ceremonial sexual event.

Finally, from yet a third perspective, if we define the hunchback not simply as an anatomical or allegorical aspect of Miss Amelia but rather as an autonomous male character, then his intervention in the fight signals the moment when, by eliminating Miss Amelia as a rival, he achieves a homosexual union with the man whom he has been trying to seduce since the moment when they exchanged their first gaze of secret complicity. In this reading, then—a reading that supposes McCullers's text to be haunted by female anxiety about male social and sexual bonding—Miss Amelia is simply the medium whose house and flesh provide the opportunity for Lymon and Marvin Macy to come together, and the mysterious cry at the end of the fight expresses their homoerotic orgasm while sending a shiver down the spines of onlookers because they realize they are witnessing a perverse and subversive event. Moreover, that the two men leave town together after destroying most of Miss Amelia's property reiterates the point that she not only is no longer necessary to them but that their union requires her obliteration.

Whether one subscribes to all or none of these readings, it is clear that at the conclusion of "Ballad" Miss Amelia has been metamorphosed from a woman warrior to a helpless madwoman. Her very body has shriveled, for she is "thin as old maids are thin when they go crazy"; her eyes emphasize her isolation because they are "more crossed . . . as though they sought each other out to exchange a little glance of grief and lonely recognition"; and her voice is "broken, soft, and sad" (70). Bereft of her once legendary physical strength, she has also lost her social, intellectual, and economic authority; her cafe is closed; her house is boarded up and all her "wise doctoring" is over, for she tells "one-half of her patients that they [are] going to die outright, and to the remaining half she recommend[s] cures so far-fetched and agonizing that no one in his right mind would consider them for a moment" (69-70). Incarcerated in a wasteland of a town where "the soul rots with boredom," she resembles not only such paradigmatic mad spinsters as Miss Havisham in Dickens's *Great Expectations* and Miss Emily in Faulkner's "A Rose for Emily" but also a female version of T.S. Eliot's wounded Fisher King.

Even the male prisoners in the novella's mysterious epilogue—a brief coda entitled "THE TWELVE MORTAL MEN"—are happier on their chain gang than is this prisoner of sex in her sad cafe, for as she sits in silence beside the one window of her house "which is not boarded" and turns toward the empty street "a face like the terrible dim faces known in dreams," their voices swell together "until at last it seems that the sound does not come from the twelve men on the gang, but from the earth itself, or the wide sky" (3,71). Even in the penitentiary, McCullers implies, men are sustained by their own community while a woman like Miss Amelia—who, even at her most powerful, never had a community of women—has been inexorably condemned to the solitary confinement such a singular anomaly deserves.

—Sandra M. Gilbert and Susan Gubar, *No Man's Land: The Place of the Woman Writer in the Twentieth Century*, vol. 1: *The War of the Words* (New Haven: Yale University Press, 1988), 108–12

B I B L I O G R A P H Y

The Heart Is a Lonely Hunter. 1940.

Reflections in a Golden Eye. 1941.

The Ballad of the Sad Café. 1943.

The Member of the Wedding. 1946.

The Member of the Wedding: A Play. 1951.

The Ballad of the Sad Café: Novels and Stories. 1951.

Collected Short Stories and the Novel The Ballad of the Sad Café. 1955.

The Square Root of Wonderful. 1958.

Clock Without Hands. 1961.

Sweet as a Pickle and Clean as a Pig. 1964.

The Mortgaged Heart. Ed. Margarita G. Smith. 1971.

Short Novels and Stories. 1972.

Sucker. 1986.

GERTRUDE STEIN

1874–1946

GERTRUDE STEIN was born on February 3, 1874, in Allegheny, Pennsylvania, the youngest of five surviving children of Daniel and Amelia Stein. She spent her childhood in Vienna, Paris, and Oakland, California, and later attended Radcliffe, where she studied under philosopher and psychologist William James.

Stein was especially interested in psychology and her first published work, "Normal Motor Automatism," cowritten with Leon Solomons, was published in the *Psychological Review* in 1896. She studied medicine at Johns Hopkins University from 1897 to 1901 but left without receiving a degree. In 1903 she moved to Paris with her brother Leo and lived there for the rest of her life. She returned to America only once.

In 1904, Stein and her brother began collecting paintings, including early works of Cézanne, Matisse, Picasso, and Braque, and started what became their famous Saturday evening gatherings frequented by members of the expatriate and French avant-garde. In 1907 Stein met Alice B. Toklas, who became her lifelong lover and assistant; they lived together until Stein's death.

Influenced by the aesthetic philosophies and styles of the artists she collected and by Flaubert's *Trois contes*, Stein wrote *Three Lives* (1909). Likewise, the cubism of Picasso—for whom Stein sat for a portrait—informs her astonishing prose-poem, *Tender Buttons* (1914). Over the next 40 years she wrote almost constantly, producing nearly 500 works, including portraits, plays, poems, and scores of books, only a few of which were published in her lifetime. While some critics hailed her stream-of-consciousness techniques as liberating and illuminating, others thought her work self-indulgent, deliberately obscure, and intellectually dishonest.

Among her best-known works are *Tender Buttons*, *The Making of Americans* (1925), and the popular *The Autobiography of Alice B. Toklas* (1932); the opera *Four Saints in Three Acts* (cowritten with composer Virgil Thomson) premiered in the United States in 1934. By the time Stein recorded her experiences in France during World War II in *Wars I Have Seen* (1945), her reputation in America was firmly established. She died on July 27, 1946.

Stein was undoubtedly one of the most influential writers of her time and was central to a significant segment of the European artistic community; Sherwood Anderson and Ernest Hemingway are among those most directly in her debt. Her experimental writing has influenced generations of poets concerned with the sound and the portrayal of consciousness.

A "famous lesbian," Stein also aroused keen interest in her sexuality; she has been the subject of a number of biographies. She herself examined the theme of lesbianism in several works: her early novel, Q. E. D. (1903), for example (published posthumously as *Things As They Are*) examines the rivalries and desires among three young women, and her *Autobiography of Alice B. Toklas* explores her lifelong relationship with Toklas. One of Stein's most intriguing works on the subject is "Lifting Belly," an extensive "encoded" poem of lesbian eroticism.

C R I T I C A L   E X T R A C T S

VIRGIL THOMSON

Gertrude not only liked people, she needed them. They were grist for her poetry, a relief from the solitudes of a mind essentially introspective.

Alice Toklas neither took life easy nor fraternized casually. She got up at six and cleaned the drawing room herself, because she did not wish things broken. (Porcelain and other fragile objects were her delight, just as pictures were Gertrude's; and she could imagine using violence toward a servant who might break one.) She liked being occupied, anyway, and did not need repose, ever content to serve Gertrude or be near her. She ran the house, ordered the meals, cooked on occasion, and typed out everything that got written into the blue copybooks that Gertrude had adopted from French school children. From 1927 or '28 she also worked petit point, matching in silk the colors and shades of designs made especially for her by Picasso. These tapestries were eventually applied to a pair of Louse XV small armchairs (chauffeuses) that Gertrude had bought for her. She was likely, any night, to go to bed by eleven, while Miss Stein would sit up late if there were someone to talk with.

Way back before World War I, in 1910 or so, in Granada Gertrude had experienced the delights of writing directly in the landscape. This does not mean just working out of doors; it means being surrounded by the thing one is writing about at the time one is writing about it. Later, in 1924, staying at Saint-Rémy in Provence, and sitting in fields beside the irrigation ditches, she found the same sound of running water as in Granada to soothe her while she wrote or while she simply sat, imbuing herself with the landscape's sight and sound. In the country around Belley, where she began to summer only a few years later, she wrote *Lucy Church Amiably* wholly to the sound of streams and waterfalls.

Bravig Imbs, an American poet and novelist who knew her in the late twenties, once came upon her doing this. The scene took place in a field, its enactors being Gertrude, Alice, and a cow. Alice, by means of a stick, would drive the cow around the field. Then, at a sign from Gertrude, the cow would be stopped; and Gertrude would write in her copybook. After a bit, she would pick up her folding stool and progress to another spot, whereupon Alice would again start the cow moving around the field till Gertrude signaled she was ready to write again. Though Alice now says that Gertrude drove the cow, she waiting in the car, the incident, whatever its choreography, reveals not only Gertrude's working intimacy with landscape but also the concentration of two friends on an act of composition by one of them that typifies and reveals their daily life for forty years. Alice had decided long before that "Gertrude was always right," that she was to have whatever she wanted when she wanted it, and that the way to keep herself always wanted was to keep Gertrude's writing always and forever unhindered, unopposed.

Gertrude's preoccupation with painting and painters was not shared by Alice except in so far as certain of Gertrude's painter friends touched her heart, and Picasso was almost the only one of these. Juan Gris was another, and Christian Bérard a very little bit. But Matisse I know she had not cared for, nor Braque. If it had not been for Gertrude, I doubt that Alice would ever have had much to do with the world of painting. She loved objects and furniture, practiced cooking and gardening, understood music. Of music, indeed, she had a long experience, having once, as a young girl, played a piano concerto in public. But painting was less absorbing to her than to Gertrude. ⟨. . .⟩

Gertrude lived by the heart, indeed; and domesticity was her theme. Not for her the matings and rematings that went on among the amazons. An early story from 1903, published after her death, *Things as They Are*, told of one such intrigue in post-Radcliffe days. But after 1907 her love life was serene, and it was Alice Toklas who made it so. Indeed, it was this tranquil life that offered to Gertrude a fertile soil of sentiment-security in which other friendships great and small could come to flower, wither away, be watered, cut off or preserved in a book. Her life was like that of a child, to whom danger can come only from the outside, never from home, and whose sole urgency is growth. It was also that of an adult who demanded all the rights of a man along with the privileges of a woman.

—Virgil Thomson, "A Portrait of Gertrude Stein," *Virgil Thomson* (1966), in *The Chelsea House Library of Literary Criticism: Twentieth-Century American Literature*, vol. 6, ed. Harold Bloom (New York: Chelsea House Publishers, 1987), 3766–67.

RANDA K. DUBNICK

Tender Buttons represents a radical change from the early prose style of *The Making of Americans* and of other works to that which ⟨Stein⟩ called poetry. From prose, with its emphasis on syntax and its suppression of vocabulary, she moved to a concern for poetry with its emphasis on vocabulary and its suppression of syntax. This change manifests itself in a shift of linguistic emphasis from the operation of combination (horizontal axis) to the operation of selection (vertical axis).

Tender Buttons attained "a certain notoriety" in the press and attracted polemical criticism, perhaps because it seemed to "veer off into meaninglessness," at least in conventional terms. But the work is more than a literary curiosity. Its marked stylistic change appears to have been a breakthrough that influenced the direction of much of Stein's future work. "*Tender Buttons* represented her full scale break out of the prison of conventional form into the colorful realm of the sensitized imagination." ⟨. . .⟩

As the concerns of Stein's writing gradually shift from an interest in orderly analysis of the world to an interest in the immediate perception of the world by the consciousness, her writing appears to deal more and more with the word itself; with the mental images called up by and associated with the word (signifieds), and with the qualities of words as things in themselves (signifiers). "Her imagination was stimulated then not by the object's particular qualities alone, but also by the associations it aroused . . . and by the words themselves as they took shape upon the page."

Perhaps coincidentally, a similar shift in emphasis was occurring in the painting of the Cubists around the time *Tender Buttons* was composed. ⟨. . .⟩

This new interest in the word itself, and especially in the noun and the associative powers of the word, was what Stein considered the essence of poetry. In *Tender Buttons* and other works that she held as poetry, the chief linguistic operation is association (given various labels by structuralists such as substitution, selection, system) and choice of words. The association of words and concepts by similarity or opposition, and the selection of a word from a group of synonyms, are operations that function along the vertical axis of language. Interestingly enough, the *Tender Buttons* style also suppresses syntax (the horizontal axis) while it is expanding vocabulary. Construction of syntax becomes increasingly fragmentary until syntax disappears altogether in some of the more extreme passages. ⟨. . .⟩

It is ironic that, in spite of Stein's intention in writing *Tender Buttons* to capture immediate experience while consciousness grapples with it, there have been so many problems in the reading of this book. One problem inherent in the work itself is the disjunction of the two axes of language making it almost impossible to read the work for conventional discursive content. Moreover, this problem leads to another: the effort of trying to "figure it out," to reconstruct the content, not only exhausts the reader, but overdistances him from the work itself. Such an effort is futile anyway, for *Tender Buttons* demands to be dealt with in its own terms. The reader is given none of the literary allusions that the reader of Pound, Eliot, or Joyce can hold on to. ⟨. . .⟩

As Sutherland suggests, perhaps what the reader of Stein is required to do is to look *at* the work, rather than *through* it. One cannot look *through* it because it is an opaque, rather than transparent, style. If one does look *at* the work, what does one see in *Tender Buttons?* He sees the word presented as an entity in its own right. By forcing the reader to attend to the word, Stein makes the word seem new, again. In this effort, she does not ignore the meanings of words, as so ma⟨n⟩y critics have claimed. However by presenting each word in an unusual context, she directs attention not only towards its sound but towards its sense as the reader is forced to grapple with each word, one at a time. One is forced to attend to the word, and to language, with a sense of bewilderment and perhaps with a sense of wonder and discovery.

—Randa K. Dubnick, "Two Types of Obscurity in the Writings of Gertrude Stein," *The Emporia State Research Studies* 24, no. 3 (Winter 1976), in *American Women Poets*, ed. Harold Bloom (New York: Chelsea House Publishers, 1986), 84–85, 87–88, 90, 94–95

CLIVE BUSH

The Making of Americans shows us the authorial voice breaking with "society" by creating a magnificent epitaph for it. For Gertrude Stein it meant a long apprenticeship, reaching a threshold of release from the tyranny of the sentence with all its implications of reality. The completeness of the break is described in her essay "The Gradual Making of *The Making of Americans*" and realized halfway through *A Long Gay Book*, written after *The Making of Americans*.

We have, of course, described the process too clearly. Gay, *déracinée*, living among bohemians *and* artists, herself exempted from "necessity," Gertrude Stein also had to escape from the pseudo-alternative of American bourgeois life: bohemianism. The *life-style* (a term as dogmatically aesthetic and significant of *behavior* as "way of life") included an interest in psychoanalysis, managing art, collecting, or, as Gertrude Stein herself said in a particularly vicious mood in "The Notebooks," teaching ballet to little girls. We should, therefore, expect from the novel a variety of tones, and indeed contradictory attitudes toward the fate of American history turning into social behavior. The movement goes between inner and outer perception, between nostalgia and hatred, ironic approval and obsessive criticism, chilly analysis and praise of courage face to face with invisible neurosis, between pride and despair. Indeed the tone of the authorial voice matches these varieties as it changes the terms of its address from "gentle reader" of Swiftian memory to "stranger" of twentieth-century nihilistic angst.

Various disciplines merge in the novel. From her training at Harvard and Johns Hopkins she brought the experimental legacy of a classificatory habit of mind, a distrust of teleologies, and a disposition toward evolutionary psychology as a model for human behavior. In Europe she immersed herself in literature and painting. The curious thing to emerge from her prodigious excursions into literature is a double leaning toward eighteenth-century novels, many written by women, and toward histories of military leaders. There is a sexual differentiation of direction toward the private and public realms. It seems as if she needed to ascertain the poles of traditional "feminine" and "male" behavior: the one expressing its conflicts in the early bourgeois novel whose class, economic, and social conflicts mythicized themselves in the Gothic romance; the other betraying her fascination with violent male power games which lasted throughout her life. Thus we may at least speculate that in the paralleling of the search for a husband with the search for glory she was looking for the historical origins of psychological types, a favorite nineteenth-century activity.

In satire she found comedy and public tragedy by characterizing human activity as behavior, and by mocking the linear continuities of idealism and destiny.

—Clive Bush, "Toward the Outside: The Quest for Discontinuity in Gertrude Stein's *The Making of Americans*," *Twentieth Century Literature* (Spring 1978), in *American Fiction 1914 to 1945*, ed. Harold Bloom (New York: Chelsea House Publishers, 1987), 82–83

LYNN Z. BLOOM

⟨By⟩ letting the reader in on the joke of the real authorship of the *Autobiography* right from the start, instead of publishing it anonymously or pseudonymously, Stein's strategy is to take the reader into league with her. Once she has him on her side as a participant in her joke, it's hard to turn against the perpetrator of it. Thus the reader is more inclined to accept Stein's image of herself (as seen by Toklas and by herself) as true than he might if he had the judgment of a bona fine intermediary biographer to question. Again Stein, through Toklas, controls the reader as well as her material.

If the subject's personality or psyche were suppressed, flattened, distorted, or falsified, some of the advantages of autobiography-by-identification would be lost. But none of these occur in *The Autobiography of Alice B. Toklas*, in which both Gertrude Stein and Alice B. Toklas are very much alive and very well. All in all, the advantages of this innovative form are manifold, and as practiced by Stein it has no conspicuous disadvantages—except unrepeatability.

Another innovative aspect of *The Autobiography of Alice B. Toklas* is that, despite its intense focus on Gertrude Stein, a biographical portrait of the alleged autobiographical subject does emerge quite clearly. The work is a double portrait, of Stein and of Toklas. The *Autobiography* is further unusual in that Stein deliberately wrote it to emulate the oral speech mannerisms of another person—in choice of words, level of language, syntax, speech rhythms—rather than precisely her own, though the two are not incompatible. Indeed, she succeeded very well, judging from Toklas' own style in *What Is Remembered*, ⟨. . .⟩ even allowing for the possibility that in the latter volume Toklas could have imitated Stein's imitation of herself. Stein always treats Toklas-as-narrator the way she evidently treated Toklas-as-intimate-lifelong-friend, with the respect that maintains Toklas' integrity and never makes her feeble or foolish, never jokes at Toklas' expense (unlike Boswell's sometimes silly sycophancy, with which Toklas is occasionally wrongly compared). Thus Alice, like her biographical creator, is a vivid, witty, personable tartly gracious presence in her own pseudo-autobiography, an enduring tribute to a friend and to a friendship, among other things.

—Lynn Z. Bloom, "Gertrude Is Alice Is Everybody: Innovation and Point of View in Gertrude Stein's Autobiographies," *Twentieth Century Literature* (Spring 1978), in *The Chelsea House Library of Literary Criticism: Twentieth-Century American Literature*, vol. 6, ed. Harold Bloom (New York: Chelsea House Publishers, 1987), 3778

MARY ALLEN

Gertrude Stein's story "Many, Many Women" is riddled with the word *one*, which appears three thousand six hundred and sixty-three times. The phrases "she is one" and "she was one" occur hundreds of times. Frequently seeking a larger whole, Stein actually perceives oneness in the smallest unit—object, word, or person. Her belief that only matter broken into its most basic components exists in its integrity has everything to do with the fragmented effect of her writings. She shatters things that are commonly stuck together—related objects, words in familiar patterns, people bound to each other—so that the individual unit may flourish. Her new arrangements emphasize formerly unexpected characteristics of the individual parts rather than the creation of new entities. While Stein's critics observe that her work falls into pieces, what is not conceded is that a sense of wholeness comes after the shattering. Like other moderns she sees that things fall apart. But for her there is virtue in this condition. Stein tenderly breaks the world into pieces, and although she sometimes tries, she never puts it back again.

Well in the American tradition of individualism, Stein does not hold to the convention that alienation and loneliness inevitably accompany that theme. The strong may earn a tough-minded pleasure in accepting the uniqueness and the aloneness that everyone inherits. The connections most desire, she sees, are too often based on destructive illusions. In combination, something is lost.

Above everything, Stein values liberty, and her idea of freedom calls for the fresh view of a child who has not yet learned to put things together. His world is new, and it is pleasingly small. Excitement comes from seeing nearby things in original ways rather than in looking far for the exotic. ⟨. . .⟩

The marvelously playful *Tender Buttons* is a logic-defying work that has received a due amount of ridicule. But where it refuses analysis, it does not refuse pleasure, yielding the fun a child gets from poking at a world he would not expect to understand. A curious enjoyment can be derived from not "understanding" *Tender Buttons*, with its conscious attempt to dislodge logic. Critics continue, however, in their efforts to establish connections in this book of non sequiturs. In *Gertrude Stein in Pieces*, Richard Bridgman observes that objects share common qualities: a tiger skin and a coin are the same color. But when a common characteristic is located, with the suggestion of a true association, the essential differentness and impossibility of connection become even more noticeable. A coin and a tiger skin are so very *unlike*. *Tender Buttons* makes sly fun of the predilection of the highly trained, logical mind in its attempt to create meaningful wholes. The fresher child's approach is to accept the individual object and to probe it for new significance. He plays with it. The art of play is the method of *Tender Buttons*, although the book is touched by a maternal tenderness for the strangely arranged "Objects," "Food," and "Rooms." Nothing in this small world, however, is grown up or dead. Things smash, but they are not destroyed. In fact, Stein had a particular weakness for breakable objects.

—Mary Allen, "Gertrude Stein's Sense of Oneness," *Southwest Review* (Winter 1981), in *The Chelsea House Library of Literary Criticism: Twentieth-Century American Literature*, vol. 6, ed. Harold Bloom (New York: Chelsea House Publishers, 1987), 3781–82

ELIZABETH FIFER

Although Stein's writing often assumes a bantering tone, it speaks movingly of the anguish of being misunderstood, of needing a reader who will participate vigorously in the act of creating meaning. Caught in a web of words and struggling to be understood, Stein must use the very obfuscating language that created her previous difficulties. In a passage from *A Sweet Tail*, she admits her need for a reader to "rescue" her meaning: "Suppose a tremble, a ham, a little mouth told to wheeze more and a religion a reign . . . that makes a load registrar and passes best . . . gracious oh my cold under fur, under no rescued reading" ⟨*Geography and Plays*, 1968, p. 67⟩. This monologue is in the conditional—"What if I were like that and no one understood?" Of course, Stein is like that. Her sexual and creative "tremble" is both emphasized and belittled by her use of the word "ham." The "little mouth," a reference to the vagina, is simultaneously the writer's mouth, "hamming it up"; and her text, told to "wheeze," is made purposefully difficult. Her lesbian love, "religion a reign," is identifiable both by its serious and its "royal" nature. The whole "load" of her sexuality must be interpreted by the reader, who either understands her garbled message by correcting it and passing it on, or who misunderstands and lets its truth "pass" unrecognized. This educational metaphor is explicit throughout Stein's difficult texts. Stein fears being unmasked, but she also fears going unrecognized. If she is not read clearly, she will become "cold," and her texts will betray their purpose. ⟨. . .⟩

Why does Stein use this difficult language? She herself gives us a partial answer in *A List.* "Change songs for safety . . . if they were . . . differently decided . . . delighted . . . accidentally relieved and repeatedly received and reservedly deceived." Stein must "change songs for safety." If she were "differently decided," if she were not a lesbian, perhaps she would write differently. Yet, in her trope of contradiction, her positive note is also clear. She claims to be "delighted" and "relieved" by both her writing and her life, indulging herself "repeatedly." She emphasizes two ideas: accident and deception (as opposed to intention) as keys to both her reception and her reserve. ⟨. . .⟩

Stein's coding strategy is a willed and intentional process, a carefully worn mask through which she artfully expresses her thoughts and feelings. But her intrusion "errors," uncensored areas of her discourse which intrude on prosaic statements and make them ambiguous, are far more frequent and far more puzzling. These intrusions seem to enter haphazardly into her texts, creating a randomized surface. It is as if parts of the message have actually appeared against her will or that Stein has no control over its development and logical direction. ⟨. . .⟩

Stein's intrusions usually occur when she is trying to rationalize the problem of sexuality. Just as she is telling us that she will not reveal herself or that it is probably better not to be associated with the idea of sexuality at all, Stein provocatively emphasizes the sexual content of her associations. In the following selection, for instance, the intrusions occur as physical descriptions of the earth, drawn from the vocabulary of mining: "It is as well to be without in their reverberation in the meantime ways which are in opening to their site do unexpectedly deliver it as in a tunnel and they attend the opening to their site do unexpectedly deliver it as in a tunnel and they attend the opening and the exit." If, in the beginning, Stein seems to be begging the question of sexuality (using "reverberation" to refer to the movement of orgasm), the very mention of this word causes the appearance of associated kinds of sexualized geological images such as the earthquake or the explosion that mining requires, in turn producing other metaphorically related words: "opening," "site," "deliver," "tunnel," "exit." These words intrude upon her originally framed denial to become a kind of contradictory approval of her original premise.

—Elizabeth Fifer, "Rescued Readings: Characteristic Deformations in the Language of Gertrude Stein's Plays," *Texas Studies in Literature and Language* (Winter 1982), in *The Chelsea House Library of Literary Criticism: Twentieth-Century American Literature*, vol. 6, ed. Harold Bloom (New York: Chelsea House Publishers, 1987), 3784–85

MARIANNE DEKOVEN

As in much impressionist and modernist fiction, narrative tone and temporal structure are at odds in *Three Lives* with the thematic content deducible from close reading and a reconstruction of linear causality. The tone and emphasis are noncommittal, cheerful, naive, at most mildly mocking; the thematic content is bitter, angry, implying a sophisticated social-political awareness and judgment. Temporal structure is preponderantly either a "continuous present" or static, yet each novella plots a classic trajectory of rise and fall. Nothing better epitomizes the contradictions of *Three Lives* than its epigraph, a quotation from Jules Laforgue: "Donc je suis un malheureux et ce/n'est ni ma faute ni celle de la vie." These lines certainly belie the narrator's cheerful innocence, but they equally belie the conclusions we can draw with excellent justification from all three novellas that a cruel "life," at least, is very much to blame for the mistreatment and death of these women.

We need no longer speculate about the psychological reasons for Stein's diverting attention, both her own and the reader's, from her anger and sadness. Richard Bridgman and Catharine Stimpson have shown with great clarity that Stein simultaneously concealed and encoded in her literary work troublesome feelings about herself as a woman, about women's helplessness, and particularly about lesbianism, still very much considered by society a "pollutant," as Stimpson puts it, during most of Stein's life ⟨Catharine Stimpson, "The Mind, the Body and Gertrude Stein," *Critical Inquiry* 3, 1977, p. 493⟩. But Stein did not merely stifle or deny her anger, her sense that she did not fit and that the deficiency was not hers but rather that of the structure which excluded her. In effect, Stein's rebellion was channelled from content to linguistic structure itself. A rebellion in language is much easier to ignore or misconstrue, but its attack, particularly in literature, penetrates far deeper, to the very structures which determine, within a particular culture, what can be thought.

Stein's anti-patriarchal rebellion was not conscious or intentional, as her denial of her own bitterness and anger in *Three Lives* suggests. But for her, as perhaps for Virginia Woolf, there is an extra dimension to the view of experimental writing as anti-patriarchal, because both writers defined themselves in opposition to the notions of women which patriarchy provides.

Stein's attitude toward her gender offers further material for speculation. ⟨. . . W⟩hen this material becomes particularly relevant to Stein's writing, her female self-hatred was such that she was psychologically compelled to identify herself as a man in order to be a happy, sexually active person and a functioning writer. While she lived with her brother Leo, she was a frequently depressed, subservient sister; when Leo left and Alice Toklas moved in, she became a generally happy, very productive husband. This male identification did not shift until the late twenties, when there is evidence that Stein began to feel better about her female identity. Throughout her radically experimental period, therefore, she essentially thought of herself as a man (there is direct evidence of this identification in the notebooks, where Stein says "Pablo & Matisse have a maleness that belongs to genius. Moi aussi, perhaps"). We might posit a speculative connection between this male identification, and the concomitant suppression of her female identity, with the shift of the rebellious impulse from thematic content to linguistic structure, where the subversive implications of the writing are at once more powerful and abstruse.

—Marianne DeKoven, *"Three Lives," A Different Language: Gertrude Stein's Experimental Writing* (1983), in *The Chelsea House Library of Literary Criticism: Twentieth-Century American Literature*, vol. 6, ed. Harold Bloom (New York: Chelsea House Publishers, 1987), 3790

JAYNE L. WALKER

In *Tender Buttons* Stein channeled the flood of concrete particulars she first tapped in *G.M.P.* to create an artfully structured composition. Its three sections, "Objects," "Food," and "Rooms," form a provocative sequence. From the external objects we see and touch, the text moves inward to the substances we ingest and, in the final section, outward again to the spaces that surround us. *Tender Buttons* describes a female world (circa 1912) of domestic objects and rituals—a world of dresses and hats, tables and curtains, mealtimes and bedtimes, cleanliness and dirt. Although a few exotic items, including an elephant and a "white hunter," make momentary appearances, the iconography of domestic life dominates the text. Concrete nouns and adjectives name a wealth of homely particulars. But in its artful rearrangement of these details, the text models a world in which objects, foods, and rooms are liberated from their normal subordination to human routines and purposes. ⟨. . .⟩

While its concrete objects are animated with human qualities, *Tender Buttons* presents human beings simply as physical objects, equal to all the others named and arranged in these "still lifes": "and so between curves and outlines and real seasons and more out glasses and a perfectly unprecedented arrangement between old ladies and mild colds there is no satin wood shining" (473). Here, as in "A Feather" and many other pieces, spatial contiguity is the ordering principle of this "perfectly unprecedented arrangement," but "mild colds" and "real seasons" mingle with the "curves and outlines" of purely spatial configurations. Sometimes the human body is reduced to a set of synecdoches, as in "Colored Hats": "Colored hats are necessary to show that curls are worn by an addition of blank spaces, this makes the difference between single lines and broad stomachs" (473). Occasionally the discourse creates shocking juxtapositions of human bodies and inanimate objects, as in "Little sales ladies little sales ladies little saddles of mutton" (475). This equation of "little sales ladies" with pieces of meat strikingly illustrates how radically the order of *Tender Buttons* refuses to privilege human meanings and purposes. In her earlier works, Stein portrayed human beings in terms of essential character, abstracted from their concrete daily life in the physical world. The radical reversal in *Tender Buttons* suggests not so much a dehumanization as a new affirmation that human existence is intimately involved with the physicality of matter and of flesh. The physical world portrayed in *Tender Buttons* includes the most intimate realities of the female body. "A Petticoat" shows "a disgrace, an ink spot, a rosy charm" (471). And a "shallow hole rose on red, a shallow hole in and in this makes ale less," an obvious trasnmutation of Alice (474). ⟨. . .⟩

⟨. . .⟩ Stein's pursuit of "reality" forced her to confront the irreconcilable difference between the order of language and the chaotic plenitude of immediate experience. ⟨. . .⟩ *Tender Buttons* claims that each of its "collections" of words "shows the disorder, . . . it shows more likeness than anything else." By the time she wrote this text, Stein's acute awareness of language as a "necessary betrayal," coupled with her continuing dedication to the "realism of the composition," had led her to conclude that, within language, "real is only, only excreate, only excreate a no since." Uniting the words creation and excretion, the verb "excreate" boldly asserts the inseparable connection between mind and matter. External to more conventional creativity, nonsense is the only viable model of the "real" that language can create. ⟨. . .⟩

In *Tender Buttons*, Stein joyfully embraced what she later identified as the "reality of the twentieth century . . . a time when everything cracks, where everything is destroyed, everything isolates itself." Later in her career she asserted that the "creator of the new composition in the arts is an outlaw until he is a classic," until the time when the "modern composition having become past is classified and the description of it is classical." From our vantage point, we can readily situate *Tender Buttons* within the historical poetics of modernism. In Yeats's "Second Coming," "[t]hings fall apart; the center cannot hold." In *The Waste Land*, a "heap of broken images" is presented as the sum of human knowledge. Fragmentation and the loss of a center have become part of our "classical description" of the themes and structural principles of literary modernism. But Stein remained an "outlaw" long after writers like Yeats and Eliot were enshrined as "classics." The playful, domesticated disorder of *Tender Buttons* is strikingly different from the apocalyptic "rough beast" presaged by Yeats's vision of chaos or the spiritual aridity of Eliot's "waste land." In *Tender Buttons* the absence of a center is presented not as a loss but as a liberation that allows limitless invention of new, purely poetic orders.

> —Jayne L. Walker, *"Tender Buttons:* 'The Music of the Present Tense,'" *The Making of a Modernist: Gertrude Stein from "Three Lives" to "Tender Buttons"* (1984), in *The Chelsea House Library of Literary Criticism: Twentieth-Century American Literature*, vol. 6, ed. Harold Bloom (New York: Chelsea House Publishers, 1987), 3791, 3794

MALCOLM COWLEY

⟨The⟩ great mystery about Gertrude Stein is how this woman with a real influence on American prose, so that her first book marks an era in our literature; this woman famous for her conversation, able to change the ideas of other writers, able to hold and dominate big audiences when she lectures, should at the same time have written books so monumental in their dullness, so many pyramids and Parthenons consecrated to the reader's apathy.

I am not speaking of her exoteric works like *The Autobiography of Alice B. Toklas* and the present volume, but rather of her experimental essay-poemnovels like *Tender Buttons* and *The Making of Americans* and *Lucy Church Amiably*. And the trouble isn't at all that these books have no meaning. If we felt they were pure nonsense, we could find some pleasure in the word patterns, the puns, the rhymes, the mere sound of it all; everything would be dada, would be good fun. The trouble is that they do have a meaning, somewhere in the author's mind: a definite subject that eludes and irritates us and sets us off on a vain search as if through a pile of dusty newspapers for an item which we are sure must be there, but which we are equally sure we can never find. ⟨. . .⟩

Wars I Have Seen starts out to give us more in the same self-centered vein: more about the early life of the very great author, more about her becoming a legend, more about how it felt to be the spoiled youngest child in a family of five boys and girls. ⟨. . .⟩ But her attention keeps being distracted by present events, much as a rheumatic twinge or the ticking of an alarm clock will intrude into a pleasant dream about the past. Soon the sleeper wakens to feel that there are intruders in the house.

The intruders, of course, are the Germans; and here in an occupied village the effects of their presence are felt in a thousand indirect ways. ⟨. . .⟩

At the beginning of *Wars I Have Seen* you are bothered by Miss Stein's American but excessively personal style, with its flatness of statement, its repetitions, its deliberate errors in grammar, and its absence of commas, except where the sense calls for a period or a semicolon. Later you become reconciled to your reading; or perhaps the style itself becomes a little simplified and humanized through the author's preoccupation with her subject. For the first time she forgets herself in her subject, and her readers forget themselves too, and forget Miss Stein, as they follow the life of a French village from day to day.

—Malcolm Cowley, *The Flower and the Leaf: A Contemporary Record of American Writing Since 1941*, ed. Donald W. Faulkner (New York: Viking Penguin, 1985), 72–75

ESTELLE C. JELINEK

Catharine Stimpson defines the problem of women at the turn of the century who were liberated intellectually but not sexually as the "feminization of the mind/body problem." ⟨. . .⟩

For women like Stein, "the feminization of the mind/body problem" created confusion over "what women might do with their bodies and what they might say about it, especially in public." For Stein, in her time and with her personality, camouflage was the only way she could write about her life. There was no way for her to coexist or synthesize her dual roles as private lesbian and public writer. Thus, fragmented anecdotes and a discontinuous chronology were necessary to conceal her true self in a genre predicated on self-revelation. And they do not contribute to a rounder or more insightful portrait ⟨. . . .⟩ Instead, they represent Stein's lack of trust and faith in a world that does not accept or allow her to write about her sexual preference. ⟨. . .⟩

It is because of this need to hide her private life with Alice Toklas that the autobiography becomes a pretense at self-portraiture, for she must exclude the only meaningful intimate relationship of her life. She hopes to distract her readers from the absence of this personal element by concentrating on amusing portraits of famous people. Nonetheless, Stein does not entirely exclude her personal life from *The Autobiography of Alice B. Toklas*. ⟨. . .⟩

If Stein had written in her own voice about Toklas's wifelike functions, her readers would probably have been shocked or disturbed. But if Toklas chooses to perform these duties, in her own voice, while the genius worked, then the audience may not even notice. Toklas's presence as the narrator legitimized Stein in a world that expected some information stereotypically associated with women in an autobiography by a woman, just as the geniuses Stein gathered around her legitimized her as a professional, if yet unrecognized, writer.

Writing her life story in the voice of her intimate companion serves yet another function. By placing Toklas in the ostensible center of the autobiography and by making her the narrator, Stein pays homage to their—her and Toklas's—personal success story. Stein makes famous the most important person in her life; she makes famous the "wife" of the genius who will one day be famous for her work. ⟨. . .⟩

Stein's need to disguise her relationship with Toklas is not surprising. During a time when most women had little choice between celibacy and domesticity, it was socially acceptable for women to share homes with one another. Jane Addams lived with another woman. So did M. Carey Thomas, Frances Willard, and Susan B. Anthony. Nevertheless, marriage was still the socially preferred relationship. Unpublished diaries and letters from the nineteenth century are filled with passionate and intense descriptions written by women to one another, sometimes explicit about physical contact but most of the time not. Physical relationships were not common until the beginning of the twentieth century because women were so ignorant of their bodies that they did not often connect sexuality with anything save procreation.

Stimpson describes Stein's motive for disguising and "encoding" her lesbian relationship in her earlier novels *Q.E.D.* and *Fernhurst*, both written between 1903 and 1905, as "the need to write out hidden impulses; the wish to speak to friends without having others overhear; the desire to evade and to confound strangers, aliens, and enemies." By 1932 the disguise was reduced to the "openness" of giving Toklas the role of narrator of Stein's autobiography. Stein did not live to benefit from the struggles of the women "who first exemplified the feminization of the mind/body problem," but she "left for contemporary women the consolation that it could be endured, even transcended."

    —Estelle C. Jelinek, "Exotic Autobiography Intellectualized," *The Tradition of Women's Autobiography: From Antiquity to the Present* (Boston: G. K. Hall & Company, 1986), 136–37, 143–45

B I B L I O G R A P H Y

Three Lives. 1909.
Portrait of Mabel Dodge at the Villa Curonia. 1912.
Tender Buttons. 1914.
Have They Attacked Mary. He Giggled. 1917.
Geography and Plays. 1922.
The Making of Americans. 1925.
Descriptions of Literature. 1926.
Composition as Explanation. 1926.
A Book Concluding with As a Wife Has a Cow: A Love Story. 1926.
An Elucidation. 1927.
A Village. 1928.
Useful Knowledge. 1928.

An Acquaintance with Description. 1929.

Lucy Church Amiably. 1930.

Dix Portraits (with English translation by G. Huguet and V. Thomson). 1930.

Before the Flowers of Friendship Faded Friendship Faded. 1931.

How to Write. 1931.

Operas and Plays. 1932.

The Autobiography of Alice B. Toklas. 1933.

Four Saints in Three Acts. 1934.

Portraits and Prayers. 1934.

Chicago Inscriptions. 1934.

Lectures in America. 1935.

Narration: Four Lectures. 1935.

The Geographical History of America. 1936.

Is Dead. 1937.

Everybody's Autobiography. 1937.

A Wedding Bouquet. 1938.

Picasso. 1938.

The World Is Round. 1939.

Prothalamium. 1939.

Paris France. 1940.

What Are Masterpieces. 1940.

Ida. 1941.

Wars I Have Seen. 1945.

Brewsie and Willie. 1946.

Selected Writings. Ed. Carl Van Vechten. 1946.

The First Reader and Three Plays. 1946.

In Savoy. 1946.

Four in America. 1947.

Kisses Can. 1947.

The Mother of Us All (with Virgil Thomson). 1947.

Literally True. 1947.

Two (Hitherto Unpublished) Poems. 1948.

Blood on the Dining-Room Floor. 1948.

Last Operas and Plays. Ed. Carl Van Vechten. 1949.

Things as They Are. 1950.

Unpublished Work (Yale ed., 8 vols.). 1951-58.

In a Garden. 1951.

Absolutely Bob Brown; or, Bobbed Brown. 1955.

On Our Way (with Alice B. Toklas). 1959.

Writings and Lectures 1911-1945. Ed. Patricia Meyerowitz. 1967.

Lines. 1967.

Lucretia Borgia. 1968.

Motor Automation. 1969.

A Christmas Greeting. 1969.

Selected Operas and Plays. Ed. John Malcolm Brinnin. 1970.

Gertrude Stein on Picasso. Ed. Edward Burns. 1970.

I Am Rose. 1971.

Fernhurst, Q. E. D., and Other Early Writings. 1971.

Sherwood Anderson/Gertrude Stein: Correspondence and Personal Essays. Ed. Ray Lewis White. 1972.

Why Are There Whites to Console. 1973.

Reflection on the Atomic Bomb. Ed. Robert Bartlett Haas. 1973.

Money. 1973.

How Writing is Written. Ed. Robert Bartlett Haas. 1974.

Last Will and Testament. 1974.

Dear Sammy: Letters from Gertrude Stein and Alice B. Toklas. Ed. Samuel M. Steward. 1977.

SYLVIA TOWNSEND WARNER

1893–1978

SYLVIA TOWNSEND WARNER was born on December 6, 1893, at Harrow-on-the-Hill, England, the only child of George Townsend Warner, a schoolmaster, and Nora Hudleston. Her parents educated her at home after they were asked to remove her from kindergarten for disruptive behavior. She had full access to her father's library and read Thackeray's *Vanity Fair* and Mackay's *Extraordinary Popular Delusions and the Madness of Crowds* before she was 10 years old. From Mackay's book she learned "spells" for raising the devil, which she practiced on her black cat—the beginning of a lifelong fascination with witchcraft.

Trained in music, Warner worked for 10 years as an editor of the multivolume *Tudor Church Music* before abandoning the study in 1926 to become a full-time writer. Her first book was a volume of verse, *The Espalier* (1925), but Warner became a critical success in England and the United States with the publication of her novel *Lolly Willowes* (1926), in which a "spinster" becomes a witch. She continued to write fiction and verse, publishing two more novels during the 1920s and a second volume of poetry, *Time Importuned*, in 1928.

During this period, Warner was introduced by mutual friends Nancy Cunard and T. F. Powys to another writer, Valentine Ackland. The two women traveled to Spain as Red Cross volunteers in 1930 and began living together in 1932. They collaborated on a collection of poems, *Whether a Dove or Seagull*, in 1933. Warner and Ackland were lovers until Ackland's death in 1969.

In 1935, Warner joined the Communist party in England; her political fervor is obvious in at least two of her subsequent novels, *Summer Will Show* (1936) and *After the Death of Don Juan* (1938). Homosexuality is another recurring theme in her novels: in *Mr. Fortune's Maggot* (1927) a homosexual missionary falls in love with a male convert, and in *Summer Will Show* a Parisian woman becomes the lover of her husband's mistress.

Warner began writing short stories during the 1930s. The first story she submitted to *The New Yorker*, "My Mother Won the War," appeared in the May 30, 1936, issue; the magazine would publish 144 stories and 9 poems by Warner over the next 40 years. She also wrote biographies, most notably of Jane Austen (1951) and T. H. White

(1967). She died on May 1, 1978, in Dorsetshire, where she had lived with Valentine Ackland.

Warner's novels are characterized by unique plots and settings, eccentric characters, and an often whimsical comic style. As a poet, Warner has been called a "feminine Thomas Hardy." She wrote frequent, charming, and witty letters; her collected letters, published in 1982, have added to her literary reputation.

CRITICAL EXTRACTS

OLIVIA MANNING

Miss Townsend Warner has been criticised and is likely to be criticised again for the fact that in her new novel, *The Corner That Held Them*, she views her fourteenth-century nuns through twentieth-century eyes. I can only feel thankful that she does. How bitter this mediaeval concoction would be without the jam of modern wit and irony! The age she covers—one that as a result of the Black Death of 1358 and the Great Plague of 1374 became so obsessed by death that it produced the Dance of Death, an hysteria possessing whole communities, sending them into the churchyards, to dig up bones and skulls, and dance until everyone fell exhausted—is not an easy one to humanise. Viewed from this distance, its quality is so macabre that it appears more alien than the heydays of Greece, Rome or even Egypt. It is, therefore, unlikely that any attempt by the writer to fit out her nuns with archaic language and thoughts would produce figures any nearer to our understanding than those of the Bayeux Tapestry.

In literature reality is relative only to our willingness to believe, and, because I can believe in them, Miss Warner's nuns are for me much more like fourteenth-century nuns than could be any tedious puppets talking pseudo-Chaucerian. As far as period details are concerned I do not know whether the novel is accurate or not, but it is something more—it is entertaining. Miss Warner's survey of thirty-three years of life in the convent of Oby is from start to finish a mild, sustained delight, never during its three hundred and ten pages jarring one by any obvious error in the drawing of her long pageant of characters. She treats them all with equal insight and interest so that, as far as importance is concerned, they are all much of a size and rouse the same sympathy. The resulting effect is slightly flat but one of complete realism.

—Olivia Manning, *Spectator* (3 December 1948), in *The Chelsea House Library of Literary Criticism: Twentieth-Century British Literature*, vol. 5, ed. Harold Bloom (New York: Chelsea House Publishers, 1987), 2898

JOHN UPDIKE

The stories of Sylvia Townsend Warner stick up from *The New Yorker's* fluent fiction-stream with a certain stony air of mastery. They are granular and adamant and irregular in shape. The prose has a much-worked yet abrasive texture of minute juxtaposition and compounded accuracies. Candles are lit in an antique shop, and "The polished surfaces reflected the little flames with an intensification of their various colors—amber in satinwood, audit ale in mahogany, dragon's blood in tortoise shell." Two old ladies reminisce: "They talked untiringly about their girlhood—about the winters when they went skating, the summers when they went boating, the period when they were so very pious, the period when they were pious no longer and sent a valentine to the curate; the curate blushed, a crack rang out like a pistol shot and Hector Gillespie went through the ice, the fox terriers fought under old Mrs. Bulliver's chair, the laundry ruined the blue voile, the dentist cut his throat in Century Wood, Claude Hopkins came back from Cambridge with a motorcar and drove it at thirty miles an hour with flames shooting out behind, Addie Carew was married with a wasp under her veil." How particular, yet how inclusive and shapely in this catalogue! Though Miss Warner can be trivial in her effects and vague in her intentions, she rarely lacks concreteness. On every page there is something to be seen or smelled or felt. ⟨. . .⟩

Her stories tend to convince us in process and baffle us in conclusion; they are not rounded with meaning but lift jaggedly toward new, unseen, developments. "Healthy Landscape with Dormouse" presents with unblinking clairvoyance a miserably married and (therefore) unrepentantly mischievous young woman, Belinda. The story's locale is Belinda's consciousness, but instead of ending there the story leaps out of her head and concludes on a village street. Some suddenly introduced bus passengers have seen Belinda and her husband fight and jump into a car: "They ran to the car, leaped in, drove away. Several quick-witted voices exclaimed, 'Take the number! Take the number!' But the car went so fast, there wasn't time." It suggests a Mack Sennett comedy; it suggests furthermore an almost compulsive need, in Miss Warner's work, for witnesses. Her world is thoroughly the horror and fatalism and hysteria of the First World War. Their quiet life and smoldering secret allegorize England between the wars. Framed by monstrous cataclysms, the diffident gallantry and fuddling ordinariness of the nation, personified by an incestuous couple, are seen as somehow monstrous—the cozy sibling idyll of Victorian mythology gone mad. The historical context is indicated; twenty years of truce pass in terms of private social strategies and public social movements. ⟨. . .⟩ The odors and occupations of *interbella* England, evoking Miss Warner's full vocabulary of flowers and foods and architectures, are suffused with the blameless decadence of the central situation. The story moves with unforced symbolism to the level of epic statement. Incest is civilization's ultimate recourse:

> Loving each other criminally and sincerely, they took pains to live together happily and to safeguard their happiness from injuries of their own inflation or from outside.

Of course, no touch of implied condemnation, or of undue compassion, intrudes upon the perfect sympathy with which this scandalous marriage is chronicled. Miss Warner's genius is an uncannily equable openness to human data, and beneath her refined witchery lies a strange freshness one can only call, in praise, primitive.

—John Updike, "The Mastery of Miss Warner," *New Republic* (5 March 1966), in *The Chelsea House Library of Literary Criticism: Twentieth-Century British Literature*, vol. 5, ed. Harold Bloom (New York: Chelsea House Publishers, 1987), 2899–2901

JOHN L. ABBOTT

The strength of Miss Townsend's stories ⟨in *The Innocent and the Guilty*⟩ lies not in their range or philosophical depth—she tells us nothing new—but in her extraordinary capacity to depict with astringency of style aspects of the human condition. Her fiction concerns itself less with actions or events and more with states of mind, malaises of the soul: it suggests reasons for the tic in the face, the gray in the hair, the stoop in the shoulders, the twist in the smile, or the stammer in the speech. A fine example, one of the longest in the volume, is "But at the Stroke of Midnight" which recounts the flight of bland Mrs. Ridpath from the bonds of a hollow marriage, an empty life. Throughout, the author gives us vivid objective correlatives of a woman's despair so that one of those sad souls one brushes by to catch the tube home takes on individuality and meaning.

Miss Townsend's writing depends for its effect not so much on manipulations of plot to create shock or surprise (though "A Visionary Gleam," surely her jeu d'esprit in the collection, produces just that) as on her ability to evoke moods, feelings, impressions, the ineffable in life. The best example of the above is a story entitled "Oxenhope," a richly evocative record of one man's return to his past and his realization that it cannot be recovered. It is, potentially, one of the most hackneyed of themes, yet Miss Townsend avoids the trite and the cliché and produces through the topography of a small world remembered and revisited an account of genuine emotion. Other stories deserve comment and praise. In "Bruno" and "The Green Torso," Miss Townsend not only provides an intelligent commentary on the world of the homosexual and the hippie but, more important, presents those subtleties of human relationships that reveal clearly man's doomed contest against the power of loneliness and worse, perhaps, against his own self-imposed definition of sexual normalcy.

A reviewer feels constrained to spare superlative, to leash hyperbole, to assume the presence of artistic imperfection. Such a stance is virtually unnecessary in Miss Townsend's case. One can fault, really, only the title of the book, a particularly inept one, surely not Miss Townsend's own, which fails to suggest the complexity of the document to come. But the text throughout proves her an artist.

—John L. Abbott, *Studies in Short Fiction* (Winter 1973), in *The Chelsea House Library of Literary Criticism: Twentieth-Century British Literature*, vol. 5, ed. Harold Bloom (New York: Chelsea House Publishers, 1987), 2898–99

JOHN UPDIKE

Lolly Willowes; or, The Loving Huntsman, her first novel, originally published in 1926 and now reissued in paperback by two different feminist presses, is the witty, eerie, tender but firm life history of a middle-class Englishwoman who politely declines to make the expected connection with the opposite sex and becomes a witch instead. ⟨. . .⟩

⟨. . .⟩ ⟨When⟩ I recommended *Lolly Willowes* to a feminist friend she scowled and said, "Of course, that's what men like to tell us. Either marry one of them or become a witch." Let us respectfully construe the word "witch" as "free woman." Freedom, in daily things, is what Lolly Willowes likes about her condition. At the novel's end, the heroine misses a bus and exults in the realization that it does not much matter if she fails to return home that night. Her landlady, Mrs. Leak, herself a witch, will not mind, nobody will mind: "Lovely to be with people who prefer their thoughts to yours, lovely to live at your own sweet will, lovely to sleep out all night!" From the claustral comforts of domestic lovingness she has escaped to an indifferent lover, Satan, and falls asleep in the liberty of "his undesiring and unjudging gaze, his satisfied but profoundly indifferent ownership." Human love—unnatural, undiabolical love—demands service in return for its ministrations, and not only Lolly in her village solitude but also Jake ⟨of Kingsley Amis's *Jake's Thing*⟩ in his rough dons' chambers renounces this service. Dons and witches alike live consecrated lives apart from that middle terrain, overpopulated by lovers and kin, between private and abstract satisfactions. Both these thoroughly British novels advance— *Jake's Thing* more clumsily and apologetically—the case for asceticism in a world without religion. In the thick of a cultural consensus whose propaganda urges amorous conjunction, they argue for detachment and celibacy, not as an ordeal enroute to a good afterlife but as a method (can it be?) of living well now.

—John Updike, "Jake and Lolly Opt Out," *Hugging the Shore: Essays and Criticism* (New York: Alfred A. Knopf, 1983), 303, 306–7

CLAIRE HARMAN

The story ⟨*Lolly Willowes*⟩ was really an elaborate way of presenting the same thesis as Virginia Woolf did in *A Room of One's Own*, published three years later, except that where Virginia Woolf's woman wants a room in which she can write fiction, Lolly Willowes's vision is of women being able to 'sit in their doorways and think.' ⟨. . .⟩ To be struggling for privacy, not power, is still not a very common view of the feminist ideal and the retiring nature of the hero-ine, Lolly, perhaps persuaded readers that it was not a very serious one either. The book seems ultimately comfortable on that score, though it was much wittier and crisper than most women's fiction of the period. The novelty of the theme, and the author's apparent imperviousness to received wisdom, ensured the book a high oddity value. Though *Lolly Willowes* set out to overturn 'the bugaboo surmises of the public' about witches, and about the single woman, that too common phenomenon of the post-war years, it amused people more than it startled them.

The novel was a great success. The Chatto & Windus press cuttings book alone include over ninety notices for *Lolly Willowes*, many of them lengthy, and all favourable. ⟨. . .⟩ The American reviewers were predominantly reminded of Jane Austen, the British reviewers of David Garnett (whose fantasy novel, *Lady Into Fox*, had been a bestseller in 1924). ⟨. . .⟩ Sylvia was ⟨. . .⟩ asked a lot of foolish questions about black magic, which she answered with a mixture of candour and flippancy, at one time suggesting that modern witches might use their vacuum cleaners instead of broomsticks for flying. There was specula-tion, too, as to whether Sylvia herself, like Lolly, was a witch, and Sylvia dined out on it for some time. ⟨. . .⟩ Sylvia had always kept an open mind on reli-gious questions. A month after *Lolly Willowes* was published, she took tea with Margaret Murray, whose study of witchcraft had been so influential. Miss Murray, an imposing elderly lady, liked the character of Lolly 'though she was doubtful about my devil', Sylvia wrote to David Garnett. ⟨. . .⟩

The sales of the book were very high. Chatto & Windus reprinted twice in one week in February 1926 (the book came out in January) and the U.S. sales 'leapt the 10,000 fence' by June. *Lolly Willowes* was selected as the first Book-of-the-Month choice of the new American book club and nominated for the Prix Femina (which was won that year by Radclyffe Hall). Sylvia had writ-ten to Charles Prentice at the end of January acknowledging receipt of an "incredibly magnificent cheque" for £16 5s 6d, more than five times her weekly salary, but such sums became so familiar that by September she was able to receive a cheque for £233 without comment. In 1926 she earned £437 from *Lolly Willowes* and in 1927, from Lolly and her next novel *Mr Fortune's Maggot*, an amazing £1284, eight and half times her Tudor Church Music income. It was the only time at which Sylvia could be considered a bestseller, and *Lolly Willowes* remains the book by which she is imperfectly remembered. ⟨. . .⟩

⟨. . .⟩ Like *Lolly Willowes*, *Mr Fortune's Maggot* is an appealing blend of cleverness, oddity and pathos, and as such seemed to fit into the voguish Twenties genre of the 'fantasy novel', typified by Garnett's *Lady Into Fox*. But there is much more to Sylvia's two novels than their oddity. Both books are rich in imagery and extraordinarily sensual descriptive prose; the author's imagination is wayward rather than whimsical. But probably her greatest achievement in the two books is her handling of the central characters; Lolly, the woman fleeing from her fate of ordinariness and Timothy Fortune, the mild man brought down by love, both mute, middle-aged English failures—the most unpromising material. Without laughing at them, glorifying them or sentimentalising them, Sylvia opens these characters up to the reader's sympathy, and in the process they acquire a reality which overflows the books which were meant to contain them.

Mr Fortune's Maggot was received enthusiastically by a public—especially an American public—whose appetite had been whetted by *Lolly Willowes*. The reviews were sometimes embarrassingly enthusiastic, the sales again good, again Sylvia just missed a prize—this time the James Tait Black—and was selected by an American book club, the Literary Guild. Sylvia now thought of herself as a writer, though it is doubtful that her colleagues on Tudor Church Music noticed, as they were working hard on William Byrd and Thomas Tallis at the time. Oddly enough, Sylvia found it soothing that Buck remained unimpressed by her literary achievements. It was a relief 'to be reduced to my common denomination again and to be treated just as an ordinary accustomed Sylvia and to have my life-long convictions recognised as extempore'—every now and then.

    —Claire Harman, *Sylvia Townsend Warner: A Biography* (London: Chatto & Windus, 1989), 64–66, 71–72

GILLIAN SPRAGGS

Even in the 1980s, the lesbian element in Sylvia's life and work is plainly capable of causing anxiety to one of her foremost critical champions. In her introduction to the Virago reprint of Sylvia's 1936 novel, *Summer Will Show*, a historical novel set in England and France just before and during the 1848

French revolutions, and finding its emotional centre in the unconventional, intense attachment that grows up between Sophia Willoughby, estranged wife of an English gentleman, and the Jewish woman, Minna, his discarded mistress, Claire Harman uneasily comments: 'Lesbianism was not Sylvia Townsend Warner's theme in this book, though at points it seems implicit', adding, with transparent relief, 'Not all women who loose themselves from being "kept"—in or out of marriage—are suddenly lesbians' (viii). Both statements are, as far as they go, impeccable: but there is a very great deal that is being left out.

In fact, lesbianism as a theme is nowhere tackled directly in Sylvia's fiction, though male homosexuality is an incidental motif in some of her stories, and also in her novel *The Flint Anchor* (1954). (It is also implicit, and central to the story, in the much earlier novel *Mr Fortune's Maggot* (1927). At the same time, it is clear that Sylvia's experience of living as a lesbian informs some of her best writing, including her fine short story, 'A Love Match', which won the Katherine Mansfield prize in 1968, and which handles with sensitivity and wit an illicit (and loving) relationship between a brother and sister. In *Summer Will Show*, Sylvia Townsend Warner chose not to make an issue of the sexual element in the relationship between Sophia and Minna. Nevertheless, although unstressed, it is certainly not unspoken; it pervades the second half of the book. ⟨. . .⟩

⟨. . .⟩ *Summer Will Show* was begun in 1932, less than five years after Radclyffe Hall's explicitly lesbian novel *The Well of Loneliness* had been banned from publication as the result of a famous obscenity trial. *The Well of Loneliness* was not published again in Britain until after the Second World War. During the 1930s it is doubtful whether any British publisher would have taken the risk of bringing out a novel that openly dealt in a serious and non-condemnatory way with a sexual relationship between two women. Nor could Sylvia Townsend Warner, whose money from writing was an important part of her income, afford to take such an open risk with her career as the independently wealthy Radclyffe Hall. ⟨. . .⟩

⟨. . .⟩ For any woman to acknowledge that she loves another woman while living in a culture in which desire for the beloved is commonly constructed as compelling and natural; mutually satisfied desire as fulfilling, enriching, necessary to the integrated life; but in which the desire of one woman for another is stigmatised as unnatural, inordinate, taboo, a dangerous personal and social contaminant: that is to experience such a sharp contradiction in the positions offered her within which to understand herself and her relations with the world that coherent discourse becomes impossible. The only creative resolution is a rejection of the accepted 'wisdom' of the culture, which is equivalent to going into exile, with all the accompanying pain. But if the beloved woman joins her, another 'country', a homeland of the heart, will be open for their joint exploration; and a new native tongue will be forged from their discourse.

The love poems of Valentine Ackland and Sylvia Townsend Warner are pioneering charts of a territory which is even now not over-trodden: which, in many respects, indeed, is still proscribed. To read them with understanding is to enter into the imagination of exiles. For some of us, it feels like coming home.

—Gillian Spraggs, "Exiled to Home: The Poetry of Sylvia Townsend Warner and Valentine Ackland," *Lesbian and Gay Writing: An Anthology of Critical Essays*, ed. Mark Lilly (Philadelphia: Temple University Press, 1990), 111, 112, 123–24

BARBARA BROTHERS

Unmarried women, until post–World War II fiction, had been allotted the spare room in the houses built by social and fictional conventions. They were visitors, onlookers at life's drama, "redundant" or "superfluous" women (as the British had so explicitly labeled them). How impertinent Sylvia Townsend Warner must have seemed in 1926 when she chose such a woman for the heroine of her novel *Lolly Willowes or the Loving Huntsman*. Tradition prescribes that Lolly be "absorbed into the household of one brother or the other" upon the death of her widowed father, given the "small spare-room . . . the handiest . . . for ordinary visitors" (2) in that household, and made semi-useful doing needle work and escorting nieces to dancing lessons. Warner depicts her heroine as literally and figuratively bound by this convention until Lolly decides at age forty-seven to escape from the Victorian household of her brother to a room of her own choosing, a room in which she brews herb teas, listens to stories about the people of the secluded village to which she has moved, and creates her own imaginative understandings of her life and their lives. ⟨. . .⟩

Lolly's age and her spinsterhood make her an unusual heroine, especially for a bildungsroman. Yet *Lolly Willowes* is revolutionary and subversive in more than its portrayal of an old maiden aunt who casts off the role society has created for her and rejects other middle-class values that define what is good and proper. Warner also mocks both social and literary conventions when she transmutes her seemingly innocent and comically realistic bildungsroman into a satiric fantasy, flouting literary conventions by combining the two types of fiction. In Part 1 of the novel, the narrator realistically details Lolly's life at Apsley Terrace, the London home of Lolly's brother, and relates in a flashback the details of the Willowes family history and the first twenty-eight years of Lolly's extended youth in Somerset. In the next two parts of the novel, she combines realism and fantasy; Lolly achieves womanhood by making a pact with the devil and becoming a witch.

Warner realizes that a radical re-visioning of Western culture and the literary tradition that expresses and imparts Western values is necessary if women are to come to know themselves and create their own stories. Anticipating Virginia Woolf's call in *A Room of One's Own* (1929), *Lolly Willowes* retells social and literary history from the perspective of a woman who refuses to cast herself as Eve. For a woman to achieve adulthood, in Warner's view, she must use her independent income to claim more than a room of her own. She must, like Lolly, challenge what Adrienne Rich has called the male prerogative of naming. The numerous literary and biblical allusions, particularly to Milton's *Paradise Lost* and the story of the fall, call attention to the fact that women, married or unmarried, have been confined not only within men's rooms but even more restrictively within man's prison house of language. Warner questions the naming and the stories of not just Milton but those before and after him in literature, in government, and in the church. To escape from the powerful scripts of the patriarchy, a woman must reinterpret what is "natural" and retell the myths of the past. Through Lolly's observations in the last two parts of the novel, Warner rewrites Milton's characterization of Adam, Eve, and Satan and his interpretation of the fall and of good and evil. In the conclusion of the novel, Lolly reaches maturity by redefining what is good and what is natural through revealing a new Satan and creating a new understanding of witchhood.

   —Barbara Brothers, "Flying the Nets at Forty: *Lolly Willowes* as Female Bildungsroman," *Old Maids to Radical Spinsters: Unmarried Women in the Twentieth-Century Novel*, ed. Laura L. Doan (Urbana and Chicago: University of Illinois Press, 1991), 195–96

TERRY CASTLE

What makes this novel ⟨*Summer Will Show*⟩ paradigmatically "lesbian," in my view, is not simply that it depicts a sexual relationship between two women, but that it so clearly, indeed almost schematically, figures this relationship as a breakup of the supposedly "canonical" male-female-male erotic triangle. ⟨. . .⟩

   ⟨. . .⟩ ⟨*Summer Will Show*⟩ is a work obsessed with "revising" on a number of counts. In the most literal sense the novel is a kind of revisionist fantasia: in recounting the story of her pseudo-Victorian heroine, Sophia Willoughby, Townsend Warner constantly pastiches—yet also rewrites—Victorian fiction itself. The opening scene at the limekiln, for example, both recalls and traduces the episode in *Great Expectations* in which Pip is dangled over a limekiln by the infamous Orlick: the "great expectations" here belong, ironically, to the observer, Sophia herself. The early episodes involving the mulatto Caspar and the uncle in the West Indies likewise rework and subvert elements from *Wuthering Heights* and *Jane Eyre*. After Sophia's arrival in Paris, a curiously erotic scene in which Minna shows her her duelling pistols (154-6) is an almost direct parody of a similar moment in *Shirley*. ⟨. . .⟩ Minna herself is a kind of revolutionary variant on a George Eliot heroine. Her Jewishness and political radicalism bring to mind characters and situations from *Daniel Deronda* and *Felix Holt;* her appearance—and passionate intelligence—may be modeled on Eliot's own. Yet she is far more deviant than any Eliot heroine is ever allowed to be. Tellingly, her very name appears to originate in the famous passage in *The Mill on the Floss* in which Maggie Tulliver declares her wish to "avenge" all the unfortunate dark-haired heroines of English literature—"Rebecca, and Flora MacIvor, and Minna, and all the rest of the dark unhappy ones." Maggie's Minna is the hapless heroine of Sir Walter Scott's *The Pirate*, abandoned by her lover on a frigid Scottish beach. By contrast, Townsend Warner's Minna—with her freedom from convention, her sexual charisma, and survivor's instinct—is at once a satirical rewrite of the first Minna and a more resilient version of Maggie herself.

But it is not only English fiction that Townsend Warner is rewriting in *Summer Will Show*. ⟨. . .⟩ ⟨It⟩ is Flaubert, obviously, and *his* novel of 1848, that Townsend Warner is most deeply conscious of displacing. Anyone who doubts the subterranean importance of *L'Éducation sentimentale* to *Summer Will Show* need only consider the name Frédéric—or Frederick—and the parodistic relationship that exists between Flaubert's antihero, Frédéric Moreau, and Townsend Warner's comic villain, Frederick Willoughby.

To invoke Flaubert's masterpiece, however, is also to return—with a vengeance—to the Sedgwickian issue of erotic triangulation. For what is *L'Éducation sentimentale* if not a classic work, in Sedgwick's terms, of male homosocial bonding? Flaubert's Frédéric, we recall, acts out his emotional obsession with his friend Arnoux by falling in love first with Arnoux's wife, then with his mistress. Townsend Warner's Frederick, by contrast, not only has no male friend, his wife and his mistress fall in love with each other. In the very act of revising Flaubert—of substituting her own profoundly "anticanonical" fiction in place of his own—Townsend Warner also revises the plot of male homosocial desire. Indeed, all of her revisionist gestures can, I think, be linked with this same imaginative impulse: the desire to plot against the seemingly indestructible heterosexual narrative of classic European fiction.

—Terry Castle, *The Apparitional Lesbian: Female Homosexuality and Modern Culture* (New York: Columbia University Press, 1993), 74, 80–82

B I B L I O G R A P H Y

The Espalier. 1925.
Lolly Willowes: or, The Loving Huntsman. 1926.
Mr. Fortune's Maggot. 1927.
The Maze: A Story to Be Read Aloud. 1928.
Time Importuned. 1928.
Some World Far From Ours. 1929.
The True Heart. 1929.
Elinor Barley. 1930.
This Our Brother. 1930.
Opus 7. 1931.
A Moral Ending and Other Stories. 1931.
The Salutation. 1932.
The Week-End Dickens (editor). 1932.
Rainbow. 1932.
Whether a Dove or Seagull (with Valentine Ackland). 1933.
More Joy in Heaven and Other Stories. 1935.
Summer Will Show. 1936.
After the Death of Don Juan. 1938.
The Cat's Cradle Book. 1940.
People Have No Generals. 1941.
A Garland of Straw and Other Stories. 1943.
Two Poems. 1945.
The Portrait of a Tortoise: Extracted from the Journals of Gilbert White (editor). 1946.
The Museum of Cheats. 1947.
The Corner That Held Them. 1948.
Somerset. 1949.
Jane Austen, 1775-1817. 1951.
The Flint Anchor. 1954.
Winter in the Air and Other Stories. 1955.
Boxwood. 1957.
By Way of Saint-Beuve, by Marcel Proust (translator). 1958.
A Spirit Rises. 1962.
Sketches from Nature. 1963.
A Place of Shipwreck, by Jean René Huguenin (translator). 1963.
A Stranger with a Bag and Other Stories. 1966.
T. H. White: A Biography. 1967.

King Duffus and Other Poems. 1968.
The Innocent and the Guilty: Stories. 1971.
Kingdoms of Elfin. 1977.
Azrael and Other Poems. 1978.
Twelve Poems. 1980.
Scenes of Childhood. 1981.
Letters. Ed. William Maxwell. 1982.
Collected Poems. Ed. Claire Harman. 1983.
One Thing Leading to Another and Other Stories. Ed. Susanny Pinney. 1984.
Selected Poems. 1985.

JEANETTE WINTERSON
b. 1959

JEANETTE WINTERSON, born in 1959, was adopted as a child by a Pentecostal Evangelical family in Lancashire, England. Groomed from an early age to become a missionary for the church, Winterson was a preacher at age 12. When she was 16, the congregation discovered her lesbianism and subjected her to public humiliation, including an exorcism; she left her church and was forced from her home. She worked in a mental hospital and a funeral parlor before studying English at Oxford University.

After her studies, Winterson embarked on an unsuccessful job search that ended when an editor, impressed with her storytelling abilities during an interview, suggested she write about her experiences. The resulting autobiographical novel, *Oranges Are Not the Only Fruit* (1985), was an immediate popular and critical success and won England's prestigious Whitbread First Novel Award. Adapted by the author for television in 1990, the series *Oranges Are Not the Only Fruit* won international awards, including BAFTA Best Drama and the Prix Italia (although her mother called Jeanette a "child of the Devil" after reading the book).

Winterson has since published five more novels, including the critically acclaimed *The Passion* (1987), which won the John Llewellyn Rhys Prize in England, and *Sexing the Cherry* (1989), winner of the E. M. Forster Award (American Academy of Arts and Letters). Her writing is noted for its combination of magic realism and sensual detail and for her ability to blend historical events with pure myth; she has been compared to modern fabulists such as Luis Borges and Angela Carter.

Winterson is adept at creating extraordinary language-dependent worlds in which narrative and character are free from the constraints of linear time; yet her experimental style does not obscure her principal themes of love, loss, ritual, and exile. As a writer of lesbian fiction, she is commonly viewed as representative of a new phase, in which the traditional emphasis on self-discovery and self-affirmation has shifted to a broader examination of the nature of humanity itself.

C R I T I C A L   E X T R A C T S

ROSALIND MILES

As the makers of the contemporary novel have explored the nature of society and sexuality and their relation to each other, a solution that has been emerging as more and more acceptable is the idea of life without men. The lesbian alternative in fact implicitly offers a radical critique of heterosexism, rejecting as it does the set of values and structures that assumes heterosexuality to be the only natural form of sexual and emotional expression, the old lie insisting that women have only sought emotional and sexual fulfilment through men— or not at all.

This alternative perspective has, however, been a long time coming. (See Jane Rule's scholarly and compelling *Lesbian Images*, 1975, and the fascinating *Lesbian Studies*, 1982, edited by Margaret Cruikshank.) Unspoken, unspeakable, underground, and invisible, lesbianism has been the perfect image of the love that dared not speak its name even more than male homosexuality. Pairs of women were invariably interpreted as friends in a passionless co-existence; woman-identified writers like Virginia Woolf, Emily Dickinson and Gertrude Stein were forced by a society at once homophobic and misogynist to adopt coded, oblique, or private languages. This in turn meant that lesbian women writers until very recently worked alone, cut off from their own history and tradition, and with little support or even hope of it from other lesbians, from other women, or from society at large. The lesbian in this situation thus became the perfect paradigm of the woman writer, suffering twice over the need to reinvent, imagine, discover, and verify everything for herself, devoid of signposts, milestones, and sustenance along the way. Our lesbian foremothers and the role-models they might have provided were not merely forgotten, but obliterated. 〈. . .〉

〈. . .〉〈But among recent writers,〉 lesbianism has become a positive image, in every variation from Rita Mae Brown's ebullient attention-seeking, to Alice Walker's wistful evocation of the love between women in *The Color Purple*, and Jeanette Winterson's original, enchanting *Bildungsroman* of a young lesbian in the prize-winning *Oranges Are Not the Only Fruit* (1985). Winterson's heroine demonstrates in the sharpest possible way that lesbian women will no longer tolerate the ignorant, condescending judgment of the heterosexual world:

> On Palm Sunday Melanie returned, beaming with an important
> announcement. She was to be married that autumn to an army man.
> To be fair he had given up the bad fight for the Good Fight, but as
> far as I was concerned he was revolting. I had no quarrel with men.

At that time there was no reason that I should. The women in our church were strong and organised. If you want to talk in terms of power, I had enough to keep Mussolini happy. So I didn't object to her getting married. I objected to her getting married to *him*. And she was serene, serene to the point of being bovine. I was so angry I tried to talk to her about it, but she had left her brain in Bangor. She asked me what I was doing.

'Doing for what?'

She blushed. . . .

She left the day after, to stay with him and his parents. Just as they were driving off . . . he patted my arm and told me he knew, and forgave us both. There was only one thing I could do; mustering all my spit, I did it. (p. 124)

'If you want to talk in terms of power' . . . In that sentence Jeannette Winterson economically sums up the growth of the lesbian novel in the last twenty years—after centuries of denial and repression, it has come into its own.

—Rosalind Miles, *The Female Form: Women Writers and the Conquest of the Novel* (London: Routledge & Kegan Paul, 1987), 177–78, 191–92

KATHY PAGE

Jeanette Winterson slips easily from the past to the present, from the plausible to the fantastic and back again. Her first novel, *Oranges Are Not the Only Fruit*, was the largely autobiographical account of her upbringing by an adoptive mother who wanted her to be a missionary. The second, *Boating for Beginners*—drawing on a wealth of biblical influence—was set at the time of the Flood. Although very different, both were characterised by the wit and agility of the story-telling voice. Neither quality is lacking in *The Passion*, but this latest novel has a concentration of purpose that sets it apart from the others. The passion in question is not Christ's, neither is there more than passing reference to any kind of organised religion, yet this novel is written with an intensity and a degree of repetitiveness that give it a strongly evangelical flavour.

The action takes place during the Napoleonic wars and spans the continent of Europe, but *The Passion* is not concerned with history. There are people with webbed feet in it, but it is not a fairy story. It's a novel about one word: the noun of the title. 'Only connect the prose and the passion and both will be exalted,' Forster wrote in *Howards End*; this essentially poetic (and evangelical) aim is the driving force of Jeanette Winterson's book.

The word passion, with its breathy 's's and connotations of illicit desire, is a pleasure to read and hear in the mind's ear. In this book you will read it, and the imagery of conquest it trails in its wake, many, many times. Passion is a demon which the two protagonists, Henri and Vilanelle share. Like Napoleon himself, it's a ruthless commander and its effects are as devastating as the scourge of Europe. The passion is of the romantic type and lurks 'somewhere between fear and sex', also 'somewhere between god and the devil'. How does it arise? What common need does it satisfy in the essentially ordinary Henri and the exotic Vilanelle? The book is not interested in such questions; it aims to convince without argument. ⟨. . .⟩

Passion, says Vilanelle, is 'sweeter split strand by strand'. For the faint-hearted—or, as Henri puts it, 'lukewarm people'—the best approach will be to take this hymn to desire strand by strand (there's a bookmark for the purpose) and read it for enjoyment of the writing. Bloomsbury have packaged it to appeal to the epicure and, in this respect, it doesn't disappoint. Jeanette Winterson has worked the narrative into a glittering setting for her ominous meditations on the nature of passion, and the language she uses, whether solemn and latinate or brief and to the point, is vivid and tightly controlled.

—Kathy Page, "Heart and Stomach," *The New Statesman* 113 (26 June 1987): 26

Nicci Gerrard

Her first two novels—*Oranges Are Not the Only Fruit* and *Boating for Beginners*—are acerbic and touching comedies. The next two, *The Passion* and, now, *Sexing the Cherry*, are slim and poetic novels of magic realism. They are arresting precisely because they are unafraid of zestful morality, and enchanting because, like The Bible, they often make imaginative metaphor literal. *The Passion* is set in the Napoleonic Wars and ranges down the labyrinths of Venice and the vast wastes of Siberia. Its web-footed heroine literally loses her heart. *Sexing the Cherry* takes place during the epic ravages of the civil war, plague and great fire. In it, the grotesque and loyal dog woman, who can hold a dozen oranges in her mouth and who sucks a gallant would-be lover into her cavernous vagina, is literally heavier than an elephant. The protagonist, Jordan, is in search of the dancer (or perhaps "the dancing part of himself") who really does float. *Sexing the Cherry*, like its predecessor *The Passion*, combines sensuous detail, magic and lovely language. And it, too, meditates religiously upon the nature of reality and of the self ("I'm not looking for God, only for myself" says the restless Jordan, "and that is far more complicated").

There are two religious roles according to Winterson, who specialises in epigrammatic virtuousity: that of the priest and that of the prophet. The priests "have all the words written out already and only have to read them". The prophets, on the other hand, "are always on the edge, crying in the wilderness—and often what they say isn't wanted. Art should be shocking—otherwise, all you are left with is entertainment—like a baby with a dummy."

So, with engaging and slightly shocking candour, the novelist sets herself up as a prophet of Hampstead Heath. And for someone who so flagrantly transgressed the laws of her native church, she speaks in strangely biblical and rapturous prose about her ideals and ambitions. When *The Passion* was translated into several foreign languages, she felt "pride, yes, but above all joy—joy that more people would read my words". When she considers modern life, she condemns its continual noise and stress which "take the hallowed time out of life". When she calls herself an "optimist" it is because she "believes in miracles". ⟨. . .⟩

There could be something faintly ludicrous about someone who thinks she is a "prophet crying in the wilderness". Yet with her quiet but almost tangible self-assurance, this "self-made" woman somehow pulls it off. Considering the question of whether or not she is arrogant, she pauses before replying: "I've always thought of arrogance as being pleased with oneself without just reason. I have reason to be pleased with myself. Of course I am pleased with myself. Against all the odds I have come from nowhere and been able to make a difference."

—Nicci Gerrard, "The Prophet," *The New Statesman & Society* 2, no. 65 (1 September 1989): 13

Hilary Hinds

Jeanette Winterson's first novel, *Oranges Are Not the Only Fruit*, is one of those success stories of which feminists feel proud. From its small-scale beginnings as a risky undertaking by the newly formed Pandora Press in 1985, through the winning of the Whitbread Prize for a first novel later the same year, to its much-lauded adaptation for BBC television by Winterson herself in January 1990, the work's reputation, like that of its author, has grown and prospered. Winterson herself is now unquestionably treated as a 'serious' author, highly praised by other 'serious' authors such as Gore Vidal and Muriel Spark; yet she is also a popular success, appearing on Clive James's television chat show and being sympathetically profiled in the popular press. The 'serious' side of the success story, her qualification as a representative of high culture, is largely dependent on her literary output: *Oranges* and, more especially, her third novel, *The Passion*; her popular success and high media exposure can be dated to the television adaptation of *Oranges*. That an author who is a lesbian and a feminist should be so successful in such contrasting contexts is seen by other lesbians and feminists as something to celebrate. Whatever misgivings may be felt about the traps and pitfalls of the mainstream, the sight of 'one of us' being given so much approval by the pillars of the establishment, whence usually comes opprobrium, is a source of enormous pleasure. ⟨. . .⟩

By the mainstream press particularly, ⟨. . .⟩ *Oranges* was not seen princi-
pally as a lesbian text: Jeanette's lesbianism was seen merely as a suitable foil
to her mother's Evangelicalism, its significance assessed in terms of humour,
narrative and 'character'. Far from confirming Winterson's own assertion that
lesbianism is at the centre of the story, on the basis of the reviews one would
think it were, as one reviewer put it, one of 'countless novels on the stands
about families, separation, and the emotional spaces people create or don't create for one another' (*Ms*, October 1985). By suggesting that Jeanette is a character with whom we can all sympathise, because lesbianism is just another
human experience, these critics aspire to a universal reading. Whilst this lib-
eral humanist reading has the advantage of being accepting and inclusive of
lesbian experience, it does deny all sense of the novel having any specificity,
whether to lesbian experience or to Northern working-class experience.
Lesbian oppression, whether in the form of violence, repression, stereotyping
or denial, has no part in such a depoliticised reading, and thus remains unac-
knowledged.

—Hilary Hinds, "*Oranges Are Not the Only Fruit*: Reaching Audiences Other Lesbian Texts
Cannot Reach," *New Lesbian Criticism: Literary and Cultural Readings*, ed. Sally Munt (New York:
Columbia University Press, 1992), 153, 157

GABRIELE GRIFFIN

Lesbians claimed cultural space in tandem with and in the wake of the women's
and the gay liberation movements. This resulted in the construction of lesbian
culture(s) which, while still acknowledging the heterosexist legacy of lesbians
as deviant in various ways, increasingly moved towards a position that was
assertive, affirmative and celebratory of lesbians. Rather than fighting negative
stereotypes, lesbians began to explore the opportunities inherent in their his-
torically-conditioned situation. ⟨. . .⟩ The refusal of negative stereotypes of lesbians increasingly informed work on/by lesbians. 'Deviant' gave way to
'defiant' and one of the new images of the lesbian in literature to emerge in the
early 1970s was that of the defiant lesbian hero.

One of the first and perhaps best-known versions of this image is the protagonist of Rita Mae Brown's *Rubyfruit Jungle* (1973), Molly Bolt, who has much
in common with the first-person narrator of Jeanette Winterson's *Oranges Are
Not the Only Fruit* (1985). Both novels portray a lesbian coming of age, literally
and metaphorically, charting her progress from childhood to young adulthood
which involves the affirmation of the protagonist's lesbian identity and her
rejection and move away from the community in which she grew up. In parallel to the uncertainty concerning the origins of lesbianism *per se*—are you
born one or do you become one—the origins of the protagonists of *Rubyfruit
Jungle* and of *Oranges* are to some extent uncertain. Both girls are adopted. ⟨. . .⟩

⟨. . .⟩ Uncertainty of origin leads to Molly being cast in the role of 'bastard' (p. 3), while the protagonist of *Oranges* says, 'I cannot recall a time when I did not know that I was special' (p. 3). Despite eliciting very different value-judgements, being a bastard and being special have the same function of setting the individual apart from the community. Molly, antagonizing everybody, appears at first destined to be a loner, Jean in *Oranges*, initially fully integrated into her community, is cast as a potential leader. Both make their mark on their respective communities from an early age.

One of the most striking aspects of both texts is that, as in Victorian novels, the identity of the individual is constructed as being established through her relation to the community of which she is a part. Being adopted, the precise nature of the protagonists' place in their community is under question from the outset. ⟨. . .⟩

In contrast to previous lesbian novels, such as Ann Bannon's, where heterosexist society functions as a backdrop intervening in the lesbian protagonist's life by stigmatizing her, in the novels of the 1970s and 1980s this situation is reversed, with the lesbian protagonists serving to highlight the inadequacies and intolerance of the communities from which they seek to escape.

—Gabriele Griffin, *Heavenly Love? Lesbian Images in Twentieth-Century Women's Writing* (Manchester, UK: Manchester University Press, 1993), 62–64

PAULINA PALMER

A stereotype and mythic image which is frequently projected onto the figure of the lesbian in patriarchal culture is that of *monster*. Society, as Pamella Farley observes, defines 'the normal' and 'the natural' in opposition to the image of 'the abnormal' and 'the unnatural'—and sees homosexuality and lesbianism as representing the latter. 'By definition heterosexuality denies homosexuality; but it both requires and suppresses the scapegoat. Her function is to be the unthinkable alternative' ⟨"Lesbianism and the Social Function of Taboo," in *The Future of Difference*, ed. Hester Eisenstein and Alice Jardine, 1980, 270⟩. ⟨. . .⟩

⟨. . .⟩ ⟨In⟩ *Oranges Are Not the Only Fruit*, ⟨. . .⟩ conventional standards of normality are again deconstructed and shown to be relative and artificial. When Jeanette is in primary school she is puzzled by the fact that the teacher criticizes the gloomy but original design of the sampler which she has made, while praising the tritely pretty piece of work produced by one of her class-mates. The incident leads her to perceive that:

> What constitutes a problem is not the thing, or the environment
> where we find the thing, but the conjunction of the two; something
> unexpected in a usual place (our favourite aunt in our favourite poker

parlour) or something usual in an unexpected place (our favourite
poker in our favourite aunt) . . . ⟨Pandora, 1985, 5⟩

This observation acquires additional significance, moving from a comic
dimension to a serious one, in the light of subsequent events—namely
Jeanette's discovery of her lesbianism and the relationship which she forms
with Melanie. Sexual passions which appear perfectly natural to the two girls
are regarded by Pastor Finch, in the context of his puritanical religious beliefs,
as decidedly unnatural.

Oranges Are Not the Only Fruit also inverts the image of monster, by assign-
ing it not to the lesbian characters but to representatives of patriarchal masculinity. Young Jeanette, on overhearing a neighbour remark that she has
married a pig, takes the comment literally. She believes that the husband
really is a pig. 'It was hard to tell he was a pig. He was clever, but his eyes were
close together and his skin bright pink. I tried to imagine him without his
clothes on. Horrid' (p. 71). This reference to the animal world is fancifully
elaborated. It shifts, in postmodernist manner, from being an image for the
repulsive aspects of male physical appearance to one representing 'men as
beasts'. This, in turn, becomes a vehicle for describing male duplicity and cun-
ning: 'And beasts are crafty, they disguise themselves like you and I. Like the
wolf in "Little Red Riding Hood" . . . Did that mean that all over the globe, in
all innocence, women were marrying beasts?' (pp. 72-3)

A motif with connotations of the monstrous which plays a central role in
Oranges Are Not the Only Fruit is the demon. The Pastor, when accusing Jeanette
and Melanie of demonic possession, employs it in a conventional manner as a
signifier of supernatural evil. However, it is subsequently transformed into a
signifier of individualism and personal freedom when the Orange Demon
unexpectedly materializes to Jeanette and engages her in conversation.
Hopping onto the mantelpiece, he cheerfully tells her that everyone has a
demon and that if she insists on keeping hers, she will have 'a difficult, different time' (p. 109).

Winterson is not, of course, the first writer to identify demons with liberation and to portray her/his protagonist conversing with them. In *The Marriage
of Heaven and Hell* (1790) by William Blake, a poet to whom Winterson alludes,
angels are associated with oppression while the denizens of Hell represent liberation. A devil, appearing to the poet in a flame, reinterprets the Scriptures
from a radical viewpoint and gives him moral counsel.

—Paulina Palmer, *Contemporary Lesbian Writing: Dreams, Desire, Difference* (Buckingham, UK:
Open University Press, 1993), 90, 94–95

PAULINA PALMER

Winterson's imaginative treatment of fairy tale and fable ⟨in *Oranges Are Not the Only Fruit*⟩, as well as being a vehicle for representing Jeanette's shifting identities and the displacements which fantasy enacts, also has literary and ideological import. From a literary point of view, the interplay of different narratives and genres which it generates creates an exercise in intertextuality, illustrating the fact that all texts are composed of grafts from earlier ones ⟨Jonathan Culler, *On Deconstruction: Theory and Criticism After Structuralism*, 1983, 134-39⟩. On an ideological level, it functions as a strategy to question and challenge the patriarchal values associated with the fairy tale. Images of femininity constructed by a male-dominated culture are interrogated and problematized. In the tale of the princess who was so sensitive that she wept for the death of a moth (Winterson 1985:9), the stereotypically feminine attributes of narcissism and sentimentality are confronted and rejected, while the story of the princes' search for a flawless woman examines male ideals of femininity and exposes their oppressive effect on flesh-and-blood women (pp. 61-7). The story of Red Riding Hood (p. 73) is transformed into a fable illustrating a young girl's feelings of anxiety about heterosexual relations and male duplicity. ⟨. . .⟩

The most important text the authority and ideology of which the novel questions and undermines is, of course, the Old Testament, the master text of Western civilization. A strategy which Winterson employs to achieve this is to place biblical motifs in new and incongruous contexts. The titles of the books of the Old Testament function as structuring devices in Jeanette's Coming Out story. Biblical episodes and themes also have their authority undercut by appearing in settings which are comically inappropriate. The text 'The summer is ended and we are not yet saved' features incongruously on a child's sampler (p. 39), while Elsie, in re-creating the episode of the Three Men in the Fiery Furnace, uses the unusual medium of *mice* (p. 31). Even bearing in mind the various weird and wonderful materials which postmodern artists employ, this must surely rank as a first. ⟨. . .⟩

Winterson's skill in interplaying different intellectual and literary approaches, illustrated by her reworking of motifs from the 1970s Coming Out novel in the light of contemporary concepts of narrativity and subjectivity, is also apparent in her treatment of lesbianism. The focus which the novel places on woman-identifed involvements reflects lesbian feminist attitudes, but its emphasis on the sexual aspect of lesbianism has more in common with the perspectives of the lesbian sexual radicals. While the network of female relationships which comprise Jeanette's life recalls Rich's theory of lesbian continuum, these relationships are not idealized or described uncritically.

Although in some episodes women are portrayed as loving, strong and loyal, in others they are depicted as weak or tyrannical, willing to oppress their sisters by colluding with the representatives of patriarchy. Jeanette's adoptive mother is portrayed in a particularly ambiguous light. Her character displays a contradictory though convincing amalgam of courage and bigotry carried out in the name of religion, though including examples of compulsory heterosexuality, extends beyond it. In the tradition of Blake, whose radical concept of morality influences the novel, it encompasses sexual repression in general.

The interest in subjectivity and narrativity which informs *Oranges Are Not the Only Fruit* is developed in Winterson's subsequently published novel *Sexing the Cherry* (1989). In the latter, however, it takes a more complex form, since the interplay of narratives revolves around not one consciousness but two— the Dog-Woman's and that of her adopted son, Jordan. An additional complication arises from the fact that identities and psychological attributes are envisaged as transcending the boundaries of time and space. Jordan and the Dog-Woman are seventeenth-century figures, and each has a twentieth-century double or counterpart who displays analogous qualities and attitudes. Or, to put it more accurately, as emerges toward the end of Winterson's novel, the two seventeenth-century figures function as alter egos for the present-day ones. The psychological and political affinities between the Dog-Woman and her present-day counterpart are described particularly vividly. While the former invests her energies in challenging religious bigotry and exterminating puritans, the latter devotes her life to ecological issues and spends her time fighting multinational companies in an attempt to stem the tide of environmental pollution. Both women are ridiculed by the general public as 'monsters'—the Dog-Woman on account of her exceptional size and strength, which are regarded as unfeminine, and the present-day figure on account of her radical views and commitment to a politics of direct action.

The relevance of these four characters, and the specular relationship existing between them, to the theme of subjectivity, is elucidated by Jordan's remark, 'The inward life tells us that we are multiple not single, and that our one existence is really countless existences holding hands like those cut-out paper dolls, but unlike the dolls never coming to an end' ⟨1990, 90⟩. Jordan also clarifies the fluid and shifting interaction between subject and alter ego which typifies the novel. Uncertain whether the dancer with whom he is infatuated and whom he spends his youth seeking is real or imaginary, he asks the pertinent question, 'Was I searching for a dancer whose name I did not know or was I searching for the dancing part of myself?" ⟨40⟩. The ambiguous relationships which some of the characters bear to reality—are they 'real' or imaginary, we are prompted to ask?—highlights one of the novel's key themes. As Winterson playfully reminds us, by drawing attention to the fictionality of the

text and the acts of representation which its construction involves, the question is ultimately meaningless since all the characters portrayed in it are fictions.
  —Paulina Palmer, *Contemporary Lesbian Writing: Dreams, Desire, Difference* (Buckingham, UK: Open University Press, 1993), 102–4

LAURA DOAN

In *The Passion* (1987) Winterson shifts from the fruit metaphor ⟨of *Oranges Are Not the Only Fruit*⟩ to cross-dressing, a cultural performance that illustrates how perceptions of external "appearance" and internal "essence" interrelate in a problematic state of flux. Villanelle, the protagonist, dresses "as a woman in the afternoon and a young man in the evenings," because "that's what the visitors liked to see. It was part of the game, trying to decide which sex was hidden behind the tight breeches and extravagant face-paste" (62, 54). Cross-dressing thus maneuvers the dresser into a position of power, not only the power of knowledge and the ability to control perception but also, and more important, the power and freedom to choose and to play with choice. For Villanelle, this choice takes the form of whether or not she should declare herself as a woman when she meets and falls in love with a masked woman (a disguise that only partially obscures identity, though highlights seductiveness) at a Venetian gaming table one evening. Venice, the city of disguises, is a postmodern city par excellence in its mutability and is thus the ideal domain for Villanelle, now accoutered with a moustache and a man's shirt to hide her breasts. As with fruit, cross-dressing emphasizes the demarcation between various possible essences (hidden, secretive, delicious, and juicy) and appearances (which may or may not be a true indication of what resides beneath the surface). While debating on whether or not to reveal that she is in fact a woman, Villanelle herself ponders how clothes are an unreliable and arbitrary source of information where sexuality is concerned: "What was myself? Was this breeches and boots self any less real than my garters?" (66) By raising this question, Winterson moves beyond the inner/outer trope to invest cross-dressing with what ⟨Judith⟩ Butler claims for drag, namely, that it "fully subverts the distinction between inner and outer psychic space and effectively mocks both the expressive model of gender and the notion of a true gender identity" ⟨*Gender Trouble: Feminism and the Subversion of Identity*, 1990, 137⟩.

For Villanelle, this gender mocking is doubly inscribed both in her choice of dress and in the fact that her body bears the marks of both sexes, at least as far as Venetian culture is concerned. Villanelle, though not a hermaphrodite, possesses the Venetian bodily equivalent through her webbed feet, a prerequisite for male gondoliers; "there never was a girl," we learn, "whose feet were webbed in the entire history of the boatmen" (51). Just as Jeanette in *Oranges* usurps her masculine power through her success in the pulpit (134), Villanelle enters the male domain because of a genetic inheritance. The oddity of webbed feet can remain hidden for years beneath boots, but there's no mistaking the implications: the search for clear-cut distinctions where gender is concerned is futile. In fact, the midwife who attempts to make a clear cut between the male and female is repelled each time she attempts to insert the knife between Villanelle's toes; the knife springs "from the skin leaving no mark" (52). Such cultural insertions, Winterson suggests, constitute a violation of nature—an apparent turnaround from *Oranges*. In the first novel cultural authority over a socially constructed nature is available for the taking (not "is a lesbian natural?" but "who is asking?"), whereas in *The Passion* it is the body or, more specifically, the double gender encoding of Villanelle's body that invites cultural confusion and unintelligibility (social [re]construction cannot alter a genetic identity). The relationship between nature and social construction is not a simple reversal from one novel to the next, though. What the reader discovers in the natural upset Winterson inscribes on Villanelle's female body (marking the masculine by the slightest tissue of skin strategically situated between the toes) or in Villanelle's probing interrogation of the "self" and the "real" is not a quest for a unified and coherent essentialized self but a consistent willingness to explore multiple and fragmented fictions of identity, that is, to engage in endless speculation. Ultimately, the essential question has far less to do with the nature of nature, for Winterson the novelist recognizes that, as Diana Fuss explains, "when [essentialism is] put into practice by the dispossessed themselves . . . [it] can be powerfully displacing and disruptive" 〈*Essentially Speaking: Feminism, Nature and Difference*, 1989, 32〉.

—Laura Doan, "Jeanette Winterson's Sexing the Postmodern," in *The Lesbian Postmodern*, ed. Laura Doan (New York: Columbia University Press, 1994), 148–50

B I B L I O G R A P H Y

Oranges Are Not the Only Fruit. 1985.
Boating for Beginners. 1985.
The Passion. 1987.
Sexing the Cherry. 1989.
Written on the Body. 1993.
Art & Lies. 1995.

VIRGINIA WOOLF

1882–1941

ADELINE VIRGINIA WOOLF (neé Stephen) was born at Hyde Park Gate, London, on January 25, 1882. Virginia was the second daughter of Sir Leslie Stephen, the editor of the *Dictionary of National Biography*, and many of the leading British intellectuals of the day were regular guests in the Stephen home. While her brothers attended prestigious universities, Virginia was taught at home. Although exceptionally learned, Woolf continued to regret—and resent—her lack of formal education.

Virginia's childhood was at times traumatic: she was molested by two of her older half-brothers, and her mother's death in 1895 transformed Leslie Stephen into a morose and imperious parent. After her father's death in 1904, Virginia, her sister Vanessa (later Vanessa Bell), and their two brothers moved to Gordon Square, forming the nucleus of the Bloomsbury Group, an intellectual bohemian community that eventually included John Maynard Keynes, Lytton Strachey, E. M. Forster, and Roger Fry, among others.

Many members of the group were homosexual, including Strachey. Subscribing to the belief, common among Victorian homosexuals, that one should marry for convenience, Strachey proposed to Virginia. She accepted, but the engagement lasted all of 24 hours. Virginia married Leonard Woolf, a heterosexual novelist, political writer, and Bloomsbury member, in 1912.

The Woolfs' marriage appears to have been a platonic relationship, however, and 10 years later, Virginia met the stately and aristocratic Vita Sackville-West, with whom she had perhaps the most important and passionate relationship of her life. Though by the late 1920s the relationship had cooled, Woolf and Sackville-West remained close until Woolf's death in 1941.

Virginia had begun writing for the *Times Literary Supplement* of London in 1905 and continued to do so until nearly the end of her life. Her first novel, *The Voyage Out*, appeared in 1915 and was followed in 1919 by a second, *Night and Day*. In 1917 she and Leonard founded the Hogarth Press, which subsequently published all of her novels. Though her first two were essentially realistic in style, she soon began to experiment with new formal techniques such as stream-of-consciousness narrative and complex, varying time scales. The unusual qualities of her third novel, *Jacob's Room* (1922), were praised by her friend T. S. Eliot, but other critics attacked the book for its lack of plot.

Woolf distinguished herself as one of the principal exponents of modernism with her critical essay "Mr. Bennett and Mrs. Brown" in 1923. Her subsequent novels reinforced this claim: *Mrs. Dalloway* (1925); *To the Lighthouse* (1927); *Orlando* (1928), a fictional biography inspired by Vita Sackville-West; and *The Waves* (1931), among others.

Woolf wrote *A Room of One's Own* (1929) based on two lectures on women in fiction she had delivered. The work is hailed as one of the earliest feminist classics. As with her previous works, it touches on the subject of lesbianism, as in the well-known "Chloe liked Olivia" passage: "Do not start. Do not blush. Let us admit in the privacy of our own society that these things sometimes happen. Sometimes women do like women."

On March 28, 1941, Virginia Woolf committed suicide, prompted by a recurrence of earlier mental illness. Along with several collections of her critical essays published after her death, her *Letters* (1975-80) and *Diaries* (1974-84) reveal much about Woolf's literary and social friendships and provide a unique glimpse into the creative processes of her mind.

C R I T I C A L   E X T R A C T S

CONRAD AIKEN

That Mrs Woolf is a highly ingenious writer has been made glitteringly obvious for us in *Mrs. Dalloway* and *To the Lighthouse* which is not in the least to minimize the fact that those two novels also contained a great deal of beauty. That she is, and has perhaps always been, in danger of carrying ingenuity too far, is suggested, among other things, by her new novel, or "biography," *Orlando.* Whatever else one thinks about this book, one is bound to admit that it is exceedingly, not to say disconcertingly, clever. In England as well as in America it has set the critics by the ears. They have not known quite how to take it—whether to regard it as a biography, or a satire on biography; as a history, or a satire on history; as a novel, or as an allegory. And it is at once clear, when one reads *Orlando*, why this confusion should have arisen; for the tone of the book, from the very first pages, is a tone of mockery. ⟨. . .⟩

⟨It⟩ is an extremely amusing and brilliant *tour de force*. It is as packed with reference, almost, as *The Waste Land*. Some of the references, it is true, are too esoteric—for one not in the enchanted circle—to be universally valid; and this may or may not be thought a mistake. One's private jokes and innuendoes are pretty apt to become meaningless, with the passage of time and the disappearance of the milieu which gave them point. This, again, is of a piece with Mrs. Woolf's general air of high spirits; of having a lark; of going, as it were, on an intellectual spree; and that there is far too little of this spirit in contemporary literature we can cheerfully admit. But here too one feels inclined to enter a protest. For the idea, as has been said, is first-rate, an idea from which a poet might have evoked a profusion of beauty as easily as the djinn was released from his bottle. Mrs Woolf does indeed give us a profusion of beauty and wisdom: but it is beauty and wisdom of a very special sort. Her roses are cloth roses, her scenes are scenes from a tapestry, her "wisdom" (that is, her shrewd and very feminine comments on men and things) has about it an air of florid and cynical frigidity, a weariness wrought into form; as if—to change the image—she were stringing for her own entertainment a necklace of beautifully polished platitudes. If only—one thinks—she could have brought an Elizabethan freshness to this admirable theme—if she could have worked her mine a little deeper, a little more honestly, a little less for diversion's sake, and a little more for poetry's; and if, finally, she were not quite so civilized, in the Kensington Gardens sense of the word, or so burdened with sophistication, or could admit now and then, if for only a moment, a glimpse into the sheer horror of things, the chaos that yawns under Bloomsbury—but then this book would not have been the charming jeu d'esprit that it is; it would have been something else.

—Conrad Aiken, *Dial* (February 1929), in *The Chelsea House Library of Literary Criticism: Twentieth-Century British Literature*, vol. 5, ed. Harold Bloom (New York: Chelsea House Publishers, 1987), 3112

STEPHEN SPENDER

Imaginatively, ⟨Virginia Woolf⟩ is I think the inhabitant of two worlds. One of these is the isolated self, her own sensibility, of which she is almost the prisoner, and of which the various female characters who are the heroines of her novels—Mrs. Dalloway, Mrs. Ramsay, Orlando—are but masks. This self is Adam-like—or since she is a woman, should I say Eve-like? Her approach to the outer world is that she is completely isolated, and unique, and that every instant—the sun shining on the leaves, the bird singing from the branches— is unprecedented, unique, and will never happen again. It has happened, like the Creation, for the first time. ⟨. . .⟩

The view opposite to Virginia Woolf's compulsive vision—from which she could not, I am sure, ever escape for a moment—is that life is a routine. The

routine view of life is that it consists of lots of precedents which have consequences. Precedents and consequences form chains of behaviour, and to live
you have to relate your own life to these tracks of connections—as you also
have to do to understand other people, to understand history, to understand
anything about behaviour at all. Everything that is achieved in the world is
achieved as the result of a routine; not just the routine itself—going to the
office every morning—but a vision of life as routine. The routine vision
extends far beyond time-tables and offices, it extends to one's ideas about the
characters and behaviour of other people. The characters in novels, for example, are for the most part hitched on going to school, falling in love, getting
married—behaving in ways which show that according to established routines
they are villains or heroes, or something a bit subtler between the two, or that
makes them both at the same time.

Virginia Woolf was aware of course of routines. But they seemed to her
strange. She stood outside them. They were also particularly associated in her
mind with the male sex. The man, rather than the woman, was a creature of
routine. The more he excelled at it the more absurd he appeared in Virginia
Woolf's eye; so that a highly successful man who became Prime Minister, or
an admiral, was like a creature with bright golden chains not only hung on him
but visibly running all through him. Some women in Virginia Woolf's world
were outside routines. They saw the world as a moment to moment flashing
on of physical and mental events which never ceased to surprise, never lost
their wonder. In order to please their men these women pretended to accept
the routine view of life; but they never really did so, and the fact that they had
to play this game with their husbands, of pretending to believe, made men
faintly absurd and certainly opaque. ⟨. . .⟩

⟨. . .⟩ ⟨Her⟩ second world was an inner world in which her family and her
friends played roles in her imagination: in which they existed, as I say, as a
group, revering one another, believing in the talents of each and all, exchang-
ing ideas, gossip and confidences. Each member of the group was a part of a
shared consciousness. There was interaction between her isolation and her
sense of friendship which gave the group the character of a work of art of relations achieved and of values intensely imagined. Communication between
them was ideal, together with the wit, the story-telling, the malice, the gossip
and the entertainment—only very thin walls dividing the rooms where they
met from tragedy. If there was tragedy, they could talk about it.

The Waves is a prose poem about the group of friends whose lives, from
birth almost, play to one another like the instruments in quartet or quintet. Yet
each member of the group has projected upon him or her Virginia Woolf's
sense of isolation. It is both a real harmony between interrelated lives and a

multi-faced mask of human loneliness. It seems to me a book of great beauty and a prose poem of genius.

—Stephen Spender, *Recollections of Virginia Woolf,* ed. Joan Russell Noble (1972), in *The Chelsea House Library of Literary Criticism: Twentieth-Century British Literature,* vol. 5, ed. Harold Bloom (New York: Chelsea House Publishers, 1987), 3111

JAMES NAREMORE

Between the Acts is built on that attempt at a masculine-feminine dialectic which is so much a part of Mrs. Woolf's fiction; the important historical events, if La Trobe can be taken as an authority, are not wars but loves. Hence the three plays that make up the "acts" of the summer pageant (they can be read as parodies of Shakespeare, Congreve, and Gilbert and Sullivan) are all at bottom the same play about love between the sexes. To underscore the sense of historical continuity, three sets of male-female relationships are established within the story proper, each representing a different period of history but each fundamentally the same. The first is contained in the eighteenth-century portraits which hang facing one another in Pointz Hall. On the one hand is an ancestor who holds the reins of his horse and seems to chafe at having to pose. ("If you want my likeness, dang it sir, take it when the leaves are on the trees.") Opposite him is an anonymous lady who leans elegantly on a pillar and leads the viewer's eye "through glades of greenery and shades of silver, dun and rose into silence." The male-female roles are characterized here as in Mrs. Woolf's other novels; even small details like the fact that the male figure "has a name" and is a "talk producer" are typical and significant. Reinforcing this statement about the elemental distinctions between the male and female, we have a nineteenth-century couple, Mr. Bartholomew Oliver, late of the Indian Civil Service, and his sister, Lucy Swithin:

> Old Bartholomew tapped his fingers on his knee in time to the tune. . . . He looked sardonically at Lucy, perched on her chair. How, he wondered, had she ever borne children? . . .
>
> She was thinking, he supposed. God is peace. God is love. For she belonged to the unifiers; he to the separatists. (p. 140)

The third couple are, of course, the twentieth-century figures, Giles and Isa—she dreamy and always murmuring fragments of verse, he, like the other males, impatient to do something. The confrontation of these two at the end represents the major "act" of the novel, the next great historical event; but that act is only about to take place as the novel ends. Indeed, even their infidelity to one another is not yet an accomplished fact.

These, then, are two important implications of the title: we are between wars and between two decisive acts in the lives of an archetypal male and female, in both cases the security of Pointz Hall is threatened, and in both cases an important event seems imminent, so that Giles and Isa continually have the feeling that the future is "disturbing our present." But there is a third and perhaps transcendent implication that helps us understand more clearly the impulses behind Mrs. Woolf's experimentation with the form of the novel. The title suggests, as Geoffrey Hartman has noted, that the book is about unfilled spaces 〈"Virginia's Web," *Chicago Review* 14 (1961): 28〉; more specifically, it is about the anxiety that grows from an effort to discover a continuity and unity in life. The great problem that animates this novel, as indeed all Mrs. Woolf's novels, is whether to deny or accept the terrible sense of separation between things. What is threatened here is not only the continuity of English civilization and the continuity of the relationships at Pointz Hall, but the continuity of life itself. By positing a world and a family hovering between acts, Virginia Woolf creates an air of uncertainty—and not only about metaphysics, for the voice that speaks like a mechanical god from the bushes at the end of La Trobe's pageant is hardly convinced of the moral value of human beings.

—James Naremore, "The 'Orts and Fragments' in *Between the Acts*," *The World Without a Self* (1973), in *The Chelsea House Library of Literary Criticism: Twentieth-Century British Literature*, vol. 5, ed. Harold Bloom (New York: Chelsea House Publishers, 1987), 3126–27

VIRGINIA WOOLF

〈The〉 Thursday evening parties 〈at 46 Gordon Square〉 were, as far as I am concerned, the germ from which sprang all that has since come to be called— in newspapers, in novels, in Germany, in France—even, I daresay, in Turkey and Timbuktu—by the name of Bloomsbury. They deserve to be recorded and described. Yet how difficult—how impossible. Talk—even the talk which had such tremendous results upon the lives and characters of the two Miss Stephens—even talk of this interest and importance is as elusive as smoke. It flies up the chimney and is gone. 〈. . .〉

〈. . .〉 The argument, whether it was about atmosphere or the nature of truth, was always tossed into the middle of the party. Now 〈Ralph〉 Hawtrey would say something; now Vanessa; now Saxon 〈Sydney-Turner〉; now Clive 〈Bell〉; now Thoby. It filled me with wonder to watch those who were finally left in the argument piling stone upon stone, cautiously, accurately, long after it had completely soared above my sight. But if one could not say anything, one could listen. One had glimpses of something miraculous happening high up in the air. Often we would still be sitting in a circle at two or three in the morning. Still Saxon would be taking his pipe from his mouth as if to speak, and putting it back again without having spoken. At last, rumpling his hair back, he would pronounce very shortly some absolutely final summing up. The marvellous edifice was complete, one could stumble off to bed feeling that something very important had happened. It had been proved that beauty was—or beauty was not—for I have never been quite sure which—part of a picture.

From such discussions Vanessa and I got probably much the same pleasure that undergraduates get when they meet friends of their own for the first time. In the world of the Booths and the Maxses we were not asked to use our brains much. Here we used nothing else. And part of the charm of those Thursday evenings was that they were astonishingly abstract. It was not only that Moore's book ⟨*Principia Ethica* (1903)⟩ had set us all discussing philosophy, art, religion; it was that the atmosphere—if in spite of Hawtrey I may use that word—was abstract in the extreme. The young men I have named had no 'manners' in the Hyde Park Gate sense. They criticised our arguments as severely as their own. They never seemed to notice how we were dressed or if we were nice looking or not. All that tremendous encumbrance of appearance and behaviour which George had piled upon our first years vanished completely. One had no longer to endure that terrible inquisition after a party— and be told, "You looked lovely." Or, "You did look plain." Or, "You must really learn to do your hair." Or, "Do try not to look so bored when you dance." Or, "You did make a conquest", or "You *were* a failure." All this seemed to have no meaning or existence in the world of Bell, Strachey, Hawtrey and Sydney-Turner. In that world the only comment as we stretched ourselves after our guests had gone, was, "I must say you made your point rather well"; "I think you were talking rather through your hat." It was an immense simplification. ⟨. . .⟩

⟨. . .⟩ ⟨But⟩ one afternoon that first summer Vanessa said to Adrian and me and I watched her, stretching her arms above her head with a gesture that was at once reluctant and yielding, in the great looking-glass as she said it—"Of course, I can see that we shall all marry. It's bound to happen"—and as she said it I could feel a horrible necessity impending over us; a fate would descend and snatch us apart just as we had achieved freedom and happiness. She, I felt, was already aware of some claim, some need which I resented and tried to ignore. A few weeks later indeed Clive proposed to her. "Yes," said Thoby grimly when I murmured something to him very shyly about Clive's proposal, "That's the worst of Thursday evenings!" And her marriage in the beginning of 1907 was in fact the end of them. With that, the first chapter of Old Bloomsbury came to an end. It had been very austere, very exciting, of immense importance. A small concentrated world dwelling inside the much larger and looser world of dances and dinners had come into existence. It had already begun to

colour that world and still I think colours the much more gregarious
Bloomsbury which succeeded it.

—Virginia Woolf, "Old Bloomsbury," *Moments of Being*, ed. Jeanne Schulkind (1976), in *The
Chelsea House Library of Literary Criticism: Twentieth-Century British Literature*, vol. 5, ed. Harold
Bloom (New York: Chelsea House Publishers, 1987), 3103–4

NELLY FURMAN

For practical reasons,—need for time and privacy—a woman's book, such as *A
Room of One's Own*, might be shorter and more concentrated. But more impor-
tantly, it could reflect woman's cultural and historical status, that is to say, her
conspicuous absence. Thus, one way of conveying woman's intrinsic experience in a patriarchal society could be through a thematics of absence. In a
short essay, "Professions for Women," Virginia Woolf recounts the difficulties
she encountered as a woman novelist. While she was able to overcome some,
she felt that she had not always succeeded in expressing herself with unre-
stricted candor on the subject of her body: "telling the truth about my own
experiences as a body, I do not think I solved." It is our contention, however,
that by creating a spatial, womb-like vacuity in her text, Virginia Woolf conveys something of woman's bodily interiority. ⟨. . .⟩

Examples of Virginia Woolf's skillful use of "absence" abound.
Conspicuously placed at the end of the Oxbridge episode, the section about
the Manx cat prepares the passage into Fernham, the transition from a world
of presence to a world of absence. The sight of the tailless cat suddenly
changes the narrator's perception of the scene around her and leads her to recognize "what a difference a tail makes." One could note that it is a missing ash-
tray which brings the narrator to the window and makes her notice the cat
without a tail, while the cigarette, which brought the narrator to the window
in order to flick the ashes, itself disappears from the text. The sight of the
Manx cat makes her realize that something else is missing and that the
amorous cooing between the sexes has ceased. As the narrator enters the
woman's college, we are made aware that it is a place defined by absence. For
not only does Fernham lack the traditions and wealth of Oxbridge, but whereas in Oxbridge the narrator faced the forbidding presence of beadles, in the
gardens of Fernham she only perceives the fleeting visions of phantoms "half
guessed, half seen," the very traces of absence. When she returns late at night
to her inn and poetically evokes the aura of the night, the last sentence of the
chapter refers to an absence; "Even the door of the hotel sprang open at the
touch of an invisible hand—not a boots was sitting up to light me to bed, it
was so late."

Just as, when talking about the alternations of work and rest, one should
interpret "rest not as doing nothing but as doing something but something

that is different," similarly absence is not to be defined simply as non-presence but as something different. For Virginia Woolf, the concept of absence and its related semantic notions—invisibility, silence, inaudibility, etc.—become the distinctive feature of woman's otherness, the locus of a woman's experience in a patriarchal society. Some women, Virginia Woolf reminds us, have been able to convey their genuinely personal woman's view. Jane Austen, for example, by steadfastly keeping to her drawing room, forced the integrity of her world and the specificity of her discourse onto man's literary tradition. The fictitious Mary Carmichael not only brings to the fore a hitherto unexplored network of relationships, such as "Chloe liked Olivia," but she almost succeeds in breaking the man-made sentence and narrative sequence. As for Virginia Woolf herself, she makes the expression of absence the signifying characteristic of her integrity as a woman novelist.

—Nelly Furman, "Virginia Woolf's A *Room of One's Own*: Reading Absence," *Women's Language and Style* (L & S Books), in *British Modernist Fiction, 1920 to 1945*, ed. Harold Bloom (New York: Chelsea House Publishers, 1987), 156–58

MICHAEL ROSENTHAL

If sheer titillation accounts for much of the public's attention, the gradual realization that Virginia Woolf was, in fact, a woman writer (or at least not a man, the androgynous theory having its own advocates) has also played a substantial role. The polemical grinder of the feminist movement has greedily devoured Woolf, spewing her forth as the appropriately committed feminist whose preoccupation with the cause is somehow the key to her fiction. Such a view of Woolf is not particularly useful. It is of course true that she was very much concerned with the economic and social plight of women, and deeply sensitive to the psychic crippling inflicted on them by a male dominated world, *Orlando. A Room of One's Own, Three Guineas*, and assorted essays eloquently testify to her involvement in these issues, as well as to the deft way she can expose the absurdities of our culture. But to focus on her fiction through any sort of politicized feminist lens is seriously to distort it. Woolf herself deplored novels that preach, and hers are conspicuously free from the proselytizing that frequently occupied her when she was not at her desk struggling with her fiction. This is not to argue that Woolf was not conscious of the assumptions of an environment which held for example, that Virginia's brothers, but not Virginia, should go to university; it is simply to protest against the reductionist view, in vogue today, that Woolf's novels speak in some essential and exclusive way to feminist preoccupations. Woolf, in fact, hated the word 'feminist' altogether—'What more fitting than to destroy an old word, a vicious and corrupt word that has done much harm in its day and is now obsolete? The word "feminist" is the word indicated,' ⟨*Three Guineas*, 1938, 184⟩ finding it divisive and inimical to the overall unity of civilized people she so desired.

The feminist claim on Woolf has lately been joined by the androgynist, which sees Woolf's novels as endorsing the splendors of the androgynous mind as a palliative to all our ills. Taking as a seminal passage Woolf's discussion in *A Room of One's Own* of the flourishing artistic imagination being able to transcend any narrow sexual role, the hunters of androgyny doggedly chase the metaphor through all of Woolf's fiction, hacking out new patterns of meaning as they go. But metaphors are better left in peace to illuminate the specific contexts in which they appear. The illustrative use of androgyny to represent the kind of wide-ranging, non-dogmatic, resonant intelligence Woolf finds admirable—and capable of producing great art—cannot be generalized into establishing Woolf's 'androgynous vision.' To discover that Woolf believes that men and women should share a complex view of reality, one as free as possible from the parochialisms of any single sex, is not to discover anything very new about her work.

If Woolf is to survive as other than a precious oddity of the modernist movement, it will be neither as a member of a coterie, a radical feminist, nor a prophetic androgynist. Sexual ideologies and exotic ambiences aside, Woolf's fiction must be able to meet the reservation still shared by many and more recently expressed by Elizabeth Hardwick: acknowledging the richness of Woolf's language and the glow of her genius. Hardwick goes on to say, 'yet in a sense, her novels aren't interesting' ⟨*Seduction and Betrayal*, 1974, 141⟩. Whatever else novels are, they should at least be interesting, and it is a fact that hers have not always been thought so. ⟨. . .⟩ For plot is indeed nothing in Woolf's fiction and character ⟨. . .⟩ not much more. Novelists who dispense with both of these staples are going to have difficult times, and Woolf has received her share of critical abuse for writing novels in which, it is argued, nothing happens. ⟨. . .⟩

The center of a Woolf novel, then, does not reside in any of those several themes frequently singled out for critical investigation—the workings of consciousness, the perception of time, the quality of personal relationships—but in her effort to orchestrate these in such a way as to make us feel how together they constitute part of the experience of living. The quest is always for the form that will embody Woolf's sense of what that experience is. From *Jacob's Room* to *Between the Acts*, every one of Woolf's novels originated not with any notion of theme or character but with some notion of the form the novel might take.

—Michael Rosenthal, "The Problem of the Fiction," *Virginia Woolf* (1979), in *The Chelsea House Library of Literary Criticism: Twentieth-Century British Literature*, vol. 5, ed. Harold Bloom (New York: Chelsea House Publishers, 1987), 3138–39

IAN GREGOR

The Waves has the effect of a book written inside out. Most novels, whether they proceed to tell their tale directly or by hints and guesses, are concerned to give the reader the sense that this is "how it was"; we feel this whether we are with Lockwood being introduced to Heathcliff or, in different circumstances, with Strether being introduced to Madame de Vionnet. But with *The Waves* we feel ourselves present at something which is already "a reading" of "how it was." We seem simultaneously to be addressed and ignored; we are both within and without the discourse; detachment and a sense of extraordinary intimacy are barely distinguishable elements in our experience.

Another way of putting this would be to say that *The Waves* does not so much speak to the reader as it speaks for him. This distinctive combination of intimacy and formality, a striking feature of the rhetorical effect made by *The Waves*, finds an analogue in the rhetoric of liturgical prayer, which combines those seemingly contrary effects as part of its nature. Precisely because *The Waves* involves the reader so intimately, our attitudes toward it can shift violently. At times we experience only its formality; we are irritatingly aware only of "words, words, words, my lord," of characters simplistically conceived, of a world without a context. At other times the novel speaks to us so immediately, so directly, that the words seem virtually giving shape to a sequence of moods, so finely, so precisely, that, as with Mrs. Ramsay reading the poem, the voice seems to create the very mood in which we ourselves are reading the novel. We recall the remark in Woolf's memoir "A Sketch of the Past" about the experience which precipitates her into writing: "We are the words; we are the music; we are the thing itself."

Such is the nature of *The Waves* that it becomes extremely difficult to do justice to these shifting effects. Either we tend to overconceptualize, and our stress is on the firmness of the novel's structure, or we overemphathize, and our stress falls on its texture, on "the prose poem," etc. But if what I have said about the shifting effect is persuasive, then it follows that to look for some kind of account which offers a better "balance" will be misguided, because such an account is too preoccupied with finding a "theme" and insufficiently concerned with the effect made by theme in the actual process of reading.

For instance, what can we say about our reaction to those interchapters? The intention would seem to be to create a world irretrievably other than that of "the voices" in the main text. Nature is to be shown as neither benign nor malignant, but simply as "other"; to project our own feelings into it, and find in the movement of the sun from dawn to evening a sardonic comment on the human condition, is sentimental. And this sense of otherness Woolf seeks to dramatize by carefully marking off the interchapters and altering the typography. But for all that, in my reading experience, the structural purpose of the interchapters is stubbornly in conflict with the effect they make.

The aim is to create a neutral voice, something to set against the human and the sentient. It is the kind of effect that Eliot sought, and so effectively achieved, in the time passages in *Four Quartets*. "Go, go, go, said the bird: human kind / Cannot bear very much reality": that notion of "saying" is so recessive that we are not disconcerted by a bird's capacity for aphorism. But the interchapters in *The Waves* are so densely textured that, far from being remotely impersonal, they come across as intensely "composed" and self-regarding, confident candidates for inclusion in an anthology of modern English prose.

—Ian Gregor, "Voices: Reading Virginia Woolf," *The Sewanee Review* 88, no. 4 (October-December 1980), in *British Modernist Fiction, 1920 to 1945*, ed. Harold Bloom (New York: Chelsea House Publishers, 1987), 167–68

ELIZABETH ABEL

When Woolf discovered how to enrich her characterization by digging "beautiful caves" into her characters' pasts, her own geological image for the temporal strata of Mrs. Dalloway, she chose with precision the consciousness through which to reveal specific segments of the past. Although Clarissa vacillates emotionally between the allure of Peter and that of Richard, she remembers Peter's courtship only glancingly; the burden of that plot is carried by Peter, through whose memories Woolf relates the slow and tortured end of the relation with Clarissa. Clarissa's memories, by contrast, focus more exclusively on the general ambience of Bourton, her childhood home, and her love for Sally Seton. Significantly absent from these memories is Richard Dalloway, whose courtship of Clarissa is presented exclusively through Peter's painful recollections. Clarissa thinks of Richard only in the present, not at the peak of a romantic relationship. Through this narrative distribution, Woolf constructs two diversified poles structuring the flux of Clarissa's consciousness. Bourton is to Clarissa a pastoral female world spatially and temporally disjunct from marriage and the sociopolitical world of (Richard's) London. The fluid passage of consciousness between these poles conceals a radical schism. ⟨. . .⟩

⟨. . .⟩ Clarissa's life in London is devoid of intimate female bonds: she is excluded from lunch at Lady Bruton's and she vies with Miss Kilman for her own daughter's allegiance. Woolf structures Clarissa's development as a stark binary opposition between past and present, nature and culture, feminine and masculine dispensations—the split implicit in Woolf's later claim that "the values of women differ very often from the values which have been made by the other sex." Versions of this opposition reverberate throughout the novel in rhetorical and narrative juxtapositions. The developmental plot, which slides beneath the more familiar romantic plot through the gap between Peter's and Clarissa's memories, exists as two contrasting moments and the silence adjoining and dividing them.

Woolf endows these moments with symbolic resonance by a meticulous strategy of narrative exclusions that juxtaposes eras split by thirty years and omits Clarissa's childhood from the novel's temporal frame. There is no past in Mrs. Dalloway anterior to Clarissa's adolescence at Bourton. Within this selective scheme, the earliest remembered scenes become homologous to a conventional narrative point of departure: the description of formative childhood years. The emotional tenor of these scenes, moreover, suggests their representation of deferred childhood desire. Clarissa's earliest narrated memories focus on Sally's arrival at Bourton, an arrival that infuses the formal, repressive atmosphere with a vibrant female energy. The only picture of Clarissa's early childhood sketched in the novel suggests a tableau of female loss: a dead mother, a dead sister, a distant father, and a stern maiden aunt, the father's sister, whose hobby of pressing flowers beneath Littre's dictionary suggests to Peter Walsh the social oppression of women, an emblem of nature ossified by language/culture. In this barren atmosphere, Sally's uninhibited warmth and sensuality immediately spark love in the eighteen-year-old Clarissa. Sally replaces Clarissa's dead mother and sister, her name even echoing the sister's name, Sylvia. She nurtures Clarissa's passions and intellect, inspiring a love equal to Othello's in intensity and equivalent in absoluteness to a daughter's earliest bond with her mother, a bond too early ruptured for Clarissa as for Woolf, a bond which Woolf herself perpetually sought to recreate through intimate attachments to mother surrogates, such as Violet Dickinson: "I wish you were a Kangaroo and had a pouch for small Kangaroos to creep to." For Clarissa, kissing Sally creates the most exquisite moment of her life, a moment of unparalleled radiance and intensity: "The whole world might have turned upside down! The others disappeared; there she was alone with Sally. And she felt she had been given a present, wrapped up, and told just to keep it, not to look at it—a diamond, something infinitely precious, wrapped up, which, as they walked (up and down, up and down), she uncovered, or the radiance burnt through, the revelation, the religious feeling!—when old Joseph and Peter faced them." This kind of passionate attachment between women, orthodox psychoanalysts and feminists uncharacteristically agree, recaptures some aspect of the fractured mother-daughter bond. Within the sequence established by the novel, this adolescent love assumes the power of the early female bond excluded from the narrative.

—Elizabeth Abel, "Narrative Structure(s) and Female Development: The Case of 'Mrs. Dalloway,'" *The Voyage In: Fictions of Female Development*, ed. Elizabeth Abel, Marianne Hirsch, and Elizabeth Langland (University Press of New England, 1983), in *Virginia Woolf*, ed. Harold Bloom (New York: Chelsea House Publishers, 1986), 247–49

Virginia Blain

⟨. . .⟩ ⟨W⟩hile it is true that Bloomsbury was in many ways a strong liberating influence in Virginia Stephen's life, releasing her from the toils of respectable bourgeois hypocrisy associated with life at Hyde Park Gate, the double-edged characterization of the two Bloomsbury figures in *The Voyage Out*—St. John Hirst and Helen Ambrose—indicates the extent of their author's unease with some of the values they represent. Both appoint themselves as Rachel's educators; both regard their own attitudes to sexuality as uniquely untrammelled by conventional hypocrisy; both assume that women can have no equal share in male sexual enjoyment. When Rachel tries to explain to Helen her sense of fear and confusion at her own abruptly awakened sexual feelings after Richard Dalloway's kiss, Helen's response is dismissive:

> Men will want to kiss you, just as they'll want to marry you. The pity is to get things out of proportion. It's like noticing the noises people make when they eat, or men spitting; or, in short, any small thing that gets on one's nerves.

This is very similar to St. John's attitude to female sexuality: that it is virtually non-existent, and certainly has nothing to do with any notion of masculine pleasure or fulfillment. Here he talks to Hewet, who is beginning to fall in love with Rachel:

> "What I abhor most of all," he concluded, "is the female breast. Imagine being Venning and having to get into bed with Susan! But the really repulsive thing is that they feel nothing at all—about what I do when I have a hot bath. They're gross, they're absurd, they're utterly intolerable!"

This is a delightfully barbed parody of the narcissistic side of male homo-eroticism; but one of its effects is to make more sinister the alliance between the female-despising Hirst and the strongly male-identified Helen. In a novel which is so largely concerned with the sexual initiation rites of a virgin girl, it is tempting to see in the characterization of these two Bloomsbury figures and their effect on Rachel a sharply personal reference to Woolf herself. ⟨. . .⟩ *The Voyage Out* is not a disguised first-person novel, as such criticism implies. Although Rachel is seen from the inside, it is not her consciousness which frames the novel, but that of Woolf's narrator, whose gender-conscious ironies operate as a constant reminder to the reader of the existence of the sex-war as a kind of grim backcloth to the romantic love story. ⟨. . .⟩

One consequence of identifying Rachel Vinrace with her author has been a denigration of the novel as the product of a prudish mind. James Naremore, despite some excellent analysis of what he calls the "submission of the narrator's ego to the world she writes about," cannot resist chiding Woolf for being "manifestly prudish" in *The Voyage Out*. In a critic who is otherwise sensitive to what he terms "the generally erotic nature of her art," this misreading (as it seems to me) smacks of a blindness to the female perspective of this particular novel. Like De Salvo, he makes too close an association between the identities of author and heroine, and projects onto Woolf the nervousness about sexuality that is characteristic to Rachel Vinrace. Virginia Woolf herself may or may not have been sexually nervous: the point I would wish to stress is that she is perfectly conscious, as author, of this quality in her heroine—it is not a case of an unconscious projection of her own secret fears.

Naremore quite rightly points to the evocative image of the old lady gardeners as one which contains overtones of both sexuality and death:

> millions of dark-red flowers were blooming, until the old ladies who had tended them so carefully came down the paths with their scissors, snipped through their juicy stalks, and laid them upon cold stone ledges in the village church.

But this is not a generalized image of a sex/death equation: it is specifically an evocation of female castrators at work, and as such carries a resonance not only in the scene where Rachel spies the old women decapitating live chickens behind the hotel, but also in the much later dream-image of her delirium: "Terence sat down by the bedside . . . Her eyes were not entirely shut . . . She opened them completely when he kissed her. But she only saw an old woman slicing a man's head off with a knife." This is a recurrent dream of hers, and, like the disgustingly oozy vaginal tunnel dream, represents an internalization by Rachel of certain male fears about women. (Particularly male homosexual fears—Terence's friendship with the homosexually-inclined St. John is left deliberately suggestive.) Naremore's misunderstanding of this important layer of meaning in the novel is underlined by the nature of his reference to Woolf's essay "Professions for Women," which he invokes in confirmation of his "author-as-prude" theory.

—Virginia Blain, "Narrative Voice and the Female Perspective in 'The Voyage Out,' " *Virginia Woolf: New Critical Essays*, ed. Patricia Clements and Isobel Grundy (Vision Press Ltd., 1983), in *Virginia Woolf*, ed. Harold Bloom (New York: Chelsea House Publishers, 1986), 236–38

SANDRA M. GILBERT AND SUSAN GUBAR

⟨. . .⟩ In one of the most famous yet most opaque passages in A *Room of One's Own*, Virginia Woolf introduces her notoriously puzzling concept of "a woman's sentence." Remarking that the early nineteenth-century woman novelist found that "there was no common sentence ready for her use," she declared that the "man's sentence" inherited by "Thackeray and Dickens and Balzac" from "Johnson, Gibbon and the rest" was as alien to her mind as "the [hardened and set] older forms of literature" were to her imagination (78-80). Her comment, like the literary history in which it is embedded, seems appealingly empirical. Those of us who wish to understand the relationship between genre and gender, Woolf seems to imply—even those who wish to examine the more ontological connection between sexuality and creativity—need merely analyze and classify linguistic structures. ⟨. . .⟩

⟨. . .⟩ Woolf continually creates characters who experience themselves as alienated from the ordinary sense of language. In *The Voyage Out*, for example, Rachel Vinrace hears her lover reading the words of *Comus* and thinks that "they sounded strange; they meant different things from what they usually meant" (326). Similarly in *Mrs. Dalloway* a skywriting airplane produces an ambiguous trail of smoke which might mean "Glaxo," "Kreemo," "toffee," or "K E Y" (29-32). Again, in *To the Lighthouse* (1927), Lily Briscoe translates Mr. Ramsay's mystifying concern with "subject and object and the nature of reality" into a vision of a kitchen table suspended among the trees and, more to the point, she thinks ironically of how his "splendid mind" struggles to explore thought which, "like the alphabet," is "ranged in twenty-six letters" (53). In *A Room of One's Own*, too, the Woolfian narrator puzzles over the "straight dark bar" formed "like the [implicitly male] letter 'I'. . . . honest and logical; as hard as a nut, and polished for centuries by good teaching and good feeding" but in whose shadow "all is shapeless as mist" (103-04). Finally, in *The Years* (1937), the sibylline Sara Pargiter insistently asks "What's 'I'?" (140) while in *The Waves*, for Rhoda, figures on a blackboard are "white loops" through which she steps "into emptiness, alone" (189), and in *Between the Acts* (1941), the mysterious Miss La Trobe imagines "Words of one syllable" rising from mud, "Words without meaning—wonderful words" (212). ⟨. . .⟩

At the same time, however, Woolf offers her heroines, and a few heroes, the benediction of fantastic new languages. In *Night and Day* (1919), for instance, Katharine Hilbery articulates her feelings through enigmatic visions of "algebraic symbols'" (300). Similarly, in *Mrs. Dalloway*, the shellshocked Septimus expresses *his* strong emotions in pictographic "writings" while an ancient woman "opposite Regent's Park Tube Station" sings a famously enigmatic song that goes "ee um fah um so / foo swee too eem oo" (122). Again, in *Orlando* (1928), Woolf's androgynous hero/heroine wires her husband a comically encoded comment on the meaning of literary achievement: " 'Rattigan Glumphoboo,' which summed it up precisely" (282) while in *The Years* the two "children of the caretaker"—descendants of the Tube Station crone—provide a fitting climax to the Pargiters' family reunion with a shrill ditty that begins

"Etho passo tanno hai, / Fai Donk to tu do, / Mai to, kai to, lai to see / Toh dom to tuh do—" (429).

Finally, throughout her oeuvre, Woolf emphasizes the fact that both the alienation from language her books describe and the revision of lexicography her books detail are functions of the dispossession of women, as well as of women's natural resources in the face of this dispossession, and she does this by presenting a dramatic succession of female figures whose ancient voices seem to endure from a time before the neat categories of culture restrained female energy. The most notable of these figures is, of course, the tube station crone in *Mrs. Dalloway*. But clearly the ancestor of this woman is the "old blind woman" who, in *Jacob's Room*, sits long past sunset "singing out loud . . . from the depths of her gay wild heart . . ." (67). And her descendants appear in *To the Lighthouse* as the force that lurches through Mrs. McNab's groaning and Mrs. Bast's creaking as they stay the corruption at work on the Ramsays' summer house.

—Sandra M. Gilbert and Susan Gubar, *No Man's Land: The Place of the Woman Writer in the Twentieth Century*, vol. 1: *The War of the Words* (New Haven: Yale University Press, 1988), 229, 248–50

B I B L I O G R A P H Y

The Voyage Out. 1915.

Two Stories (with Leonard Woolf). 1917.

Night and Day. 1919.

Kew Gardens. 1919.

Monday or Tuesday. 1921.

Jacob's Room. 1922.

Stavrogin's Confession, by Fyodor Dostoevsky (translator, with S. S. Koteliansky). 1922.

Tolstoi's Love Letters (translator, with S. S. Koteliansky). 1923.

Talks with Tolstoy, by A. D. Goldenveizer (translator, with S. S. Koteliansky). 1923.

Mr. Bennett and Mrs. Brown. 1924.

Mrs. Dalloway. 1925.

The Common Reader. 1925.

To the Lighthouse. 1927.

Orlando: A Biography. 1928.

A Room of One's Own. 1929.

Street Haunting. 1930.

On Being Ill. 1930.

Beau Brummell. 1930.

The Waves. 1931.

The Common Reader: Second Series. 1932.

A Letter to a Young Poet. 1932.

Flush: A Biography. 1933.

Walter Sickert: A Conversation. 1934.

The Years. 1937.

Three Guineas. 1938.

Reviewing. 1939.

Roger Fry: A Biography. 1940.

Between the Acts. 1941.

The Death of the Moth and Other Essays. 1942.

The Moment and Other Essays. 1942.

A Haunted House and Other Short Stories. 1944.

The Captain's Death Bed and Other Essays. 1950.

A Writer's Diary: Being Extracts from the Diary of Virginia Woolf. Ed. Leonard Woolf. 1953.

Virginia Woolf and Lytton Strachey: Letters. Ed. Leonard Woolf and James Strachey. 1956.

Hours in a Library. 1958.

Granite and Rainbow: Essays. 1958.

Contemporary Writers. Ed. Jean Guiget. 1965.

Nurse Lugton's Golden Thimble. 1966.

Collected Essays. Ed. Leonard Woolf (4 vols.). 1966.

Stephen versus Gladstone. 1967.

A Cockney's Farming Experiences. Ed. Suzanne Henig. 1972.

Mrs. Dalloway's Party: A Short Story Sequence. Ed. Stella McNichol. 1973.

The London Scene: Five Essays. 1975.

Letters. Ed. Nigel Nicolson and Joanne Trautmann (6 vols.). 1975.

Moments of Being: Unpublished Autobiographical Writings. Ed. Jeanne Schulkind. 1976.

Freshwater: A Comedy. Ed. Lucio P. Ruotolo. 1976.

The Waves: The Two Holograph Drafts. Ed. John W. Graham. 1976.

The Diary. Ed. Anne Olivier Bell and Andrew McNeillie (5 vols.). 1977.

Books and Portraits: Some Further Selections from the Literary and Biographical Writings. Ed. Mary Lyon. 1977.

The Pargiters: The Novel-Essay Portion of "The Years". Ed. Mitchell Leaska. 1978.

Women and Writing. Ed. Michele Barrett. 1979.

Melymbrosia: An Early Version of The Voyage Out. Ed. Louise A. Delsalvo. 1982.

Virginia Woolf's Reading Notebooks. Ed. Brenda R. Silver. 1982.

Pointz Hall: The Earlier and Later Typescripts of Between the Acts. Ed. Mitchell A. Leaska. 1983.